Therapy after Terror

Therapy after Terror examines the impact of the 2001 World Trade Center attack on mental health professionals in New York City, and on the field of mental health. The events of 9/11 quickly were identified as an unprecedented public mental health crisis, and urgent demands for psychological treatment ensued. In response, thousands of mental health professionals volunteered their services on the scene, while uncounted others provided treatment in their regular clinical settings. Yet few mental health professionals were experienced in assisting survivors of trauma, let alone of a violent catastrophe of this magnitude. Moreover, like other New Yorkers, many therapists were 9/11 victims themselves, if only indirectly.

Based on interviews with New York City mental health professionals, *Therapy after Terror* depicts therapists' strikingly varied activities after the attack. This detailed study of the post-9/11, mental health crisis recounts the rapid organization and delivery of psychological services in schools and corporations, in restricted locations such as the Lexington Avenue Armory, Family Assistance Center, and Ground Zero Respite Centers, and in therapists' private offices. It also closely examines the attack's psychological effects on therapy patients, its unanticipated personal and professional consequences for therapists, and its extraordinary challenges to conventional clinical theories and methods.

In addition, *Therapy after Terror* investigates the social and political dimensions of mental health concepts and practices. Critically analyzing shifting notions of trauma, the subjective aspects of psychiatric diagnosis, the increasing medicalization of behavior, and the state's management of the national mood, this book raises questions concerning the politics of psychotherapy after 9/11.

KAREN M. SEELEY, MSW, PhD, is trained in clinical social work and in cultural psychology. She is a lecturer in the Anthropology Department at Columbia University and teaches in the Psychology Department at Barnard College. Dr. Seeley is also a psychotherapist with a private practice in New York City. She has published numerous articles on culture and mental health and is the author of *Cultural Psychotherapy: Working with Culture in the Clinical Encounter*.

Therapy after Terror

9/11, Psychotherapists, and Mental Health

KAREN M. SEELEY

Columbia University

CAMBRIDGE
UNIVERSITY PRESS

CAMBRIDGE UNIVERSITY PRESS

Cambridge, New York, Melbourne, Madrid, Cape Town, Singapore, São Paulo, Delhi

Cambridge University Press

32 Avenue of the Americas, New York, NY 10013-2473, USA

www.cambridge.org

Information on this title: www.cambridge.org/9780521884228

First published 2008

Printed in the United States of America

A catalog record for this publication is available from the British Library.

Library of Congress Cataloging in Publication Data

Seeley, Karen M.

Therapy after terror : 9/11, psychotherapists, and mental health / Karen M. Seeley.

p.; cm.

Includes bibliographical references and index.

ISBN 978-0-521-88422-8 (hardback)

1. September 11 Terrorist Attacks, 2001 – Psychological aspects.   2. Post-traumatic stress disorder –
Treatment – New York (State) – New York.   3. Crisis intervention (Mental health services) – New
York (State) – New York.   4. Disaster victims – Rehabilitation – New York (State) – New York.

I. Title.

[DNLM: 1. Stress Disorders, Traumatic – therapy.   2. Crisis Intervention – methods.

3. Mental Health Services.   4. Professional Role – psychology.   5. Professional-Patient Relations.

6. September 11 Terrorist Attacks – psychology.   WM 172 S452t 2008]

RC552.P67S394   2008

616.85′21–dc22   2007030542

ISBN   978-0-521-88422-8 hardback

For Hayley, Brigitte, and Tyler

Contents

Acknowledgments

My biggest debt is to the therapists who participated in this research and who, with great eloquence, candor, and insight, discussed the personal and professional impacts of their post-9/11 clinical work. I cannot thank them enough for inviting me into their consulting rooms and revisiting the profoundly taxing weeks and months after the World Trade Center attack.

I owe special thanks to David Stark for pulling me into the original research project on which this book is based (cf. Foner 2005); to Sema Gurun for indispensable support; to Monique Girard, comrade in all matters related to 9/11; and to journalist Akiko Morikawa, who clarified the culturally specific features of Americans' responses to the attack. Monica Bernheim, Melissa Brown, June Feder, Melinda Fine, Georgina Gatch, Carmen Grau, Diane Mirabito, Alan Roland, Matthew Silvan, Marjie Silverman, and others provided me with introductions to New York City therapists who offered psychological care in the aftermath of the attack. Ghislaine Boulanger, Mary Marshall Clark, Margaret Klenck, Madelyn Miller, Alan Roland, Sally Satel, Ann Stoler, and Nina Thomas helped me think through notions of trauma and their political implications. Susan Agrest, Gerard D'Alessio, Jean Maria Arrigo, Mary-Jo DelVecchio Good, Peg Hoey, Setha Low, Karen Meiselas, Sherry Ortner, Adela Pinch, Aileen Seeley, and Robert Seeley read and responded to earlier versions of this work. So did therapists at the Furman Counseling Center at Barnard College, where I was on staff, and students in my Columbia University class on "Trauma." I thank the Russell Sage Foundation for funding my initial research, Nancy Foner for providing editorial support, and Eric Schwartz of Cambridge University Press, whose guidance and calm helped bring this book to completion. Portions of this book previously appeared as

"The Psychological Treatment of Trauma of Psychological Treatment: Talking to Therapists About 9/11" in *Wounded City: The Social Impact of 9/11* (Seeley 2005b), and as "Trauma as a Metaphor: The Politics of Psychotherapy After September 11" in *Psychotherapy and Politics International* (Seeley 2005c).

I am especially grateful to my family – to my children, Hayley, Brigitte, and Tyler, and to my husband, Brinkley Messick – for lovingly standing by me and giving me the space to complete this project.

Introduction

❦

LIKE PHANTOM LIMBS that still can be felt even though they no longer exist, the twin towers of the World Trade Center continue to haunt New Yorkers, who – in the words of cartoonist Art Spiegelman (2004) – now live "in the shadow of no towers." During the first years of their absence, accounts of the attack – including journalistic, governmental, academic, fictionalized, and cinematic portrayals – proliferated. The multiplication of accounts is entirely warranted, given that no single version can fully describe the attack's antecedents, manifestations, and ramifications. Instead, the task of clarifying, classifying, calculating, and perhaps explaining the myriad causes and consequences of 9/11 can only be realized through the accumulation of a range of political, historical, national, disciplinary, and professional accounts.

Therapy after Terror tells the story of 9/11 from the distinctive perspectives of New York City mental health professionals who treated the psychologically wounded following the World Trade Center attack. Therapists, whose role it is to reflect on the problems of human experience, and to ease individuals' suffering, provide an unusual vantage point on one of the major catastrophes of our lifetime. Due to widespread fears that the attack would precipitate a large-scale psychiatric crisis among residents of New York City and the surrounding areas, these specialists in the workings of the mind rapidly became involved. Tens of thousands of local therapists offered their services, tending to the injured in family service centers, schools, corporate boardrooms, community centers, and firehouses, and later, for a fee, in private offices. Starting on 9/11 and continuing for months and years, thousands of therapists listened for countless hours as individuals discussed their personal experiences of the attack and its aftermath. This clinical work made therapists privy to uncommonly rich information concerning the varying ways people took in, made sense of, and responded to the events that unfolded that day. Indeed, New York City mental health professionals' accounts of their post-9/11 activities provide a view of the psychological consequences of this enormous act of violence that is not available from any other source. Their reports of their work, which are the substantive foundations of this book, add fresh insights into the accumulating portrait of the attack and provide new ways of assessing and conceptualizing its profound and far-reaching repercussions.

Therapists' reports of their post-9/11 work are significant not only because of what they tell us about how terror affects the mind but also because they include detailed depictions of the layout, operations, and atmosphere of settings that were off-limits to the general public after the attack. Mental health professionals were among the few civilians permitted to enter the Lexington Avenue Armory, the Family Assistance Center on Pier 94, Respite Centers at Ground Zero, and other sites located in "red zones" below Canal Street, "frozen zones" where streets were closed, "hot zones" where fires burned, and newly militarized sections of New York City that were patrolled by the National Guard. Therapists' accounts of delivering psychological assistance to the bereaved, the displaced, the unemployed, escapees, and rescue and recovery workers convey the workings, tone, and feel inside these highly restricted spaces.

In addition to examining their professional activities following the attack, *Therapy after Terror* takes a look at the therapists themselves. Prior to 9/11, very few mental health professionals were prepared to respond to a tragedy on this scale. Surprisingly few had been trained to treat survivors of interpersonal trauma, let alone of a massive and devastating attack. Therapists were uncertain how to determine which groups were most at risk, which individuals required treatment, which treatments would be most effective, and when and where they should be provided. Those who sought guidance from their professional associations, or from the clinical literature, discovered that their disciplines, including social work, clinical psychology, psychiatry, and psychoanalysis, lacked adequate models for responding to acts of mass violence. Even those who specialized in disaster mental health, including the staff of the American Red Cross, were ill equipped to address the unique aspects of the attack, as they lacked experience in mobilizing for an "urban metropolitan disaster relief operation" and for a "WMD/T (weapons of mass destruction/terrorism) response that involved high security" (Hamilton 2005:626). As a result, after the 2001 attack on the World Trade Center, mental health professionals often found themselves delivering services they had not been formally trained to provide, to populations they had not been trained to treat, in a catastrophic situation for which they had not been prepared.

Of course, mental health professionals were not the only ones who were unprepared for this catastrophe. Even after the 1993 World Trade Center bombing, the 1995 bombing of the Murrah Center in Oklahoma City, and several attacks on American interests abroad, the lack of preparedness for a major terrorist incident was strikingly widespread. Instructors at flight schools across the nation were unprepared to report students who were training to become pilots, but who had no interest in learning how to take off or land a plane. Security personnel at airport checkpoints in Washington, D.C., were not prepared to thoroughly inspect hijackers who set off alarms at metal detectors. Air traffic controllers at the Federal Aviation Agency were not equipped to handle multiple hijackings, so that when regional managers were advised of a second hijacked aircraft heading toward the World Trade Center they "refused to be disturbed" (9/11 Commission Report 2004:22). The North American Aerospace Defense Command (NORAD), which was established in 1958 to defend American and Canadian airspace against Soviet attacks, employed outdated protocols that were "unsuited in every respect" (9/11 Commission Report 2004:18). The city government of New York was unprepared for an attack that demolished its Office of Emergency Management, the agency responsible for responding to attacks. The Fire Department of New York, the New York Police Department, and the Port Authority Police Department were unprepared in "training and mindset" (9/11 Commission Report 2004: 315), lacking both the capability and the inclination to coordinate rescue operations. The Centers for Disease Control and Prevention, unlike comparable agencies in other countries, did not have specific codes for classifying deaths that were caused by terrorism (National Center for Health Statistics n.d.).[1]

This book examines not only mental health professionals' lack of preparedness to work with individuals who were injured on 9/11 but also their failure to anticipate the attack's extensive repercussions for therapeutic encounters, including altered clinical dynamics, the transmission of virulent affects between patients and therapists, and the emotional difficulties experienced by those who provided psychological care. While therapists generally are able to defend themselves against patients' instability, anxiety, and despair, some who work closely with trauma survivors, and continually hear their accounts of violation and brutality, have proven susceptible to their mental states; a number of them have suffered vicarious or secondary trauma (cf. Figley 1995; McCann & Pearlman 1990).[2] The fact that persons who endured the horrors of the World Trade Center attack, or who were instantly bereaved by it, were advised to discuss their experiences immediately in the name of mental health meant that many therapists were repeatedly exposed to patients' raw and gruesome narratives. These exposures exacted an immense emotional toll. Some therapists were newly traumatized, while others relived agonizing personal incidents of victimization and abuse. Such reactions were exacerbated by the fact that, after 9/11, New York City therapists were in the unusual clinical predicament of treating numerous individuals who were wounded by the same catastrophic events that had also injured them. *Therapy after Terror* describes the unanticipated costs for therapists of what I refer to as simultaneous trauma.

In addition to examining the attack's psychological consequences for individuals, and its professional and personal impacts on therapists, *Therapy after Terror* uses the specific case of 9/11 to critically investigate prevailing mental health theories and practices. It explores fundamental contradictions between conventional theories of psychopathology, which underplay the extent to which social and political events inflict psychological damage, and notions of psychic trauma, which stress their life-shattering effects. The fact that notions of psychic trauma had long been controversial within the several mental health disciplines and professions, were not routinely included in clinical training programs, and were not broadly endorsed by therapists at the time of the attack complicated the delivery of the requisite trauma-related mental health treatments after 9/11. This book also interrogates standard psychiatric diagnostic categories and procedures, paying special attention to shifting definitions of posttraumatic stress disorder (PTSD) over the past few decades, and to the multiple factors fueling diagnoses of PTSD after the attack.

Moreover, *Therapy after Terror* analyzes the mental health response to 9/11 through social and political frames. Challenging accepted conceptions of psychological disorders as internally generated phenomena, it describes the numerous and dynamic intersections of the intrapsychic, the collective, and the political after the attack. By examining ties between individuals' internal and external worlds, and by identifying various parties with evident interests in naming and assuaging suffering, *Therapy after Terror* illustrates that the mind, emotional states, and psychiatric disorders are inextricably entangled in politics and society. Of particular interest in the 9/11 context is the rapid emergence of mental health discourses as a preferred and legitimate mode of explaining and expressing reactions to the attack. When persons who subsequently felt frightened, bereaved, or disoriented were identified as suffering from anxiety disorders, depression, and other mental illnesses, and were then advised to undergo mental health treatment, the attack was effectively medicalized. This book assesses the consequences of medicalization for individuals who were encouraged to experience their distress in terms of psychiatric symptoms. Since the federal government rapidly poured $155 million into mental health treatments, thereby promoting clinical solutions to an act of international political violence, this book also examines medicalization's broader societal ramifications. Where the explosion of the Chernobyl nuclear reactor created "biological citizens" (Petryna 2002) who were defined by, and dependent on, the state, this book asks whether the events of 9/11 have resulted in new forms of "psychological citizenship." Such questions merit continuing attention given that American soldiers who now are returning from the war in Iraq are likely to be diagnosed with PTSD and other mental disorders.

Finally, *Therapy after Terror* documents the overall and ensuing impacts of the attack on the field of mental health. Just as the events of 9/11 have triggered significant transformations in American society, international politics, and the collective imagination, they have indelibly marked the mental health professions. Therapists who delivered mental health services to persons utterly destabilized by the attack routinely confronted the limitations of received clinical theories and methods. In response, many began to reconsider the primary purposes of psychological treatment, to modify their customary practices, and to reassess their social roles and political responsibilities. This book presents mental health professionals' urgent personal and institutional efforts to prepare themselves and their field for a world in which acts of mass violence that engender severe and extensive psychological damage are no longer unimaginable.

In critically analyzing the mental health response to 9/11, *Therapy after Terror* diverges from accounts that focus selectively on therapists' successes, celebrate their valor, and emphasize lessons learned. However reassuring to mental health professionals, such laudatory portraits run the risk of concealing rather than illuminating a series of events that may still be too painful to take in. By recounting the missteps, gaps in knowledge, disorganization, and overall lack of preparedness that compromised therapists' postattack work, this book offers a more realistic portrait of a profession assaulted by 9/11 and in transition after it. Further, by exploring the social and cultural dimensions of mental health discourses, it seeks to identify the links between individual and collective suffering, the means by which this society makes and feels its ills, and the various parties involved in shaping the emotional life of the nation.

ABOUT THE RESEARCH

The research for *Therapy after Terror* took place from September 2002 to July 2004. In the initial stages, I examined the attack's effects on New York City mental health professionals by interviewing 35 psychotherapists, including psychologists, social workers, and psychiatrists. Approximately half had additional training in psychoanalysis; two who had been trained as psychoanalysts lacked related academic degrees. Almost all of them had private practices, and all worked in New York City. The interviews were taped, and I quote from them extensively to show therapists' views, theoretical observations, and their personal images and metaphors. In some cases, I returned on multiple occasions to further develop the materials of the original interviews. To uncover the widest range of accounts of 9/11, I interviewed mental health professionals who delivered brief crisis treatments to survivors and to victims' families immediately after the attack, as well as those who were still working with such patients more than two years later when this research was in progress. In addition, in the fall of 2002 I attended a number of meetings for mental health professionals that addressed the attack's psychological impacts and the therapeutic community's response. The searching discussions that typified these meetings, and their heightened emotional tone, revealed the professional and personal issues that preoccupied this population in the aftermath of 9/11. Throughout this book, I count on the accuracy and veracity of the information contained in therapists' firsthand accounts of their experiences. Given my reliance on their accounts, which are inherently subjective, portions of this book may be seen as an oral history of September 11 as told by New York City mental health professionals.

Most of the therapists I interviewed were quite experienced; the vast majority had practiced for more than 15 years when 9/11 occurred. Two were new to the field, however, and found themselves thrown into extremely demanding clinical work in an early stage of their careers. I interviewed therapists who were available to me immediately, and I did not attempt to control for differences in their training, theoretical perspectives, or other such variables. For the purposes of this book, I do not generally distinguish among psychologists, social workers, psychiatrists, and psychoanalysts; instead I refer to them using the broad categories of "therapist," "psychotherapist," and "mental health professional." Although there are significant variations in educational formation among different kinds of mental health professionals, many of those I interviewed were involved in similar kinds of relief work following the attack. Conversely, individual practitioners within the same profession may employ contrasting therapeutic models. Of equal importance, I do not mention interviewees' specific professions in order to maintain their confidentiality. Other identifying information pertaining to individual therapists and to the patients they discuss also has been changed. I use terms such as "mental health treatment" and "psychological services" to refer to approaches ranging from crisis treatments to lengthy talk therapies, supplying more specific information about particular therapeutic orientations and interventions where it is necessary to my analysis. In light of the vast mobilization of psychological services following the attack, anything like a complete documentation of the mental health hotlines, initiatives, programs, service settings, studies, and articles that emerged is beyond the scope of this book.[3] The same is true of discussions of the attack on the Pentagon in Washington, D.C., and of the crash of Flight 93 in Shanksville, Pennsylvania that same day.

As this book was going to press, there were several key developments related to the attack. The search for remains was reopened, and that, along with improved DNA identification technologies, seemed to promise that the number of 9/11 victims who were positively identified would continue to rise (Dunlap 2006d; *Sept. 11th victim IDed*, 2007). Further, for the first time, New York City's chief medical examiner certified that a woman's death, which occurred five months after the attack, was caused by respiratory ailments due to exposure to World Trade Center dust (DePalma 2007b). Several thousand rescue and recovery workers who put in long shifts for many months at Ground Zero have developed similar illnesses (DePalma 2007a). As city officials reconsider questions concerning "Who is a 9/11 victim?" (Zadroga 2007:1), and try to determine which additional casualties qualify for inclusion in this category, the death toll may also rise. The number of casualties and the number of victims whose remains were identified that are cited in *Therapy after Terror* reflect those that were current at the time of its publication.

Since the time of Freud, mental health professionals have debated the relative psychological benefits of varying treatment approaches, and have tried to identify the underlying mechanisms by which talk therapies heal. In addition to wondering what is curative in their work, they have sought to determine whether, in actual therapeutic encounters, they employ the theories and techniques that they endorse in the abstract. Like their predecessors, contemporary therapists continue to ask, "Do we do what we think we do" (Silvan 2004:945)? As both a practicing therapist and an academic, such questions are of central importance to me, and I previously have examined them in the context of intercultural treatments (cf. Seeley 2000).

When the attack on the World Trade Center occurred, the intense involvement of mental health professionals presented an unusual opportunity to investigate these questions from another angle. Because situations of crisis invariably fracture the habits and routines of everyday life, they expose the structures and assumptions that otherwise lie hidden beneath the surface. At the same time, they facilitate the emergence of new perspectives and courses of action. By looking at therapists' accounts of this crisis, I hoped to make explicit what has been implicit in clinical work; I also hoped to examine how clinical premises and practices that were normally taken for granted were suddenly called into question as a result of the attack. This book thus provides instructive data on what therapists think they do, what they actually do, and what they have done differently since the unprecedented events of 9/11. In doing so, it intends to strengthen and enrich the mental health professions.

On a more personal note, I should state that I am a devoted and committed New Yorker – one who had a long and complex relationship with the twin towers, and who has felt strangely bereaved by their disappearance. Only recently did I realize that plunging headlong into this material offered me a way to face the injury to my beloved city. Accordingly, this book is not only a critical study of psychotherapy and of the broader mental health field but is also a work of mourning and an act of memorialization.

The Chapters

The first chapter provides the conceptual background for *Therapy after Terror*. It examines the identification of 9/11 as a mental health crisis, therapists' rush to volunteer their services despite their lack of relevant clinical training and experience, and the the establishment of Project Liberty in the context of shifting notions of trauma in twentieth-century psychology. After considering various explanations for therapists' long-standing inattention to psychic trauma, it assesses the consequences of this failing for mental health service delivery after the attack. Chapter 2 recounts therapists' efforts to provide psychological relief to direct victims of the attack on the day of 9/11 and throughout the following weeks. It begins by describing the chaos at New York City Red Cross headquarters, where thousands of therapists clamored to volunteer. Using the accounts of individual therapists, it documents their wanderings around the city in search of people to help and their frustration while waiting at hospitals for survivors who never arrived. It also discusses both the rapid organization of service centers and Respite Centers and the acute pressures on therapists at these sites, whether they were speaking to families of the missing on telephone hotlines or interacting with recovery workers at Ground Zero. Chapter 3 traces the growing demands for structured psychological services shortly after the attack, and the varied interventions of the psychotherapists who supplied them. It closely follows the experiences of a psychotherapist assigned to a corporation that lost hundreds of employees; a therapist who worked at an elementary school a few blocks from the World Trade Center; a therapist in attendance at ceremonies where New York City Mayor Rudy Giuliani's aides handed out containers full of ash to kin of the deceased; and a therapist who worked with a minority community hard hit by 9/11. Chapter 4 turns to therapists in private practice who delivered ongoing psychological treatments after the attack. It details the professional challenges they faced as they confronted numerous unfamiliar clinical situations, while also examining the attack's impact on therapeutic relationships and conventional theoretical premises. Many therapists themselves became unhinged after treating scores of individuals who were bereaved or severely traumatized by the events of 9/11. This is the subject of Chapter 5, which investigates the factors that put therapists at emotional risk, making them susceptible to patients' violent emotions, to secondary trauma, and to reliving personal traumatic experiences. In this context, I examine the phenomenon of simultaneous trauma where, after 9/11, New York City therapists faced the novel clinical situation of treating individuals suffering from a specific catastrophic event that they, too, had experienced. I then inquire into the possible effects of therapists' traumas on the treatments they delivered and on their patients.

Chapter 6 investigates diagnostic practices after 9/11. After examining disagreements among mental health professionals as to how patients injured in the attack should be diagnosed, it considers the ways in which their personal histories, theoretical allegiances, subjective interpretations of diagnostic criteria, and social contexts affected the choices they made. Because most such disagreements concerned the category of posttraumatic stress disorder, this chapter looks at historical circumstances in which members of specific groups commonly were diagnosed with PTSD. It also addresses the professional and political entailments of PTSD diagnoses after 9/11. Chapter 6 concludes by examining the medicalization of 9/11, and the transformation of collective reactions to an act of terrorism into individual mental disorders.

Because mental disturbances are political and historical as well as psychological and biomedical phenomena, Chapter 7 examines connections among psychotherapy, politics, and history. It first considers the ways therapy depoliticizes experience, reducing social and political history to the psychic experiences of separate individuals. It then explores the political implications of turning victims of September 11 into psychological patients to be treated in the privacy of a therapist's office, asking whether the privatization of suffering discouraged political action and forms of public witnessing and awareness. This chapter closes by considering the widespread diagnosis of PTSD after 9/11 as a metaphor for the victimization of the nation.

Chapter 8 charts the uncertain, and still untallied, effects of 9/11 on the field of mental health, its theoreticians, and its practitioners. It examines shifts in the mental health landscape as the result of the attack, describing the ways therapists have reevaluated clinical practices, models, concepts, and training programs, as well as their social and political responsibilities, to prepare for a world in which terrorist attacks are viewed as inevitable. In conclusion, I raise questions regarding future mental health responses to acts of mass violence, while also proposing fundamental reformulations of the therapeutic project.

CHAPTER I

Trauma Histories

ॐ

I N THE HOURS AFTER the 2001 attack on the World Trade Center, New York City hospitals prepared to receive the wounded. Outside St. Vincent's Hospital in Greenwich Village, gurneys dressed in clean white linens were neatly arrayed along Seventh Avenue. Doctors stood at the ready, awaiting a deluge of injured survivors. But the hospital beds remained empty. Due to the impact of the airplanes, the heat of the flames that engulfed Trade Center offices, the thickness of the smoke inside them, the debris that rained down from the towers, and the sheer force of their collapse, most injuries were fatal, so that persons with physical wounds never materialized in great numbers.[1a] In lieu of bodily injuries, many of those who escaped from the immediate vicinity of the World Trade Center attack – like scores of others less directly exposed to it – suffered wounds that were psychological. As the loss of life, the property damage, and the terrorist threat were measured, and as the shock and fear settled in, attention quickly turned to the public's mental health.

Concerns about widespread psychological injuries escalated, especially once the attack was officially declared a federal disaster.[2a] Disasters are events of such magnitude and severity that they exceed the capacities of local governments and organizations to cope with them and to provide for the recovery of all whom they affect.[3] Events that fall into this category are known to cause extensive psychological harm (Norris et al. 2002; Vlahov 2002). But some types of disasters are particularly debilitating. Those that are unanticipated and that heavily damage the economy, property, and the environment engender higher rates of mental disturbance. When disasters are humanly caused and are intentional, consist of acts of mass violence, and present continuing threats – all key features of the World Trade Center attack – they produce pervasive and incapacitating distress (Norris 2002). Terrorist attacks, which are deliberately designed to provoke intense fear, shock, and intimidation among the population at large, are perhaps the most psychologically harmful of all disasters (Collogan, Tuma, Dolan-Sewell, Borja, & Fleischman 2004).[4]

Following the deadliest terrorist attack ever to take place on American ground, experts in public health anticipated that rates of mental disorder would be staggeringly high. Because the unprecedented nature of the attack made it impossible to foresee exactly how many individuals would be psychologically injured, these experts generated a range of predictions. Some public health officials extrapolated from rates of mental disorder produced by the 1995 Oklahoma City bombing and estimated that 34% of those who were "most exposed" – including those injured in the attack, families of the injured and the deceased, rescue workers and their families, and World Trade Center employees and their families – or approximately 528,000 persons would develop post-traumatic stress disorder (Herman, Felton, & Susser 2002a).[5] They further projected that an additional three million New York metropolitan area residents would experience other psychiatric illnesses, such as anxiety or depressive disorders (Herman et al. 2002b). Others in public health were considerably more pessimistic; they expected mental health problems to develop not only in the 12.7 million residents of New York City and its surrounding counties but also in every resident of New York State (Jack & Glied 2002). Despite their divergent predictions, public health officials generally agreed that the attack had triggered a "looming mental health crisis" (Cohen 2005:25) of unparalleled proportion.

Early studies seemed to support the view that persons who escaped the towers, civilians who directly witnessed the attack, uniformed service personnel who responded to it, friends and relatives of the 2,749 people it killed, rescue and recovery workers at Ground Zero, and all other inhabitants of the New York City area were psychologically vulnerable.[6] These studies showed that rates of PTSD and depression had almost doubled among Manhattan residents (e.g. Galea et al. 2002). When taken together with other research that found that consumption of cigarettes, alcohol, and marijuana had increased after the attack (Vlahov et al. 2002) and that prescriptions for sleeping pills and antidepressants had risen by 17% and 28%, respectively (Harvard College 2002), they added to growing fears of an impending mental health emergency.[7]

Even before public health officials had predicted widespread psychological disorder, and before studies documenting it had been published, thousands and thousands of New York City mental health professionals mobilized. Considering themselves uniquely qualified to come to the aid of individuals injured in the attack, therapists instantaneously transformed themselves from private practitioners to public servants. Many who had spent their careers behind the closed doors of clinical consulting rooms, treating patients upset by more personal matters, thought it their civic duty to deliver emotional relief. Some fashioned themselves as first responders, like firefighters, police officers, and emergency medical technicians, and they immediately rushed to the scene. Others contacted disaster relief organizations and their professional associations to learn how they might help. Although they were not yet fully certain what had occurred and may have been fearful of additional attacks, approximately nine thousand mental health professionals made their way – frequently on foot, because the attack had damaged the subways and disrupted public transportation – to the New York City chapter of the Red Cross (Sommers & Satel 2005).[8] A few mental health professionals warned their colleagues against providing interventions that were too hastily conceived; yet thousands clamored to be on the frontlines in responding to a national catastrophe.

Beginning on September 11 and continuing for the next several months, therapists volunteered their services. Disaster relief organizations such as the Red Cross, as well as numerous government agencies, arranged for the delivery of psychological assistance at various sites around the city, and assigned mental health professionals to staff them. Therapists worked in the Armory on Lexington Avenue, comforting countless persons who arrived searching for the missing; on telephone hotlines, providing information to callers who could not locate their relatives; at Pier 94 on the Hudson River, consoling families of the deceased; at social service centers, providing monies for shelter and food to the displaced and unemployed; and at Respite Centers at Ground Zero, supporting rescue and recovery workers. Other therapists reached out to groups and individuals they believed to be at risk. In local firehouses, community centers, schools, and corporate boardrooms, as well as in their private offices, they listened as evacuees, witnesses, firefighters, police, and relatives of the deceased told their stories. Although there are no precise counts of either the number of psychotherapists who delivered mental health services in the wake of the 2001 attack on the World Trade Center, or of the number of individuals who sought psychological care, in the following weeks and months, therapists seemed to be everywhere. Many found that after 9/11, their telephones never stopped ringing. As one therapist asked, with little sense of exaggeration, "Was there ever a time when everyone in New York City wanted treatment?"

A variety of factors encouraged the influx of new psychological patients. Among the most important, within weeks of 9/11 the New York State Office of Mental Health unveiled Project Liberty, a mental health program designed to address the epidemic of psychiatric disorders that public health officials had predicted. Prior to the attack, state mental health personnel had failed to develop emergency plans for an incident of this size, and were unfamiliar with the

Federal Emergency Management Agency (FEMA) and the disaster relief moneys it disbursed; yet, they quickly applied for government funding (Oldham 2004). Their efforts were successful. FEMA granted them more than $155 million in funding, the largest amount the federal government had ever awarded for either crisis counseling or disaster mental health services (Donahue, Lanzara, Felton, Essock, & Carpinello 2006). Project Liberty's aims were twofold; to provide short-term mental health services,[9] and to educate the public about common psychological responses to the attack so that people could identify key symptoms in themselves, their children, spouses, friends, colleagues, and employees (Felton 2002). To achieve its second goal, Project Liberty embarked on a massive publicity campaign, advertising heavily on television and radio. The New York City Department of Health and Mental Hygiene pitched in, hiring "a savvy New York City media firm" (Felton 2004:151) to hone Project Liberty's message, create appealing products, reach out to various communities, and secure celebrity endorsements.[10] Ads promoting Project Liberty, which urged the public to "feel free to feel better" by speaking with trained psychological counselors, soon covered city subways and buses and were posted on the Internet. Project Liberty also distributed more than twenty million brochures in over a dozen languages offering free mental health services wherever people desired to have them (Danieli & Dingman 2005a).[11] As the result of these extraordinary efforts, by September 2002, more than half of all New Yorkers were aware of Project Liberty's mental health programs (Felton 2004).

Supplementing Project Liberty's advertisements were additional publicity campaigns conducted by a wide range of organizations, including the National Institute of Mental Health (NIMH) and other federal agencies, the American Red Cross and other nongovernmental agencies, and the Center for Modern Psychoanalytic Studies and other private mental health institutions. These organizations saturated the New York metropolitan area with flyers informing individuals of the emotional difficulties they might experience as a result of the attack. The American Red Cross posted flyers to help people "recognize your feelings and physical symptoms" in order to "reduce your stress and to begin the healing process." The Center for Modern Psychoanalytic Studies, a private training institute, posted flyers listing "normal stress reaction[s] to the Trade Center disaster." Several flyers encouraged parents to look for signs of distress in their children, and many recommended seeking professional treatment to alleviate the expected psychological suffering.

Not only were mental health services heavily advertised, but they were made exceptionally accessible. When the attack produced the "largest single expenditure for mental health services in history" (Stone 2005:il), the usual financial barriers to treatment were eased. Barriers to brief treatment all but disappeared

when Project Liberty offered free crisis counseling to everyone who was emotionally wounded on 9/11. Its four thousand mental health practitioners sometimes worked out of conventional clinical settings serving as Project Liberty
sites, but frequently met with individuals, families, and groups in private homes,
schools, parks, workplaces, and community centers to make services more con-
venient (Danieli & Dingman 2005a). Abundant funds for mental health services
came from other sources as well. The Red Cross and private charities – including the New York Community Trust and the United Way, which established
the September 11th Fund (Lowry & McCleery 2005) – collected more than a
quarter of a billion dollars for the psychological care of individuals affected by
the attack (Sommers & Satel 2005). Some private insurance companies, in a fit
of generosity, also eased access to treatment. Persons who had been employed
in the World Trade Center and its immediate vicinity had had comparatively
high rates of insurance coverage for mental health treatment. In cases where
the primary policyholder was killed in the attack, many insurance companies
agreed to continue covering surviving family members (Jack & Glied 2002).[12]

As a result of these factors, uncounted numbers of New Yorkers – whether
under Project Liberty's auspices, in agency or institutional settings, or in private practitioners' offices – began new courses of psychological treatment, or
extended existing ones, after the attack. Incoming patients included individuals
who had narrowly escaped the towers, who had tried to rescue others, and who
had lost relatives and friends, as well as those less directly affected who struggled
to grasp this unfathomable act and its significance for their lives. Whether all
of those who sought treatment were upended by the events of 9/11, or whether
the attack provided a "socially acceptable way to get psychological help" for
unrelated matters (Sommers & Satel 2005:201), psychological services suddenly
were in broad demand. Indeed, it is likely that never before had so many people
sought psychological services to relieve the adverse emotional consequences of
a major disaster, let alone of a terrorist attack.

There were several indications that the demand for such services would
persist long after 9/11. For one, at the time of the 2001 World Trade Center
attack, the American Red Cross still was delivering psychological services to
persons injured in the Oklahoma City bombing, which had occurred more than
six years earlier. That particular disaster had convinced Red Cross workers that
some people required long-term treatment to cope with acts of mass violence
(American Red Cross in Greater New York 2004a). Mental health professionals
concurred. The *Diagnostic and Statistical Manual of Mental Disorders* (DSM),
the official catalog of psychiatric illnesses, previously had established extended
timetables for both the onset and the duration of severe psychological wounds.
This handbook unequivocally stated that the full impact of traumatic incidents

and their most debilitating symptoms could take months or even longer to emerge (American Psychiatric Association 2000). Not only could their onset be delayed, but disturbances such as posttraumatic stress disorder, other anxiety disorders, and depression – the same disorders that were expected to afflict millions of New Yorkers after the attack – often were viewed as recurrent or lifelong conditions that required ongoing treatment (M. Miller 2003). In addition, although Project Liberty was in compliance with the 1974 Robert T. Stafford Disaster Relief and Emergency Assistance Act, and thus initially restricted the use of federal funds to brief, crisis-oriented interventions, the federal government later took the unusual step of covering long-term treatment in cases where it was deemed clinically necessary (Felton 2004).[13] Finally, the growing sense that psychological services would be required on more than a short-term basis grew out of common conceptions of disasters. Disasters are seen as protracted events with multiple phases, the deleterious effects of which unfold over time and persist long past the moment of impact (Myers & Wee 2005). Accordingly, when more than two years later, the Red Cross described the Trade Center attack as "not just one event, but an evolving series of needs" (American Red Cross 2004), the implications for mental health professionals were clear: their involvement with persons injured on 9/11 would be a lasting project.

TREATING THE UNNAMABLE

Despite urgent attention from various quarters concerning the psychological consequences of 9/11, and despite therapists' eagerness to do whatever they could to help, no one was fully certain exactly how to proceed. Such uncertainties deepened when the attack demonstrated the resistance to linguistic expression that some consider the hallmark of atrocities, abuse, and other malicious acts of violence (Caruth 1995b). In a clear expression of this resistance, the attack soon was referred to by numbers rather than names, so that "9/11" became the "universal shorthand" for a series of staggering occurrences (Rosenthal 2002:28). Like many others around them, therapists had difficulty labeling "our loss, the attack, the disaster, the catastrophe, the act of war, what should we call it (Dimen 2002:451)?" This poverty of language was especially distressing for members of a profession that placed the highest value on verbalizing experiences, no matter how agonizing or terrible, and on saying the unsayable. After September 11, psychotherapists, uncharacteristically, were at a loss for words.

Not only were the events of 9/11 beyond the reach of everyday language but their psychological consequences also defied classification in the specialized categories of the mental health professions. None of the hundreds of diagnostic categories contained in the most up-to-date edition of the *Diagnostic and Statistical Manual* – each with its crisp clinical language and neat lists of symptoms (American Psychiatric Association 2000) – adequately captured the intricate combinations of horror, rage, anguish, incomprehension, disorientation, excitement, shock, fear, and bereavement that many individuals experienced. As noted above, mental health professionals were not alone in finding it impossible to put these events into words; but for this particular community, the inability to classify the attack's psychological effects had serious practical implications. How could they help persons injured in ways that were overwhelmingly painful, but that defied psychiatric categorization? Without clear ways to grasp the emotional damage wrought by the attack, how could therapists determine what kinds of aid to provide? And how were they to identify the sufferers themselves?

Lacking clinical precedents, therapists likened individuals wounded in the attack to previous patients who had been devastated by catastrophes. Some saw them as survivors of a disaster, like people who had lost everything to hurricanes or floods. Others viewed them as families of crime victims, like those who had lost loved ones to murder. Still others compared them to victims of, or witnesses to, horrifying atrocities. But even therapists with expertise in these areas felt unprepared to treat those who were deeply wounded on September 11. Therapists who had helped persons hurt by natural disasters and accidents were unsure how to aid victims of a deliberate act of mass violence. Those who specialized in bereavement were uncertain how to assist persons who had no body to bury, whose losses could be counted in dozens, whose private losses were strangely public, or whose relatives were killed by members of a previously unheard of international terrorist organization. Those who had treated individuals with histories of trauma, including survivors of abuse, victims of torture or genocide, and veterans of Vietnam, had not been trained to work with persons harmed by a current catastrophe – one that maintained an ominous presence long after the towers had fallen.

The utter novelty of these circumstances was compounded by the fact that, after 9/11, New York City psychotherapists found themselves in the extremely rare clinical situation where they and their patients had been psychologically wounded by the same calamitous events. On September 11, therapists lost friends and relatives in the attack; some lost long-term psychotherapy patients. They stood on street corners watching the towers burn and collapse; they fled lower Manhattan in states of numbness or panic; they desperately tried to determine the safety of their kin; they raced to pick up their children from school; they walked home covered in ash. Their apartments were contaminated and damaged; they lost access to their offices in the "frozen zone" downtown;

they breathed air that was loaded with poisons; they thought they were going to die. As they engaged in clinical work following 9/11, many New York City therapists felt as victimized and destabilized as their patients. In consequence, they could no longer depend on the usual, unquestioned distinction between "a patient with psychopathology and a physician with a cure" (McGlaughlin 1981:642).

TRAUMA THEORIES IN MENTAL HEALTH

While some mental health professionals continued to believe that the psychological sequelae of September 11 defied classification, others began to assimilate them to existing psychiatric concepts and categories. Many settled on the term "trauma" to describe them. Freud (1920/1961:33) had applied this rubric to "excitations" so overpowering that they breached the "protective shield" that normally defended the mind against events in the world outside, thereby gravely compromising "the functioning of the organism's energy." In more recent years, trauma has emerged as the "master term in the psychology of suffering" (Hoffman 2004:34). It commonly has been invoked in situations where horrific acts of violence, interpersonal abuse, deadly accidents, and large-scale atrocities and catastrophes have overwhelmed human coping capacities. The term "trauma" and its variants have been heavily employed since the 9/11 attack. The events themselves have been labeled "traumatic," and persons wounded by the attacked have been described as "traumatized" and as vulnerable to "retraumatization" should further calamities occur. Moreover, individuals who experienced a particular amalgam of reactions, including flashbacks, intrusive memories, numbing, and nightmares, frequently have been diagnosed with posttraumatic stress disorder – the diagnostic category many mental health professionals consider to best describe "the way the mind responds to overwhelming trauma" (van der Kolk 2002:390).

The increased interest in trauma in connection with 9/11 tends to obscure the fact that psychological theories linking exposure to traumatic incidents with debilitating mental distress have gone in and out of fashion over the past century or so (cf. Boulanger 2002a; Herman 1997; McNally 2003; Shephard 2001; Young 1995). During this period, mental health professionals have vacillated between claiming that traumatic experiences were the key causes of psychiatric disorders and dismissing such ideas entirely. Like so many foundational features of the mental health field, this pattern was initiated by Freud. His first published scientific paper, "The Aetiology of Hysteria" (Freud 1896/1998), introduced the seduction theory. In this paper, Freud fervently argued that children who had been sexually violated were at psychological risk, and that repressed memories of premature seductions produced psychopathology in adults. But a few years later, with equal fervor, he retracted this seminal theory. Evidently, Freud came to realize that his highly esteemed senior colleagues were uncomfortable with the portrayal of rampant incest and sexual abuse in bourgeois European society. They rejected his theoretical statement and, in doing so, ostracized him. To regain his standing in the medical community, Freud revised his views. Instead of treating patients' stories of childhood sexual violation as factual, he reinterpreted them as fictions, and, more important, as evidence of unconscious fantasies and desires. Freud's followers and disciples expunged all traces of the seduction theory from his writings and correspondence to safeguard his reputation (Masson 1998). Succeeding generations of psychoanalysts supported the later Freudian line. Attuned primarily to the unconscious and to intrapsychic conflict, they were not inclined to emphasize the injurious mental consequences of catastrophic real-world experiences. Less orthodox psychotherapists reproduced the Freudian pattern, first discovering the profound psychic damage caused by traumatic experiences and then, for various reasons, eradicating such notions. Because they neither elaborated theories of trauma, nor designed treatments for traumatic injuries, nor taught courses concerning trauma in professional training institutions, for much of the twentieth century, the concept of psychic trauma was forgotten or overlooked in mainstream mental health.

There are additional explanations for this remarkable lapse. For one, mental health professionals' shared "episodic amnesia" (Herman 1997:7) pertaining to trauma may reflect the enormous emotional costs of maintaining a steady focus on the kinds of disturbing occurrences to which this concept refers. Alternatively, the inattention to trauma may mirror society's wishes to keep material of this nature out of collective awareness. For both individuals and communities, incidents that produce psychological trauma, whether hurricanes, earthquakes, assaults, sexual violence, torture, acts of terrorism, mass shootings, or war, simply may be too horrible, and too psychologically menacing, to engender sustained attention. As a result, impulses to closely examine them often have been superseded by stronger impulses to look away, to minimize their impacts, or to question their basis in fact. This common aversion to trauma also has had the effect of discouraging individuals who have endured traumatic experiences from speaking up about them. Unlike those who claim that traumatic incidents are inherently unspeakable, and that the silence that typically shrouds them results from the impossibility of putting those experiences into words (Caruth 1995b), others assert that this silence largely derives from the absence of an audience that is willing to hear about them. Such refusals to listen, which have been termed "conspiracies of silence" (Danieli 1984:24), have quieted individuals whose stories of sexual violation, of showers filled with poison gas, or of vicious wartime massacres have been dismissed as fabrications (Hoffman 2004). They have also quieted entire societies, as in Germany's failure to address the bitter suffering of civilians following relentless Allied bombing during World War II (Sebald 2003). Refusals to listen have been predominant in clinical consulting rooms as well, as when psychotherapists who treated Holocaust survivors and their descendants prevented them from recounting tales of genocide (Danieli 1984).

Further, therapists' attention to trauma has proved difficult to maintain absent societal contexts that defined particular kinds of injuries as exceptionally harmful, undeserved, and unjust and that offered protections to those who sustained them. In twentieth-century America, theories of trauma resurfaced in specific historical eras when social and political movements identified new precipitants of suffering and new categories of sufferers (Herman 1997). During periods of armed conflict, and especially in the presence of antiwar movements, therapists treating soldiers who were severely incapacitated by the brutality of combat invoked notions of stress and trauma to classify wounds of war (Kardiner 1941; Lifton 1978). Similarly, when the feminist movement drew attention to high rates of violence against women and to the psychological ruin it caused, therapists labeled these assaults and their consequences traumatic. Yet as soon as peace ensued or when relevant social movements declined, therapists again lost sight of psychic injuries related to trauma and stress (Davoine & Gaudilliere 2004; Shephard 2001).

Psychotherapists' repeated abandonment of concepts of psychic trauma might also be due to the fact that these concepts contradicted established theories of psychopathology. Such theories attributed mental disturbances to various flaws in the individual interior – either to intrapsychic conflicts or to marked deficiencies in early relationships, developmental processes, constitution, or character (cf. Boulanger 2002a). Clinicians trained in these theories have dominated the mental health field. Their insistence on the importance of internal and imagined experiences has prevented them from considering the potentially devastating psychic impacts of actual disasters and violence that occurred in the external world.

Conventional clinical theories not only conceived of the mind as a self-contained entity that was fundamentally separable from the interpersonal relationships, cultural surrounds, social structures, and political conditions constitutive of daily life, but they also held that mental functions were best understood in this decontextualized state. For Freud (1917/1961), ridding psychoanalytic encounters of external elements was no less crucial than cleansing surgical theatres of toxins. In his view, the mere presence of such contaminants posed threats to the project at hand and compromised patients' safety. The presence of external elements in psychoanalytic sessions had the additional disadvantage of tainting mental processes that otherwise were pure, in the sense that they were unaffected by context. To fortify the split between the internal and the external, therapists directed patients to produce specific kinds of material, such as fantasies, dreams, and wishes, which they thought would reveal the intricate workings of their private psychic worlds. Moreover, they fashioned their consulting rooms as containers tightly sealed against exterior contingencies. Therapists reassured patients that the information they disclosed in the course of the clinical hour would not leak outside these spaces and that external impingements would not seep into them. Both members of the therapeutic dyad relied on the firmness of these boundaries to keep their encounters secure. At the same time, shutting out the exterior world intensified therapists' emphasis on the imaginings of the psyche.

Toward the end of the twentieth century several movements in psychoanalysis sought to widen the clinical frame, for example, by encouraging therapists to pay more attention to patients' actual relationships (cf. Aron 1996; Mitchell 1997). Yet they continued to guard against the intrusion of social and political events. Patients who were interested in discussing such matters in treatment were likely to discover that their therapists preferred to examine the intrapsychic meanings of these events rather than the events themselves (Seeley 2000). While therapists doubtless believed that these sorts of clinical conventions provided the surest means of alleviating patients' distress, conventions of this nature also protected them. Privileging the intrapsychic allowed therapists to spend their days exploring patients' unconscious fantasies and desires, thus sparing them confrontations with disturbingly real accounts of repellent acts of cruelty and of brutal social and political conditions that caused psychological harm (Prince 1998).

Failures to elaborate comprehensive and enduring psychological theories of trauma – especially theories concerning the impacts of acts of mass violence – also speak to the political security and insularity of American mental health professionals. For several decades prior to 9/11, the United States had succeeded in fighting its wars abroad and in nearly eliminating attacks at home. This long period of domestic peace had given therapists little incentive to conceptualize the negative psychic effects of civilians' exposure to warfare, terrorist strikes, and threats of ongoing violence, to develop literatures addressing them, to build them into diagnostic systems, to develop treatments that relieved them, or to plan for the delivery of mental health services following large-scale calamities. Terror and war were prevalent in numerous other societies, but most American mental health professionals exhibited little interest in studying the psychic impact of atrocities that occurred outside their national borders. The *Diagnostic and Statistical Manual* was equally parochial. Despite its claims to be world-wide applicable, this manual was created in the United States, represented Western biomedical perspectives, reflected the lives and concerns of narrow segments of American society, and paid insufficient attention to the suffering others experienced in the face of life-threatening, humanly perpetrated horrors.

Before the World Trade Center attack took place, there were signs that such trends would continue. By the late 1990s, interest in trauma had so diminished that one mental health professional predicted that the next and fifth edition of the *Diagnostic and Statistical Manual* (DSM-V), to be published in 2010, would omit the diagnostic category of posttraumatic stress disorder altogether (International Society for Traumatic Stress Studies n.d.). The general disinterest in psychological trauma prior to 9/11 was also on display in a preliminary volume laying the groundwork for the upcoming DSM-V. This volume, which was prepared by the American Psychiatric Association and the National Institute of Mental Health, identified key questions confronting practitioners. But of its nearly 300 pages, only a few paragraphs addressed trauma-related disorders. The fact that two of these paragraphs were in chapters on culture and diagnosis suggested that mental health professionals sought to fill in existing gaps in knowledge pertaining to other societies' experiences of, and reactions to, terror, war, and disaster. However, the lack of attention to trauma elsewhere in this volume also seemed to affirm entrenched assumptions that trauma-related mental disorders – especially those caused by overpowering political violence – were primarily of relevance to "special populations" and those outside the United States (Kupfer, First, & Regier 2002:289).

Genealogies of Trauma

As a result of this irregular history, trauma did not emerge as the umbrella term for the similar psychic injuries produced by various kinds of catastrophes until relatively recently. Therapists who previously treated populations that now would be labeled as traumatized, including victims of crimes, abused women and children, and survivors of natural disasters, did not apply this term, nor did they draw comparisons across outwardly disparate groups. Instead, as they worked with individuals subjected to situations of extremity, they focused on the distinctive elements of their plight. Many who had handled such exceedingly challenging cases during their careers volunteered their services after 9/11, hoping to adapt their skills to persons who were wounded by the terrorist strike. The following genealogy of trauma, which considers the prior clinical experiences of these 9/11 volunteers, shows how current notions of traumatic injury, as well as contemporary trauma interventions, grew out of their early practices and gradually took hold.

Numerous therapists who were volunteers after 9/11 began their careers in mental health treating individuals who had been exposed to violence and abuse. One had assisted women who were targets of domestic violence – and were then known as battered women – when they first received public attention in the early 1970s. Rather than working in an agency office, as was customary, she was posted to police stations. Because there was a dearth of services for aiding this population, she designed new treatment models, visiting women in their homes, setting up drop-in centers that offered them safety, leading support and educational groups, connecting them with local resources, and listening to their stories when they came into the precinct station to drink coffee and read the newspaper. A few years later, another therapist had begun to deal with victims of abuse; her patients were women who had experienced childhood sexual violation or incest. Her work intensified in the early 1980s, when for the first time, television and radio programs broadcast the personal narratives of individuals with such histories. These programs encouraged listeners to discuss similar incidents, which they formerly had kept secret, not only on the air but also in the office of a mental health professional. Because many of this therapist's colleagues refused to take on patients who had suffered sexual assaults, her practice filled rapidly. Around this time, following the increasing provision of government assistance to victims of crime, a third therapist had worked for Victims' Services. She noticed that surviving family members, while not directly harmed by the crime, were under tremendous stress after having suffered a sudden and violent loss, identified relatives' bodies, and interacted with the criminal justice system. In response, she developed innovative programs for families of homicide victims that addressed the emotional difficulties common to indirect and "invisible" victims (National Crime Victims' Rights Week n.d.). During the same period, a fourth therapist – a physician from the Middle East who later trained as a mental health professional – was spending the first part of his medical career working in a prison where numerous inmates were tortured because of their political views. Inmates' accounts of being trapped in cells with perpetrators for weeks and months on end drew attention to the effects of protracted traumatic stress and to the role of political beliefs in mediating its impact.

Also among the mental health professionals who volunteered after 9/11 were those who had previously treated individuals harmed by acts of mass violence and war. One therapist had worked with veterans of the Vietnam War. It was not uncommon for her patients to spend their hourly sessions recounting gruesome massacres and nightmares; sometimes, as they described them, they experienced flashbacks in front of her. The fact that some veterans were less disturbed by the violence they had witnessed than by the killings they had committed alerted her to the psychological damage sustained by perpetrators of atrocity. Another therapist had assisted persons affected by the "Troubles," the 30-year period of terrorist violence between the Irish Republic and Northern Ireland. Many of them had been exposed to recurrent bomb scares and deadly explosions over the course of three decades. Moreover, those with relatives in the Irish Republican Army were subjected to state harassment, and their homes were repeatedly raided by the police. Some coped by drinking alcohol or by bullying their families. As most were unfamiliar with psychotherapy, rather than holding formal sessions with them in an office, this therapist took them out to lunch or accompanied them on errands. She saw it as her task to educate them about traumatic reactions and to suggest healthier coping strategies. A third therapist had worked with survivors of the 1993 World Trade Center bombing. In contrast with persons directly affected by the 2001 attack, these survivors received little government assistance; more than ten years later, victims' claims for compensation remained unresolved. Yet some of this therapist's patients remained so terrorized that they never returned to their jobs in the towers. Despite years of mental health treatment they failed to recover, and she watched their lives deteriorate. Other therapists had worked for international relief organizations prior to 9/11. When these organizations first were formed, they rarely offered psychological interventions. But numerous physicians and mental health professionals vigorously lobbied for them to include such services, whether they were responding to natural calamities or to political violence (Breslau 2000). As a result of their efforts, global humanitarian programs began to routinely supply mental health treatments alongside medical services, shelter, and food, and international trauma relief projects attracted many Western donors (Summerfield 1999). One therapist who had participated in these efforts, delivering psychological interventions to victims of warfare in the former Yugoslavia, was among those who donated her services after 9/11.

Finally, additional therapists who volunteered after the World Trade Center attack had earlier provided psychological aid in the wake of natural disasters in the United States. One had worked with persons affected by Hurricane Andrew in the early 1990s. Although numerous individuals she encountered experienced persisting emotional difficulties after the hurricane destroyed everything they owned, she found that many of them were wary of mental health professionals and preferred to take assistance from local religious organizations. Still, mental health services became central components of American disaster relief programs (Breslau 2000).

A number of common themes marked the delivery of mental health services to populations in situations of extremity. For one, despite wide variations across the groups themselves, and in the causes of their distress, their members were found to share various characteristics. Most were identified as being psychologically vulnerable following exposure to catastrophic events, incidents of brutality, or structural oppression. Victims of violence frequently were stigmatized, and many lacked access to money, social supports, and political power. When natural disasters struck communities impartially, those who were already the most susceptible, and who had the fewest resources, tended to suffer the greatest damage. The claim that mental health professionals' interest in trauma required the support of a political movement is relevant here (Herman 1997). In the 1960s and 1970s, grassroots movements promoting feminism, pacifism, civil rights, and crime victims' rights designated groups at risk, offering them shelter, legal protections, and financial compensations. Because these movements also drew attention to their psychological scars, they attracted mental health professionals not only as healers but also as witnesses to individuals' suffering and as advocates for their rights.

Moreover, therapists who treated members of these groups increasingly came to recognize that traditional psychological theories did not address their wounds and that established therapeutic methods failed to bring sufficient relief. In response, they devised alternative models of treatment; indeed, innovative therapeutic approaches were key features of early trauma work. These approaches were not driven by abstract concepts. Instead, they were closely based on therapists' actual clinical experiences with specific patient groups, and were designed to meet their particular emotional and practical needs. In developing such interventions, and in delivering them outside traditional mental health settings, therapists broke new clinical ground. However, at the same time, they renounced long-established and deeply cherished professional assumptions and conventions. They also parted ways with colleagues who preferred to limit themselves to customary patient populations, theories, and methods.

Clinical work with populations who had endured brutality and violation entailed a variety of occupational hazards that were both significant and unanticipated. Above all, therapists treating persons who had been subjected to deliberate cruelty did not remain unscathed. For example, the therapist who had worked with battered women was devastated to discover that one of her patients had been murdered, and the therapist who had aided Irish dissidents herself became a target of the state. In addition, these therapists often felt ostracized by their professional communities, as if they had taken on the stigma attached to victims of crimes and abuse. Many felt demeaned by public accusations that mental health professionals implanted false memories of physical or sexual assault in their patients (Lamprecht & Sack 2002). The fact that mental health professionals who responded to acts of mass violence and natural disasters frequently worked as unpaid volunteers further diminished their standing.

More distressing for therapists was the discovery that regularly confronting patients' accounts of merciless human cruelty took an emotional toll on them. Mental health professionals who worked with victims of violence, whether it had been inflicted in the suburban homes of America or in the villages of Vietnam, were continually exposed to detailed narratives of horror. Because many of their colleagues refused to accept such cases, a minority of therapists had practices full of patients who had been profoundly terrorized. Some gradually lost their capacity to listen to stories of violence, while others developed psychological symptoms resembling those of their patients. Haunted by "the shadow presence of the perpetrator" (Herman 1997:141), they grew vulnerable, mistrustful, and cynical or had gruesome nightmares, fantasies, and flashbacks; those with personal histories of brutality sometimes were retraumatized after listening to patients' accounts. Unaware of correlations between the number of victims they treated and the number of symptoms they experienced (Schauben & Frazier 1995), they did not immediately grasp the reasons for their distress. Not until the early 1990s, when colleagues coined terms like "secondary trauma" and "vicarious trauma" to describe the psychological injuries therapists sustained as the result of constant contact with survivors of violence and calamity, did they realize the necessity of limiting their exposure to traumatized patients (Figley 1995; McCann & Pearlman 1990).[14]

Several years before such terms were coined, mental health professionals who gathered at national and international conferences had noticed that survivors of diverse catastrophic stressors displayed marked similarities in clinical presentation. They soon established "trauma" as the dominant term and framework both for the devastating events themselves and for the particular wounds they caused. According to a therapist who attended these conferences, mental health professionals first grouped together various traumatic incidents with certain core resemblances. For example, they identified humanly perpetrated violence, encompassing sexual assault, incest, physical abuse, and torture, as well as large-scale acts of violence like the Holocaust and the Lockerbie terrorist attack, as a single subcategory of trauma. They later identified other subcategories, such as massive accidents and natural disasters, after observing that they induced equivalent psychological disturbances. By 1995, when the Oklahoma City bombing and the Tokyo Sarin gas attack occurred, therapists versed in such notions expected that some portion of those who survived these events would experience traumatic reactions. For many mental health professionals, the discovery that victims of widely varied stressors were similarly affected was a key scientific advance. They hoped that these new understandings would stimulate sophisticated research on the biology of trauma, rapid identification of trauma victims, and improvements in clinical treatments.

Having established important connections among atrocities, disasters, and specific kinds of psychological damage, mental health professionals helped found a number of trauma-related organizations. The International Society for Traumatic Stress Studies, which aimed to promote trauma research, enhance trauma treatments, and decrease traumatic stressors, was founded in 1985, and it published the first volume of the *Journal of Traumatic Stress* in 1988 (International Society for Traumatic Stress Studies n.d.). In 1996, the National Association of Social Workers established the Disaster Social Work Committee, which regularly held meetings to train and support mental health professionals who treated traumatized persons. Two years later, four psychiatrists launched Disaster Psychiatry Outreach (DPO). This organization prepared psychiatrists – who typically did not receive instruction in trauma or disaster mental health in medical school – to assist victims of large-scale catastrophes all over the world. Originally formed to help families of passengers who perished in an airplane crash, DPO later sent volunteers to El Salvador after an earthquake and to Sri Lanka following the tsunami in 2004 (Disaster Psychiatry Outreach n.d.).

As these new organizations took shape, older volunteer relief agencies also increased their attention to disaster mental health and trauma. The American Red Cross, which was founded in 1881 to offer food, shelter, first aid, and other basic services in the aftermath of natural disasters and accidents, began to offer mental health services in 1989. Its original disaster mental health programs were meant for Red Cross volunteers who became psychologically disturbed as a result of their work in unusually stressful circumstances; only later did the Red Cross provide crisis intervention services, and referrals for long-term psychological help, to actual victims of disasters (Howell 2005). Since their inception, these services have expanded dramatically. From 1992 to 2003, the number of volunteers involved in Red Cross disaster mental health programs grew from fewer than 100 to more than 3,400 (Hamilton 2005).

Central to the formation of organizations concerned with trauma was the construction of a new diagnostic category called posttraumatic stress disorder (PTSD). PTSD first entered the *Diagnostic and Statistical Manual* in its third edition, published in 1980 (American Psychiatric Association 1980), and was created primarily to classify the emotional wounds of soldiers returning from Vietnam. Previous editions of the DSM had included disorders caused by overwhelming stressors, including combat, but had characterized them as immediate and transient; these disorders were thought to emerge right after the traumatic incident occurred and to vanish as soon as it ended. But for Vietnam veterans, debilitating symptoms often set in, and persisted, long after they left the battlefield. Because no existing diagnostic category described the distinctive features of their suffering, veterans' highly charged memories of war sometimes were mistaken for psychotic delusions. Many veterans were misdiagnosed with schizophrenia and were prescribed antipsychotic medications that were severely incapacitating (Young 1995).

Although PTSD was designed to capture the specific psychic plight of Vietnam veterans, many therapists considered this category a breakthrough for the broader field of mental health. First, by officially acknowledging that persons' actual experiences in the external world could cause grave and enduring emotional problems, it both upset the customary calculus attributing psychopathology to internal conflict or deficiency and provided a vital alternative. Therapists were quick to see PTSD in survivors of other horrors, including concentration camps, natural disasters, and sexual assaults, as a means of explaining, and legitimizing, their psychological devastation (McNally 2003). Second, this new diagnostic category concretized psychic trauma, transforming vague notions of mental injury into a distinct psychiatric syndrome with a list of easily identifiable symptoms. Its core features included symptoms of "intrusion," in which the traumatic event was involuntarily reexperienced through recurring memories, dreams, or flashbacks; symptoms of "constriction," including numbness, apathy, or alienation; and symptoms of "arousal," such as excessive alertness, survivor guilt, impaired memory and concentration, and avoidance of activities that recalled the original event (American Psychiatric Association 1980).

The fact that PTSD could not be diagnosed in the absence of a specific, external stressor obliged the DSM to define the kinds of incidents capable of evoking posttraumatic reactions. Various editions of this manual have defined such incidents differently. The original definition of PTSD in the DSM-III underscored these incidents' objective and universal properties, describing them as "recognizable stressors" that would produce significant distress in "almost everyone" (American Psychiatric Association 1980:238). But these recognizable stressors were thought to have another essential characteristic, which was incorporated into the diagnostic criteria when the revised DSM III-R was published seven years later: they were incidents so extraordinary as to fall "outside the range of usual human experience" (American Psychiatric Association 1987:247). Some mental health professionals found this definition overly limiting – if strictly interpreted, it would exclude sexual assaults, which were common enough to fall well within the range of women's usual experiences (Brown 1995). Accordingly, the next and fourth edition of the DSM replaced this stringent criterion with a looser one, which acknowledged individuals' varying capacities to tolerate atrocities and disasters and to withstand horror, helplessness, and fear (American Psychiatric Association 1994).

Having defined traumatic stressors, the DSM then had to specify the kinds of exposure to them that would qualify individuals for diagnoses of PTSD. While the DSM-III required that persons experience devastating events firsthand, the DSM III-R extended this diagnosis to persons whose friends or kin had been harmed or who had witnessed or learned of others' involvements in physical violence or accidents (American Psychiatric Association 1980, 1987).[15] Further, in contrast with the DSM III, the DSM III-R and DSM IV no longer required that individuals sustain life-threatening injuries, but only that they had been exposed to "serious threats" to their lives or "physical integrity" (American Psychiatric Association 1987:247, 1994:424).

These changes – which made subjective perceptions of stressors, indirect exposure, and threats of injury sufficient bases for diagnoses of PTSD – significantly expanded the concept of psychological trauma. While these more inclusive definitions may have better reflected actual diagnostic practices (Young 2001), the resultant "conceptual bracket creep" (McNally 2003:231) also guaranteed that higher numbers of persons would be diagnosed with PTSD. Rising rates of diagnosis, in turn, attracted public and professional attention and stimulated research on the disorder. From 1987 to 2000, the number of scientific articles published annually on PTSD jumped from just over 100 to nearly 600 (Lamprecht & Sack 2002).

The above sections seem to suggest that there was a broad resurgence of interest in trauma-related disorders among American mental health professionals toward the end of the twentieth century. However, despite the clear proliferation of psychological constructs, categories, publications, organizations, and interest groups focused on psychic trauma, it remained peripheral to basic mental health training. Though a small group of mental health professionals was drawn to volunteer after 9/11 because of previous work treating persons who had endured disasters, wars, violence, or abuse, most had no such expertise. Many therapists who were otherwise highly skilled and experienced had little understanding of the ways in which violent incidents affected the mind. The shortage of qualified therapists after 9/11 was exacerbated by the fact that some disaster relief organizations refused to take on practitioners who had responded to prior catastrophes, but who had not completed their specific training programs. Similarly, managed care companies were reluctant to refer patients to therapists who specialized in trauma, but who did not belong to their provider networks (J. Miller 2002).

Further, even though some mental health professionals were experienced in delivering trauma treatments, or in responding to disasters, they had never encountered an event like 9/11. Therapists who had treated veterans of Vietnam had addressed horrors in a distant past, and in a faraway place, from which they were safely separated. Those who had assisted relatives of homicide victims had dealt with shock and fury, but on a drastically smaller scale. Therapists who had worked with survivors of torture or abuse were unaccustomed to patients who lacked intimate contact with those inflicting pain, while those who had aided hurricane victims in rural areas were unsure how to handle persons wounded by a terrorist strike in the heart of New York City. Although they tried to adapt their knowledge to fit the situation at hand, they recognized their short-comings in addressing the attack's immediate and persisting repercussions for both individuals and communities. Indeed, even when trauma emerged as the favored term for describing 9/11's psychological effects, and even when mental health professionals – as well as public health experts, general practitioners, disaster responders, the media, local government officials, and federal agency personnel – strongly urged New Yorkers to enter psychological treatment, most therapists on hand lacked the conceptual and practical tools to effectively treat their distress.

CONTROVERSIES IN TRAUMA

The lengthy neglect of psychic trauma in the field of mental health contributed to a lack of consensus among therapists on this topic. In fact, a number of key disagreements concerning the causes, characteristics, and treatment of trauma had yet to be resolved when the World Trade Center attack occurred. At the most basic level, mental health professionals did not agree as to how broadly or how narrowly trauma should be defined. As discussed earlier, conflicting ideas regarding the central features of traumatic stressors, exposures, and injuries resulted in shifting diagnostic criteria for posttraumatic stress disorder from one edition of the *Diagnostic and Statistical Manual* to the next. Yet no matter how these criteria were altered, they invariably drew complaints from practition-ers. When the DSM III-R (American Psychiatric Association 1987) introduced PTSD criteria that were significantly broader than those in its predecessor, the DSM III (American Psychiatric Association 1980), some mental health professionals called for additional expansion; they contended that the new list of stressors and symptoms still covered no more than "the tip of the iceberg" (Lamprecht & Sack 2002:232). In contrast, many of their colleagues complained that the revised diagnostic criteria made notions of trauma too elastic, engen-dering "careless overuse" (Boulanger 2002a:19). They insisted on reserving this term for circumstances so extreme that individuals who were subjected to them feared annihilation. Moreover, they rejected standardized notions of trauma that reduced traumatic reactions to a preset list of distinct symptoms. In their view, such reactions were not discrete aspects of personal experience, but rather constituted a totalizing loss of self. For psychiatrist Robert Lifton, who studied survivors of Hiroshima and veterans of the Vietnam War, extraordinarily traumatic experiences cleaved the self in two, creating "a second self" (Caruth 1995a:137) that was entirely dissimilar from the one that existed before. Put differently, experiences of this nature entailed "the death of the self" (Langer 1997:56). Having "perforate[d] the psyche," they caused a "radical break in being" (Tarantelli 2003:916) and destroyed the individual's sense of continuity, predictability, agency, efficacy, and safety (Boulanger 2002b; Thomas 2002). The result was a "life within death" (Tarantelli 2003:916) where there was no longer any boundary between being alive and being deceased (Langer 1997), where trust in others was obliterated, and where pain and danger were ever present.

In spite of therapists' objections that more inclusive notions of trauma trivialized the term, the DSM III-R and subsequent editions further enlarged their scope by adding the provision that direct, personal experiences of traumatic stressors were unnecessary to qualify for diagnoses of PTSD (American Psychiatric Association 1987, 1994, 2000). This new provision, which held that individuals could be traumatized by learning about, or witnessing, close associates' stressful experiences, stimulated interest in indirect psychic trauma. It also led to the conceptualization of several specific varieties of indirect trauma, some of which were transmitted from one individual to another and others that tended to spread across particular social groups. In "intergenerational trauma," parents who had been affected by interpersonal violence or atrocities unintentionally inflicted their injuries on their children by continually exposing them to their suffering (Danieli 1998). In cases of "vicarious trauma" or "secondary trauma," emotional wounds spread horizontally through close relationships, moving from husbands to their wives or from patients to their therapists (Figley 1995; McCann & Pearlman1990; Pfefferbaum et al. 2002). "Insidious trauma" involved the proliferation of psychological symptoms within disempowered populations that were constantly subjected to assaults, discrimination, and oppression (Brown 1995; Miliora 2000), whereas "collective trauma" entailed the traumatization of entire communities following mass exposure to warfare or catastrophe (Dickson-Gomez 2002; Erikson 1976, 1995). Such innovative conceptions aggravated disputes surrounding the definition of trauma. Although therapists who were interested in widening the range of persons who could be identified as traumatized readily accepted these new conceptions, they were anathema to those who sought to clearly distinguish events that were merely distressing from those that shattered the self (Boulanger 2002a).

A second area of disagreement among mental health professionals concerned which particular individuals were most likely to sustain traumatic injuries after experiencing catastrophic stressors. Research had showed that a minority of adults developed psychiatric disorders as the result of such events; one study found that, of the nearly 90% of Americans exposed to traumatic incidents, only 14% suffered from full-blown PTSD (McNally 2003; Yehuda 1999). Yet, successive editions of the *Diagnostic and Statistical Manual* failed consistently to specify which individuals were more likely to develop traumatic reactions; for example, whether individuals with preexisting psychiatric conditions (American Psychiatric Association 1980, 1987), or whether those who were physically closer to calamities were at greater psychological risk (American Psychiatric Association 1994).

While the editions of the DSM were equivocating, mental health professionals with varying theoretical orientations were taking firm, and opposing, positions on the subject. According to therapists who thought that mental disorders in adults resulted from childhood wounds, persons whose coping capacities had been compromised by early assaults and catastrophes were most likely to develop PTSD. In their view, no matter how overpowering the stressor, how direct its impact, or how prolonged the exposure, individuals without histories of emotional damage would not be seriously affected (Boulanger 2002a). Other therapists disagreed, contending that everyone had "a breaking point"; that even individuals without prior psychological injuries had limited capacities to tolerate extraordinary stress and could be severely wounded by devastating events (Lamprecht & Sack 2002:225). Contesting both these perspectives were mental health professionals who linked differential risk for PTSD to preexisting susceptibilities that were physiological or neuroanatomical rather than psychological. They argued that just as some people were predisposed to cardiac disease because of malformed hearts, others were vulnerable to traumatic stress because of abnormal brains (Young 2001). Research suggesting that PTSD ran in families, and that people with PTSD were born with smaller hippocampi, the part of the brain involved with emotion and memory, or had lower baseline levels of cortisol, the hormone released at times of stress to prevent the formation of frightening memories, provided putative evidence for this disorder's biological and genetic bases (McNally 2003; Yehuda 1999, 2000).

Determining which particular persons or populations are most susceptible to PTSD clearly has critical implications for service delivery following disasters and atrocities that affect hundreds or thousands of people. Such knowledge allows for targeted interventions to those who are most at risk for traumatic injuries and is of special value where mental health resources are limited. Yet ongoing debates concerning the etiology and probabilities of traumatization represent more than practical concerns. Conflicting positions and views also reflect divergent moral assumptions regarding the nature of human beings and the responsibilities of societies. When conventional psychological theories propose that children who resolve unconscious conflicts, enjoy secure attachments, develop basic trust, receive positive reinforcement, and, above all, do not suffer assaults or abuse will be sufficiently prepared to handle the calamities they confront as adults, they outline possibilities for preventing emotional harm. However, these theories fail to acknowledge that larger social factors, from discrimination to endemic violence, inflict psychological damage. New neurobiological theories of PTSD also reaffirm traditional views. By locating the causes of traumatic reactions in the tissues and transmitters of the brain, they associate PTSD with individuals' internal deficiencies rather than with destructive social and political environments. These conceptions make some mental health professionals uncomfortable because they challenge PTSD's fundamental premise: that powerful external events, in and of themselves, produce lasting mental distress (Yehuda 1999).

Whether the recent emphasis on the organic rather than the sociopolitical reflects the experiences of mental health professionals who have not faced continual violence, and whose safety has not been regularly threatened, cannot be determined here. But the consequences are clear. Theories of traumatic injury that look inward emphasize individuals' psychological or biological fragilities rather than the harm caused by occurrences in their social and political worlds. Accordingly, such theories offer less incentive to reduce the prevalence of violence, to modify deleterious social conditions, or to hold governments responsible for injuries that citizens sustain on the nation's behalf – whether in warfare or as the result of various acts of mass violence.

Lingering disagreements regarding which persons are more likely to develop trauma-related disorders perhaps are also linked to the fact that, as noted above, most people who are exposed to life-threatening stressors either maintain their emotional stability or experience minor problems from which they recover rapidly without professional help. Those who point to such findings often claim that it is less important to understand susceptibilities to traumatic injuries than it is to promote psychological resilience. There has been little research on this topic, and some mental health professionals have called for more extensive studies of the protective and adaptive mechanisms that permit individuals to withstand extremely stressful events (Bonanno 2004; Lamprecht & Sack 2002; Sommers & Satel 2005).

In addition to mental health professionals' conflicting views concerning how trauma should be defined and who is most likely to be traumatized, they also disagree as to how traumatic injuries should be treated. At the time of the 2001 attack, there was little definitive evidence either supporting or refuting the effectiveness of specific psychological interventions for victims of large-scale assaults and disasters (Ballenger et al. 2002). The National Institute of Mental Health (NIMH), the government agency charged with protecting the nation's psychological well-being, had acknowledged that, in the decade preceding 9/11, rising numbers of Americans had been exposed to school shootings, workplace shootings, and other acts of mass violence. However, it had yet to systematically evaluate the various kinds of mental health treatment that typically were provided following such events (National Institute of Mental Health [NIMH] 2002), including critical incident stress debriefing, supportive therapy, psychoeducation, cognitive behavioral therapy, exposure therapy, eye movement desensitization and reprocessing, and psychotropic medications (cf. Chemtob, Tolin, van der Kolk, & Pitman 2000; Foa et al. 1999; Foa, Keane, & Friedman 2000; Mitchell 1983; van der Kolk 2002; Yehuda 2002; Zoellner, Fitzgibbons, & Foa 2001).

The failure to assess these interventions is somewhat understandable. Identifying the best mental health practices depends on systematic data collection from a series of carefully designed and implemented randomized, controlled trials (NIMH 2002). Yet there are substantial logistical barriers to executing such trials in chaotic crisis situations in which injuries are widespread, as well as ethical concerns that potentially traumatized persons who have just survived a catastrophe will be psychologically wounded by participating in research (Collogan et al. 2004). Accordingly, although the NIMH recognized that mental health professionals had "key roles to play" on disaster and mass violence management teams, it still had not determined the most basic features of a mental health response, including "what should be done and why?" and "what should not be done and why?" (NIMH 2002:6). Moreover, it appeared to be more interested in evaluating existing interventions than in creating new models suited to an international terrorist attack of 9/11's magnitude.

In consequence, after the 2001 World Trade Center attack, there were no established guidelines as to the kinds of mental health interventions that should be provided, when they should be provided, whether routine screenings for posttraumatic stress disorder and other mental illnesses would inhibit or hasten the onset of psychiatric symptoms, the kinds of follow-up services that were required and for whom and for how long, whether particular interventions might increase psychological harm, and what kinds of expertise mental health professionals who delivered services should have (NIMH 2002). Such questions were to be addressed at a workshop sponsored by the U.S. Departments of Defense, Justice, and Health and Human Services (including NIMH); Veterans Affairs (which included the National Center for PTSD); and the American Red

Cross and scheduled for October 30, 2001, seven weeks after the September 11 attack.

The lack of consensus in the mental health field concerning the most effective clinical models for treating trauma survivors resulted not only from the absence of evidence-based guidelines but also from wide variations in therapists' professional training and theoretical orientation. The field of mental health is multidisciplinary. Composed primarily of psychiatrists, psychologists, social workers, and psychoanalysts, it has neither a central professional organization, standardized training programs, a unified body of theory, nor uniform modes of practice. Instead, each discipline is based on distinct types of theories and bodies of knowledge, and each teaches particular sets of skills.[16] Not only are there substantive differences across professional groups, but individual therapists within them may use dissimilar clinical approaches, in some cases because they have had additional, more targeted training. After 9/11, mental health professionals' varying approaches to trauma hinged to a large extent on whether or not they had been formally trained in this area. Many who lacked such training were unfamiliar with or dismissive of specialized trauma treatments, and they employed conventional, insight-oriented techniques when treating trauma survivors. These techniques aimed to increase patients' understandings of the ways their responses to recent incidents were shaped by earlier, and thus more psychologically crucial, traumatic experiences. They included analyzing patients' wishes and fantasies, exploring their childhood histories, and interpreting the unconscious meanings of stressful occurrences. Insight-oriented therapists also encouraged patients to verbalize traumatic events and emotions, because they considered symbolization and the creation of narrative to be essential components of psychological healing.

Although commonly used in work with survivors of trauma, insight-oriented techniques contradicted basic principles of trauma treatment. Therapists who specialized in trauma asserted that, no matter how well people understood their reactions to catastrophes, such approaches were inadequate because they neglected to address the underlying biological mechanisms that automatically were triggered in response to overwhelming stress. These specialists also were concerned that encouraging patients to verbalize catastrophic experiences without first establishing a sense of safety and a trusting clinical relationship could be counterproductive, causing them to become retraumatized or emotionally flooded (Herman 1997; van der Kolk 2002). In contrast with insight-oriented therapists who interpreted patients' responses to new stressors primarily in terms of early childhood injuries, trauma therapists emphasized the psychic damage inflicted by recent events. Moreover, while insight-oriented therapists analyzed the deeper meanings of intrusive memories, nightmares, and flashbacks, therapists who specialized in trauma were more likely to view these symptoms as neurobiological reactions that were devoid of psychological significance. Lastly, where traditional therapists examined patients' unconscious motivations – for example, exploring whether women subjected to domestic violence wished to be abused – trauma therapists flatly rejected any suggestion that patients were to blame for the brutalities they suffered. Rather than offering interpretation and analysis or seeing current disturbances chiefly through the lens of previous ones, therapists who specialized in trauma taught patients specific techniques for separating the past from the present, diminishing physiological reactions, and identifying the circumstances that triggered them.

The existence of fundamentally divergent approaches to trauma-related disorders, combined with the absence of reliable data on effective trauma interventions, impeded resolution of key disputes on the treatment of psychic trauma. James L. Stone, who was Commissioner of the New York State Office of Mental Health at the time of the attack, deplored the "disappointingly low" level of consensus as to how best to intervene. He stated that such disagreements among mental health professionals were "unpalatable under the best of circumstances," but "verge[d] on irresponsibility" at a time of a national catastrophe (Stone 2005:xlviii). In practical terms, the low level of consensus meant that New York City therapists who embarked on frantic searches for clear and dependable information on the best clinical models to use in assisting persons who were injured in the World Trade Center attack were unable to find it. As a result, multiple and contrasting treatment approaches, none of which were grounded in hard evidence and many of which were delivered by therapists without relevant clinical training and experience, flourished after 9/11.

THE MEDICALIZATION OF 9/11

Although the mental health field had paid insufficient attention to trauma, had few practitioners trained in trauma, and lacked a reliable base of knowledge on the treatment of trauma survivors, trauma became the hottest topic in the field of mental health soon after 9/11.[17] In response to the anxious suffering they observed in patients, to rapidly published studies showing elevated rates of PTSD symptoms among New York City residents (Galea et al. 2002; Goodnough 2002; Schuster et al. 2001), and to forecasts of further terrorist strikes, metropolitan area therapists and their professional organizations quickly put together numerous conferences, lectures, courses, workshops, seminars, and trainings on trauma and PTSD.[18] At the same time, several mental health professionals announced their "self-proclaimed expertise" in this area

(Danieli & Dingman 2005a:3). As one therapist observed, suddenly "every Tom, Dick and Harry was setting up some kind of trauma center." Without a centralized bureau of mental health statistics, it is impossible to ascertain exactly how many individuals received trauma-related diagnoses following 9/11. Yet there is no doubt that within mental health circles, and in the larger public domain, concepts of trauma were predominant in describing the suffering caused by the attack.

In some sense, widespread usages of concepts of trauma and of other categories of mental disorder after 9/11 should not have been surprising. The voices of the injured, where not rendered fully mute, cannot emerge from catastrophes until they find ways to articulate the wounds they have sustained. That they do so by "anchoring their discourses" to existing "genres of mourning and lamentation" (Das 2000:205) speaks to the role of cultures in transforming affects and experiences that are chaotic, incomprehensible, and unbearable into socially recognized constructs and symbols (Obeysekere 1985). Whether or not the United States truly is "one nation under therapy" (Sommers & Satel 2005), mental health professionals in this country – and most famously in New York City – have made it their vocation to take the measure of troubling states of mind; to give them formal classifications and names; to assess their precipitants, gravity, and chronicity; to enumerate their key features; to determine their impacts on being and relationship; and to provide socially acceptable remedies. With its authoritative vocabularies of illnesses, symptoms, and pains, the field of mental health, to a far greater degree than other fields, provided a set of ready-made discourses to articulate the emotional agonies the attack engendered.

But these usages had obvious drawbacks. By defining terrorist attacks as "primarily mental health emergencies" (Danieli & Dingman 2005a:5), their myriad and collective economic, social, and political impacts were subsumed under the frameworks of psychiatric disorders. Similarly, by diagnosing people destabilized by this devastating attack with PTSD and other individual mental disorders, and by recommending professional treatment, an international act of mass violence was reduced to a personal medical event.

To be sure, medicalization – the process whereby people who experience a wide range of emotional, social, moral, existential, and behavioral difficulties are turned into patients with psychiatric illnesses (Kleinman 1988:26) – did not originate on September 11, 2001. Throughout the past 100 years, the parameters of psychiatry have been radically expanded, medicalizing ever larger portions of the human behavioral repertoire. Toward the end of the 19th century, medical doctors began to focus on notions of normal functioning and on returning malfunctioning bodies to "normal working order" (Foucault,1963/1994:35).

Psychiatrists readily took up this project. As they constructed new standards of psychological normality and identified deviations from them, the number of illness categories multiplied. From the 19th century to the end of the 20th, behaviors and states previously attributed to evil, eccentricity, passion, or possession increasingly were viewed as symptoms of mental diseases. At the beginning of this period, psychiatrists in the United States and Europe recognized only a handful of mental disorders; when the DSM IV-TR was published in 2000, it contained roughly 300 varieties (American Psychiatric Association 2000). And while the second edition of the *Diagnostic and Statistical Manual*, published in 1968, had fewer than 150 pages, the DSM IV-TR has nearly one thousand. Since the end of the 1980s, there has been a growing tendency to medicalize individuals' responses to natural disasters, and to diagnose those who are psychologically devastated with PTSD (Breslau 2000). More recently, acts of mass violence also have been medicalized. After the 1995 bombing of the Murrah Building in Oklahoma City, many mental health professionals viewed the abject grief of those whose friends and relatives perished in the attack as a symptom of PTSD, rather than as an appropriate emotional reaction to a horrifying, earth-shattering loss (Linenthal 2001). Yet not all mental health professionals approved of medicalizing the World Trade Center attack. Therapists' objections are discussed in Chapter 6, and the broader political implications of medicalization are examined in Chapter 7.

Despite advancing medicalization, the prevalence of such discourses related to PTSD and other psychiatric disorders could not conceal the extent to which government mental health agencies were unprepared to respond to a large-scale terrorist attack in a densely populated urban environment. The deployment of basic vocabularies of psychological injury could not compensate for an underdeveloped mental health infrastructure, for inadequate emergency mental health plans, or for the shortage of mental health professionals who were experienced in trauma or in community mental health, disaster mental health, and public mental health. Indeed, in the immediate wake of the attack, the New York State Office of Mental Health had to organize service delivery, set up disaster mental health trainings for thousands of therapists, design public educational materials, create data collection procedures, and develop treatment protocols "from scratch" (Felton 2004:152).

New York City mental health professionals who wanted to help relieve the emotional misery caused by the attack found themselves in similar positions. Working as volunteers in unfamiliar settings, and in an unprecedented and catastrophic situation, they lacked suitable ways to intervene. As they struggled to comfort the terrorized, the disoriented, the numbed, and the bereaved, many felt that they had no choice but to "make it up as we went along." "None of the old models worked," one therapist said. "We were just going by the seat of our pants." Some attempted to acquire relevant knowledge and skills as rapidly as possible. They surfed the Internet for information on how survivors of prior disasters were treated, looked at psychological research on the Oklahoma City bombing, read everything they could find on crisis intervention, and signed up for crash courses in trauma.

Although some mental health professionals keenly felt their lack of preparedness after September 11, they did not let it interfere with their wish to help. And while many of them claimed that they offered their professional services for the good of their city and their country, mental health professionals also may have seen opportunities in this profound community and national crisis. American society commonly is portrayed as saturated in the psychotherapeutic (Ingleby 1995; Sommers & Satel 2005), yet in the decade before the attack, many mental health professionals had fallen on hard times. They had witnessed the demise of foundational Freudian theories, the decline of long-term psychotherapies, the sharp reduction in insurance coverage for psychological treatments, and the hugely successful marketing of psychotropic medications as faster acting, more effective, and less expensive than talk therapies. But 9/11 resulted in a rare public validation of therapists' distinctive expertise. The Bush administration, which before the attack had paid scant attention to mental health, was suddenly promoting it on a grand scale. The federal government identified 9/11 as a mental health crisis, recognized mental health as a key component of public health, openly acknowledged psychiatric illnesses such as posttraumatic stress disorder and depression, provided moneys to educate people about them, and supplied an array of services to treat them. Government endorsements of mental health treatments to alleviate the suffering caused by the attack created new, and newly legitimate, demands for psychological services. New Yorkers in distress were urged to get themselves to a therapist.

Whether motivated by altruism or self-interest, or whether they simply saw themselves as the occupational group "professionally involved with horror" (Sebald 2003:81), therapists discovered ways to be of service after the attack on the World Trade Center. If there really are "eight million 9/11 stories" in New York City (Rich 2002), then uncounted numbers of local psychotherapists have listened repeatedly, over long periods of time, to many of the most traumatic. The following chapters contain the stories of the therapists themselves, as well as the larger story of mental health after 9/11.

CHAPTER 2

Volunteers for America

⟳

O N THE MORNING OF September 11, 2001, the individuals and organizations that should have known the most about unfolding events, so that they might have had the chance to influence their course, were often the least informed. New York City air traffic controllers did not know that airplanes had been hijacked and were heading their way; their New England colleagues had failed to notify them (Dwyer & Flynn 2005). Government employees, even those directly concerned with national security, were not advised about the first plane that hit the Trade Center by specialized intelligence agencies; instead, they learned about it by watching the Cable News Network (9/11 Commission 2004). First responders who rushed to the scene also lacked critical information. Firefighters standing at the bottom of the north tower could not see the enormous gash near its top, some ninety floors above them; those who ran inside the building were cut off from breaking news because their radios malfunctioned in skyscrapers. Police officers who were aloft in helicopters circulating the tower, and who had a clear sense of the devastation, failed to warn firefighters about it. People inside the towers, whose offices were on the floors that were closest to the airplanes' impact, often knew little about what had happened. Though they were knocked off their chairs by the force of the crash, or were deafened by sounds of screeching metal, or felt heat so intense it singed papers on their desks, or felt the building sway, or saw people falling through the sky past their windows, many learned what had hit them only after speaking to friends and relatives – some of whom were thousands of miles away – by telephone (Dwyer & Flynn 2005).

Mental health professionals learned of the attack in a variety of ways. Many who were at work when the first plane hit at 8:46 in the morning heard the news from patients who arrived for their appointments, or from patients who called to cancel them fearing that further attacks would occur. Some therapists witnessed the attack firsthand. One therapist saw both planes hit the towers from a corner outside his downtown apartment. After the first tower collapsed, he immediately joined the masses of people walking silently uptown to get as far away from the catastrophe as possible. A second therapist who worked a few blocks from the Trade Center heard the crash and felt its impact. When he looked out his window, he saw a hole in a tower that was on fire; when the tower fell, and the air filled with smoke and debris, he saw soot pile up "like a bizarre kind of snow." A third therapist arrived at her office near the Empire State Building to see people clustered on Fifth Avenue, pointing toward the towers. When her office was evacuated because of a bomb threat, she walked miles to her apartment in Brooklyn. While crossing the Manhattan Bridge she turned around and saw the towers burning, but could not believe her eyes. A fourth therapist was walking to work in Greenwich Village when she saw a woman running down the street and shouting, "They hit the Pentagon, we're under attack! New York is under attack!"

Once they learned of the attack, therapists responded in different ways. Some locked up their private offices and raced to find their children. One walked 70 blocks uptown to pick up her daughter from school, passing through streets where throngs of people moved "like mummies," where city buses carried passengers who were bloodied, where shops and restaurants already were shuttered, and where the National Guard was out in force. Therapists who were too frightened to stay at work, or who wanted to be with their families, called all their patients to make sure they were safe before canceling their sessions and heading home. But other therapists thought that they had an obligation to be of assistance to their patients, or to the larger metropolitan community, in a time of profound crisis and uncertainty. As one therapist said, "This is my specialty. If I don't do this, who is going to do it?" A therapist who specialized in trauma added, "I was one of the few people in the city who really knew what was needed."

VOLUNTEERS FOR AMERICA

Perhaps the majority of the 9,000 therapists who went to the Red Cross of Greater New York on the morning of 9/11 to volunteer their services similarly thought that they knew what was needed. Even those who lacked specialized disaster mental health experience, or expertise in the treatment of trauma, acute stress, or bereavement, claimed that their basic clinical skills qualified them to intervene. So did their personal characteristics; they described themselves as "tough" or "level-headed" or "effective in crisis." However, their motives for volunteering went beyond pure altruism. Several therapists volunteered not only because they wanted to help others but also because they thought that it might benefit them. Some simply wanted to witness "the most significant event in our nation's recent history." Others saw volunteering as a personal test; it was a way to expand "your vision and your empathy, your capability and your insight," and they wanted to be "changed by it." Intervening in the wake of this crisis also offered therapists an unusual sense of power and gratification. Unlike the long-term psychotherapies they provided, where patients often progressed at a crawl, in disaster relief work "you can very quickly see some results for what you're doing." One therapist noted her "Statue of Liberty complex – you know, give me your tired, your poor, I'm going to rescue everybody" – thus voicing the common "illusion" that mental health professionals could magically heal individuals' devastating injuries (Frawley-Odea 2004:86). Still others were drawn to volunteer by the "lure" of traumatic events (Thomas 2002:1). They thrived on being in the thick of catastrophes, especially when it made them "feel like a part of something big." Those who were "addicted to adrenaline" enjoyed the "energy around crisis," and found situations of extreme stress "a high." There is a "pleasure component" in trauma, one said. "There is an excitement" that "buoys you up" due to the instantaneous connections, shared sense of purpose, and heightened group identifications that surface in the wake of disasters.[1]

Moreover, given that the scope of the disaster was incomprehensible, many therapists realized that the only way to grasp what had happened was to get as close to it as possible. As one therapist said,

"I knew that if I went and I sat and I listened and I talked to the fire-fighters and the cops I could understand better what happened. It would help me, selfishly, process what had happened."

They also sought to manage their personal emotional reactions. Immersing themselves in the psychic pains of others allowed mental health professionals to ward off their own panic, shock, and anguish – they preferred to "take action," rather than to "stand back" and face their despair. The therapist who had seen the entire attack from his nearby Tribeca apartment said that his work had "sort of a driven quality," which was "about staying out of my own head for a while." Assuming roles as professional helpers gave therapists a great sense of control and diminished their feelings of vulnerability; if they were capable of helping others, then they could be sure that they were not seriously damaged.[2] Finally, therapists viewed the opportunity to serve as volunteers as a boon for their beleaguered field. For once, mental health professionals, "who were usually under rocks as far as everybody is concerned," were in a position to contribute to the well-being of their society, and to be publicly recognized for it.

Although many mental health professionals were proud of their field's swift and generous response to the World Trade Center attack, not all of them agreed either that they had the capacity, or that it was their duty, to donate their services to the community following this unexpected act of mass violence. One therapist doubted her ability to help others, since "I was just as traumatized as the next person." A second insisted that before rushing in with psychological assistance, it was crucial to sort out "just what is the appropriate response of a trained mental health professional in a situation of vast public import." While acknowledging that, "if you didn't get on board and want to do outreach . . . and think of people as being terribly traumatized, you were such an outlier," he continued,

"My response was, I don't know what the hell happened . . . I honestly didn't feel any responsibility to do anything publicly. And I wasn't sure how it affected me . . . I wasn't on the edge emotionally, but I was thinking, If this is a war, what am I going to do? What risk am I in? . . . I wanted to figure out what was going on."

Another therapist was "horrified" by the swarms of "undisciplined" mental health professionals who were determined to assist the psychologically wounded when they lacked the relevant clinical qualifications, were themselves emotionally destabilized, or were incapable of listening to individuals' accounts of the attack "without going and blabbing to someone else."[3] And a third compared mental health professionals who traded stories of atrocities to soldiers who swapped tales of war; in both cases, telling such stories was meant to convince their audience of their special abilities and grit. Whatever their motivations, for legions of mental health professionals, September 11, 2001, clearly was a day when "tragedy became a draw" (Thomas 2002:2).

THE RED CROSS SCENE

The Red Cross describes its response to the World Trade Center attack as immediate and efficient. It states that by 11:00 A.M. on 9/11, the Disaster Service staff had launched the first part of its response, and that the staff of the Red Cross in Greater New York was activated for emergency service (American Red Cross in Greater New York 2004b). Many therapists who rushed to Red

Cross headquarters on Amsterdam Avenue, however, encountered quite a different scene, which they described as disorganized and chaotic. Although the building's outside plaza and internal offices had filled rapidly with psychologists, social workers, and psychiatrists clamoring to volunteer their services, "there was nobody who could tell you what to do." One therapist noted that "they had far too many therapists, and they didn't have a clue how to use them."[4]

The chaos that therapists found on Amsterdam Avenue was partly due to the fact that the Red Cross – whose mission is to help people "prevent, prepare for, and respond to emergencies," and which mobilizes relief for more than 70,000 disasters per year in dozens of countries – was not prepared for a catastrophe of this scale. The organization constantly improves its training programs and services so that its more than one million volunteers can better respond to future calamities (American Red Cross n.d.; Charity Wire n.d.). Yet even Red Cross officers who were responsible for conceiving of, and preparing for, new kinds of disasters "never imagined anything" like 9/11 in terms of victims' emergent and long-range needs (Lower Manhattan Info n.d.). The chaos at Red Cross headquarters also stemmed from the fact that New York City airports, bridges, and tunnels were closed on September 11, preventing national Red Cross leaders, including its most seasoned disaster responders, from getting into town. Senior management from national headquarters in Washington, D.C., could not arrive until September 13, when a train loaded with emergency supplies, which was donated by Amtrak, brought them to the city. An additional 467 staff members and volunteers from all over the country did not arrive until the following day (American Red Cross in Greater New York 2004b). As a result, the New York City chapter of the Red Cross, which lacked experience in responding to massive disasters, was responsible for providing relief in the attack's immediate aftermath. To further complicate matters, sending psychotherapists to deliver mental health services to direct victims of catastrophes was something of a departure for the Red Cross. In the past, it had mobilized mental health professionals primarily to aid its own workers when they became anxious or overwhelmed while serving at disaster sites.

Because of their inexperience with situations of this nature, local Red Cross leaders were unable to quickly determine the kinds of mental health services that were needed, how and where to provide them, or how to use the thousands of therapists who had suddenly appeared on their doorstep. When they identified sites in need of mental health professionals, they could not readily determine which ones to send. With "everybody and his uncle claiming to be an expert on trauma," they could not always distinguish between therapists who had expertise in responding to massive catastrophes, or in treating traumatized individuals, and therapists who did not. Moreover, standard Red Cross procedures called for them to accept only mental health professionals who had completed its particular crisis intervention training programs. But in this case of extreme emergency, and under pressure from therapists who were begging to be used, the Red Cross began "relaxing its rules" and accepting anyone with a valid state license. This requirement still posed disadvantages, as it eliminated therapists who specialized in trauma but whose licenses had expired, as well as psychoanalysts with pertinent skills who did not have a license.[5] One psychoanalyst who had treated traumatized patients for more than 20 years noted that he was rejected as a volunteer, while freshly licensed clinical novices were accepted; he likened this situation to "going to the dentist's office and having the secretary drill your teeth." Not only did the Red Cross dispatch therapists with insufficient training and experience but it also had no means of controlling the interventions they offered, leaving open the possibility that they would exacerbate rather than ease individuals' reactions to the attack.

As local Red Cross leaders frantically struggled to determine which mental health professionals to send, where to send them, and how to get them to their destinations – this itself was a challenge as the subways had been halted, numerous roadblocks had been erected, and streets near the World Trade Center were impassable – therapists stood around for hours, "signing a lot of forms" and waiting impatiently for assignments. Most of all, they waited to be given a Red Cross badge. Therapists coveted this badge because it granted them access to highly restricted locations, including the areas closest to the Trade Center. But they wanted it for another reason as well. The Red Cross enjoyed a good reputation among police officers, firefighters, and other first responders. By wearing the badge and identifying themselves as Red Cross workers, therapists instantly gained credibility with those who otherwise might have avoided them. In the end, their perseverance paid off; while at first therapists had to be "persistent" to get a badge, before long, in desperation, Red Cross staff "started giving us badges and then assigning us."

THAT DAY

Even therapists who secured Red Cross badges, and who were sent to specific locations, were not guaranteed opportunities to assist injured civilians. Like everyone else who responded to the catastrophe, the Red Cross could not accurately determine the lethality of the attack, the number of survivors, the nature and severity of their wounds, or the routes they would take to escape. As a result, their decisions about where to place therapists, and about the kinds of mental health services to provide, were flawed. Some therapists were directed to destinations that were unreachable because streets all over town had been barricaded. Others were sent to sites that already had been evacuated, or where the people they were supposed to serve never appeared. Although hundreds of thousands of people were thought to be in acute distress, therapists who were sent out on Red Cross assignments were not always able to find them.

One therapist and five of his colleagues had headed to the Red Cross shortly after learning of the attack, hoping to offer assistance in the neighborhood of the twin towers. The Red Cross first put them on a van going to the World Trade Center, but as that area grew increasingly chaotic, they were reassigned to Pennsylvania Station. From their posts in this transportation hub, they were expected to help commuters who were injured, in shock, and trying to get home. They asked the Red Cross representative on site how they should proceed, but "she didn't know what we were supposed to be doing" and told them "to figure it out for ourselves." Anticipating thousands of survivors, these therapists developed a plan; they would assess individuals' physical and mental status, help them contact their families, and "defuse the tremendous anxiety that would have built up around the catastrophe." They also aimed to help survivors "sort through" what had happened, although "we were sorting it through for ourselves at pretty much the same time." Indeed, they knew less about the smoke and the fires, the falling bodies and debris, and the collapse of the towers than those they intended to help.

As they roamed around Pennsylvania Station searching for World Trade Center survivors, they spotted only a few. They learned to identify them by looking down at their feet, because those who escaped the area had white dust on their shoes. But contrary to Red Cross expectations, Pennsylvania Station was virtually empty. Those who survived the attack had fled immediately, walking over bridges or hopping on trucks and ferries to get out of Manhattan as quickly as possible. Few were in Penn Station taking their usual commuter trains, because "no one relied on traditional transportation." After a half- hour in the station, these therapists had seen so few survivors that they concluded that it was "a waste of time" to remain there. Frustrated that the Red Cross had failed to connect them with people who needed help, they decided that they would no longer take its direction. Yet they continued to identify themselves as Red Cross volunteers, and to show their Red Cross badges, because "frankly, it just gained us admittance."

After an unsuccessful attempt "to wrestle down an ambulance to bring us to the Trade Center," these six therapists set out in search of the wounded, walking through streets where "nothing was moving," and where sirens were the only sounds that interrupted the silence. After deciding that those who were injured in the attack would be taken to nearby hospitals, they walked from one hospital to another, past the garbage trucks blocking their entrances, and offered psychological assistance. Though their offers were rejected repeatedly, in the mid-afternoon they arrived at a small hospital whose emergency medical personnel had responded to the attack. One of its paramedics was missing, and one of its ambulances had been destroyed. Several workers were wounded, and others who had run for their lives when the towers had imploded were in a state of shock. For the next few weeks, at the hospital director's request, they worked with a group of 35 staff members; many told them that this was the only place where they could talk about what they had witnessed and how it affected them.

Around 1:00 that afternoon, another therapist who for 30 years had specialized in treating catastrophic trauma walked 40 blocks from her office to Red Cross headquarters. On arriving, she found "a mob" of willing volunteers; she went upstairs, where she found "another mob." When Red Cross workers learned of her expertise in trauma, they sent her and another therapist to a pier on the Hudson River that had quickly been transformed into a morgue for victims of the attack. A Red Cross mental health officer stationed the two therapists in the makeshift morgue's reception area, instructing them to wait for victims' family members, to escort them to the doors of the morgue, and to stay there until they emerged. The therapists waited hours for ambulances transporting the deceased to arrive, at times standing on a balcony that faced downtown and watching thick smoke curl over the city. By 8:00 in the evening no ambulances had appeared, and they went home. Later that evening, the Red Cross worker who had assigned them to the pier phoned the trauma specialist and told her not to come back the next day. Only then did she realize that no ambulances had come to the morgue because "there were no bodies."

Other therapists spent September 11 waiting to tend to the wounded at various hospitals around the city, and growing frustrated and unnerved when so few of them arrived. Rather than being inundated with wounded survivors, city hospitals were flooded with friends and relatives of persons who had been in or near the World Trade Center that morning, and who had not been heard from since. One therapist who went to help at her local hospital found numerous individuals in a "desperate search" for their kin. She became acutely aware of what they refused to see; they were "not seeing the gurneys, the empty, white, beautiful, clean linens on these tens and tens of gurneys on Seventh Avenue," and they were "not seeing that there were no victims." She noticed the flyers they carried, which featured photographs and descriptions of the missing, in case the attack had left them so disoriented and dazed that they no longer knew who they were, or where they were, but might be found and guided home. She heard them repeating the missing person's description again and again to everyone they encountered. Although she listened to their descriptions and tried to lift their spirits, she had come to a different conclusion. "I just knew they were all dead," she said.

Setting Up Services

Despite its difficulties organizing the delivery of mental health services earlier that day, by the evening of September 11, the Red Cross had set up 13 shelters for people whose homes were damaged or inaccessible, or who were stranded in the city. By the morning of September 12, the Red Cross had set up phone banks at the offices of WNET, a local television station, as well as a 24-hour Emergency Communications Center at its headquarters, for callers seeking information on the safety of their kin. Also that morning, the City of New York opened the Compassion Center in the Armory on Lexington Avenue where New Yorkers could register missing friends and relatives (American Red Cross in Greater New York 2004a). The Center was heavily trafficked; approximately 2,500 people were "processed" in one day (Hill 2002). Traffic increased a few days later, when people began to arrive from out of town. Those whose kin were still missing brought toothbrushes, combs, and clothing containing their DNA so that their remains could be identified. They also brought missing persons flyers; hundreds of them were taped to a wall outside the Armory, which seemed strangely alive with smiling faces (American Red Cross in Greater New York 2004b).

Mental health professionals were assigned to all of these sites, yet few of them were sure of their roles, and they received minimal instruction in disaster mental health. Some had expected to deliver traditional psychological treatments, but soon realized that such approaches were inappropriate. "This is not psychotherapy," one therapist stated. "You don't walk into this situation and say, 'Tell me your feelings.'" Therapists who were accustomed to treating small numbers of familiar, long-term patients in 45-minute sessions were called on to interact for a few moments with scores of strangers, who were in crisis or in shock, and who did not always want to speak with them. Their job was not to explore individuals' internal worlds, family patterns, or psychological conflicts. Instead, they were instructed to listen to persons' stories only if they volunteered them, to educate them about normal reactions to catastrophic events, to escort them from one place to another, and to serve them cookies and tea.

Therapists who staffed telephone hotlines for callers who were hoping to locate their kin found the work pressured and emotionally taxing. One hotline was located in Red Cross headquarters, which was evacuated twice due to bomb scares. The sheer number of callers was daunting; by the end of the first day, volunteers had answered approximately 43,000 calls from persons all over the country (American Red Cross in Greater New York 2004b). So were the callers' emotional states; many were sobbing, or angry, or frantic for information about friends and relatives they had not yet heard from. One therapist fell apart at the end of every call, because "people were calling and wanted help, and I didn't know where to send them." Although some therapists privately doubted that those who were still missing would be found, Red Cross policy required them to wait for an official announcement that there were no more survivors before confirming callers' worst fears. Therapists were told,

> "'Don't say you think the people are dead – even though they probably are dead – just say you don't know.' So two nights in a row it was, 'we don't know, we don't know, we don't know, we don't know, yeah, it's really tough not to know.'"

When they finally received authorized lists with the names of World Trade Center survivors, each contained slightly different information. As a result, therapists sometimes misinformed callers, for example, assuring them that their friends and relatives were alive even though they had perished in the attack.

At the Lexington Avenue Armory, mental health professionals met face to face with masses of people searching for their loved ones. They sat on one side of a table, holding the lists with the names of survivors, while friends and family members sat on the other side and priests circulated around them. Therapists were instructed "to break the news that the name wasn't on the list...as tactfully as possible." It was in the course of such conversations that many people first realized that their fiancé, or son, or mother was dead. At that point, therapists were supposed to ask them what they were going to do next, if there was anyone at home, and if they needed assistance getting there.

Many therapists were grateful that the Red Cross had taught them "what to say, what not to say, and how to engage people" in these settings. But others strongly objected to its approach to mental health. One therapist insisted that individuals who were injured or bereaved required more intensive psychological treatment than the brief and basic support provided by the Red Cross. Another rejected the Red Cross emphasis on typical responses to disasters, stating that it was imperative to examine how individuals' personal histories and psychologies shaped their emotional reactions. Yet some of their colleagues were more concerned that mental health professionals overstepped their bounds, either by imposing therapeutic contact on persons who simply wished to learn the whereabouts of their relatives, or by "trying to do far too much, when all you can do is just be there, listen, and anticipate the next few days."

NEW SERVICES

In the week after 9/11, as more and more services were offered, they were consolidated in a number of metropolitan locations.[6] Also during this period, the individuals who were affected most directly by the attack, and who were thought to be most in need of help, were sorted into different categories. "The families" referred to persons who had lost relatives in the attack, "the victims" included those who had evacuated the towers or the Trade Center area, along with those who had lost jobs or apartments, and "the rescue and recovery workers" referred to police officers, firefighters, and construction crews on duty at Ground Zero. Soon there were three new kinds of service centers, each catering primarily to persons in one of these categories.

FAMILY ASSISTANCE CENTER

The Compassion Center originally was located in the Lexington Avenue Armory, but this space quickly proved too small to accommodate everyone who poured into New York City to register missing family members and friends; at times, it was so overcrowded that masses of highly emotional people waiting to enter the building stood on lines measuring eight blocks long in four directions (Federation Reference Centre for Psychological Support n.d.). On September 17, the Compassion Center moved to a larger space, where it was combined with a host of other services and renamed the Family Assistance Center (FAC) (American Red Cross in Greater New York 2004b).

The FAC was owned by the City of New York and managed by the Mayor's Office and the American Red Cross. Erected in just a few days by an events management company that built facilities for trade shows, it was set up near West 54th Street, on Pier 94 on the Hudson River. Therapists were amazed to see this 40,000 square foot building go up "on the fly. It was incredible the amount of money that went into there, and the amount of energy," one said. The space was rapidly outfitted with plush carpeting, truckloads of computers, and private booths for people seeking updated information about their kin. Thousands of teddy bears flown in from Oklahoma City were displayed along one wall, and missing persons posters covered a wall outside. Adjacent piers held temporary government offices, and tents for the media were set up across the street (Federation Reference Centre for Psychological Support n.d.).

Open 24 hours a day, the FAC was principally designed to help "the families"; the spouses, children, parents, siblings, more distant relatives, and domestic partners of those who were known to be deceased or who still were missing.

People requesting help included not only the legal spouses of those who were lost but also the mistresses they supported "who would arrive with their children – and full evidence that these were their children – and the families didn't know anything about them." Hundreds of volunteers and city employees from more than 50 agencies provided family members with regularly scheduled briefings; legal aid; information on collecting DNA samples; assistance with the Internal Revenue Service; interpretation and translation services in Cantonese, Mandarin, and Spanish; child care; spiritual counseling; food; and free long-distance telephone service (FEMA, "Family Assistance Center," n.d.).[7] An International Family Assistance Program aided citizens of other countries who had lost relatives in the attack. It offered them airline tickets to New York as well as food and lodging in the city, and it reimbursed them for moving expenses, for funeral services, and for the repatriation of remains (Federation Reference Centre for Psychological Support n.d.). Services soon were added for individuals who had lost their homes and jobs, or who had been in the thick of the attack before escaping the Trade Center area.[8]

As many as 80 mental health professionals, including employees of city, state, and federal mental health departments and agencies, delivered psychological services at the FAC. In addition, there were numerous therapists who volunteered, like the one who had temporarily left her private practice after deciding that "if I could sit through an eight-hour shift and sit with 50 families, that was more important than seeing six patients that day." Some occasionally had the chance to provide crisis intervention, bereavement counseling, or psychiatric evaluations, but others "ended up handing out cookies, because they wanted to do something and there wasn't enough to do." Therapy animals – trained dogs, cats, and birds that were meant to comfort those who "were not inclined to interact around their losses on a verbal level" (Hill 2002) – also were on site.[9] All of these mental health services were available not only to families who were bereaved but also to mental health professionals who required psychological help at the end of their grueling shifts (Federation Reference Centre for Psychological Support n.d.; FEMA, "Advocacy Needs," n.d.; Mirabito & Rosenthal 2002).

One psychiatrist who cancelled his vacation to volunteer at the FAC spoke of the "steep learning curve" involved in delivering mental health services to vast numbers of people in crisis. Working out of makeshift offices that resembled "a field clinic," and seeing scores of devastated individuals in quick succession, made him keenly feel his lack of experience in disaster mental health. At first, he had difficulty determining which interventions would be most helpful for each particular person, as well as which might have harmful effects. He also worried that he had been "too aggressive" with people for whom it was "too early" to talk about the horrific events they had witnessed. Indeed, his inexperience had led to mistakes. For example, he had encouraged one Trade Center evacuee to tell his gruesome story immediately. Although this seemed to benefit him, it destabilized the colleague who accompanied him, as it "exposed him to the trauma he didn't need." It took a while for this psychiatrist to learn to be "more careful."

Therapists had to learn to be careful not only in asking individuals what they had witnessed but also in masking their personal reactions to an environment that they found "morbid," "bewildering," and "depressing." Their job was to shore up families who came daily to the FAC to study the latest lists of survivors, or who traveled from hospital to hospital looking for their relatives, before returning to the pier with their photographs and asking, "Have you seen my family member?" When families remained optimistic that their kin had survived the attack, and were waiting to be discovered beneath the ruins of the towers, or in a safe corner of the field of debris, therapists had to conceal their lack of hope.

But if therapists had to support families when their hope was still alive, then they also had to be available to them when they finally admitted that their relatives were lost. One therapist recalled a brother and sister who had come to the FAC to examine the lists of survivors every day for a week. On the eighth day, the whole family arrived.

> *"They came with a picture ... and they looked at the lists again, and they said, 'we went to all the hospitals, they don't have him.' And they just started to cry."*

There was a long red cloth on the floor of the pier that stretched from one end to the other, with red velvet ropes on each side. According to one therapist, whenever people walked down that line,

> *"It was when they had said, 'I know that my family member is dead, and now I want to go and see a lawyer and start the process.'"*

The process involved drawing up death certificates, which proved unusually complicated. As a rule, the New York City Medical Examiner's Office required physical evidence of a body to issue a death certificate. But in the first few weeks after the attack, little evidence was found.[10] Mayor Giuliani realized that death certificates were necessary for families to submit claims for insurance and other benefits, and that they also served an important psychological function. He assured family members who acknowledged that their relatives were dead, but who lacked the requisite proof, that they would quickly receive these certificates. In turn, the Medical Examiner's Office created special procedures to grant them (Jones 2005; Langeweische 2002). Hundreds of workers from the New York State Department of Health were sent to New York City, in part to expedite this process (Rosner & Markowitz 2006). At the same time, the National Center for Health Statistics, whose classification systems at the time of the attack did not have codes to specify terrorism as the cause of death, also instituted emergency procedures. It established a workgroup on the Classification of Death and Injury Resulting from Terrorism, which quickly developed a range of new codes to identify deaths due to terrorist acts. Given that so few intact bodies were recovered from the World Trade Center, the precise nature of each individual's fatal injury – whether it was a head wound, lacerations, severe burns, or smoke inhalation – often could not be ascertained. Consequently, the death certificates of numerous 9/11 victims were coded as "homicide, terrorism, by destruction of aircraft" (National Center for Health Statistics n.d.).

SERVICE CENTERS

While Pier 94 was intended primarily for families who were bereaved, the second week after the attack saw the opening of three new service centers offering assistance to "the victims," including people who had escaped from the towers, who had lost their jobs or their apartments, or who were having difficulty coping with the disaster. These centers provided them with cash for meals, temporary lodging, rent and mortgage payments, other living expenses, and psychological care. In contrast with Red Cross reports stating that service centers functioned efficiently (American Red Cross in Greater New York 2004b), therapists on site observed a variety of problems. For one, the service centers were so overcrowded that people in need of shelter and food sometimes waited outside all day without getting in. Confronting "the bureaucracy and the red tape" made them feel that they were "running into brick walls, which was just adding to their pain."[11] Moreover, service center staff and volunteers had no way to keep track of the "thousands and thousands of people, with thousands and thousands of needs." The lack of centralized data systems, combined with the high turnover of relief personnel, meant that individuals who returned to the center for additional assistance had to deal with new workers who did not know what kinds of compensation they were entitled to, or which paperwork they had already completed. Further, the traditional Red Cross model, which calls for helping people in the immediate crisis and then referring them to local resources, was ill suited to this situation because many city resources were overwhelmed by the attack.

Such problems intensified the pressures on mental health professionals who volunteered at these sites, and who confronted misery and devastation on an unimaginable scale. Therapists were uncertain how best to respond to the thousands of individuals, including the poor as well as the wealthy, who spoke "every language in the world," and who stood on line for hours, often in great anger and distress, to tell them,

"'I'm living on the streets, I'm stuck. I have lost all of my papers, I have lost everything, all of my identity in the World Trade Center'. Or 'I was stuck in an elevator.' Or 'I got down the stairs, and now I can't breathe... Can you give me $500, can you get me a hotel room, can you help me with my creditors?' Or 'I have no apartment, I can't get into my apartment in Battery Park City.'"

One therapist found that weeks after the attack, "an amazing number of people" had not told anyone what they had experienced, but still were utterly preoccupied by having seen Trade Center elevators full of flames, or by having been trapped in a burning lobby, or by having dodged bodies falling out of windows a hundred stories overhead. Although she thought that in these cases formal therapy sessions were advisable, she found that most people did not want them. Instead, it was necessary for mental health professionals to

"suspend all that you've ever learned about how to be in the perfect setting with the two chairs properly placed and the pristine office with the box of tissues available."

Another therapist determined that to be most helpful to people standing in endless lines, rather than waiting for them to approach to her,

"You should just work the room, which is not what any of us are trained to do... In this case, I just worked the waiting room. I just went from one person to another to another to another to another to another to another, and I would talk to 30 people in the course of four hours. And if anybody was really breaking down, or saying things that were too much for other people to handle, or talking too loud... you would pull them aside."

Yet if the experience of one New York City therapist who was on the receiving end of these services is typical, the service centers' psychological benefits derived from more than mental health professionals' specific interventions.

This therapist and his family had been severely affected by the attack: his daughter was injured, his apartment near the Trade Center was ruined, and his business was badly damaged. Every Wednesday for several weeks, he and his wife went to a service center to request financial relief. At first, he found the process "a nightmare"; "it was like a soup kitchen line, and there we were from Battery Park City – what are we doing in this line?" After standing in line for hours, they would finally get to speak with a Red Cross worker who "would literally be crying" when they described what had happened to them. The emotional power of their story evoked generous offers of help. One Red Cross worker from Texas who appeared to be a "tough guy" simply asked, "'Okay, what do you want, how much?'" After several weeks of such treatment, the therapist and his wife found themselves "weirdly looking forward to Wednesday." While they had found temporary lodging in an apartment on the Upper East Side, their new neighbors "didn't want to get near us, because we were the unwanted memory of what happened." The service center was the only place in town where they didn't feel like "outsiders," and where others struggling to cope with similar wounds were interested in their story. The therapist remembered one terrible Wednesday after the agencies had established new procedures. On arriving at the center, he and his wife were informed that they would be "maxed out," and that they no longer needed to return. This was intended as a convenience, but for them it meant losing their sole supportive community. Although their daughter had not fully recovered, their apartment was in shambles, and the business remained unstable, it was at the service center that they had begun to reconstruct their lives, their social ties, and their identities. "You mean we don't get to see you any more and come down here to the disaster center any more?" the therapist asked Red Cross workers. "Where are we going to go now?"

GROUND ZERO RESPITE CENTERS

The opening of two Respite Centers, where Ground Zero rescue workers could rest and "recharge" in the course of their 12-hour shifts at the site, occurred in the third week of September. These centers contained televisions, showers, cots, and Internet and telephone services; the Red Cross and local restaurants provided workers with meals (Lower Manhttan Info n.d.). Mental health professionals were on hand to offer crisis counseling to the police officers, firefighters, National Guard members, Army personnel, ironworkers, FBI agents, hazardous materials (HAZMAT) experts, emergency management personnel, dockworkers, and demolition specialists laboring at Ground Zero.

The Respite Centers were open all day and all night because the mammoth job of removing the ruins of the World Trade Center went on 24 hours a day.

The remains of the seven buildings that had been destroyed in the attack stood in mounds up to five stories high and penetrated six stories below the ground. This landscape of peaks and valleys, composed of shattered glass, shredded steel, and densely compacted debris, was known as "the pile." Work on the pile was exceedingly treacherous. Its hills concealed voids that were vulnerable to cave-ins; its air was made toxic by the dust of decimated buildings and their contents, and by the smoke from fires that would burn until January.[12] This work was also emotionally brutal and gruesome, as it involved the recovery of human remains, tens of thousands of which had to be painstakingly culled from the rubble (Langewiesche 2002).

Not only was their task a dangerous one, but tensions ran high among the various groups working on the pile. Firefighters resented construction crews – in their eyes, mere civilians – whose technical expertise gave them control over the cleanup, while construction crews resented firefighters' privileges at the site. Police officers were angry at firefighters because the media had cast them as heroes, and firefighters were incensed with the police for having failed to warn them that the north tower was near collapse, perhaps causing the deaths of scores of their "brothers." Moreover, the diverse groups laboring on the pile had different conceptions of their task. Construction crews viewed the site as a place full of wreckage. They wanted to clear it as quickly as possible to get New York City back on its feet.[13] Their work was a sign of their patriotism, which simultaneously broadcast their professional skills. For firefighters, the task was more personal. Almost all of them had numerous friends who were missing, and their primary aim was to rescue them. They wanted to work slowly and carefully so that they would not inadvertently injure those who remained trapped in the debris. When the rescue operation officially ended on September 29, and the search for survivors became a search for the dead, firefighters still insisted on moving slowly. They were driven to recover the bodies of all 343 of their brethren, who were lost somewhere in the pile, to give them proper burials. Firefighters used rakes and shovels to sift through small patches of rubble for fragments of tissue and bone. They were bent on preventing construction crews – who removed massive pieces of tangled steel and tall piles of pulverized concrete with 180,000-pound diesel excavators – from carting away these remains with the rest of the debris. Police officers, like firefighters, seemed to be most intent on locating their own, and both groups had their own morgue; when firefighters discovered a colleague's remains, they conducted special ceremonies. In contrast, construction crews were chiefly interested in recovering the remains of civilians who had perished in the attack. Disputes as to which of the dead were most worthy, and whose remains deserved the best treatment, led to physical fights between the groups at the site (Dwyer & Flynn 2005; Langewiesche 2002).

For therapists who were assigned to Ground Zero Respite Centers to provide psychological services to these warring factions, simply getting there proved onerous. Shortly after the attack, the Red Cross had moved its New York headquarters to Brooklyn. This meant that therapists who lived downtown within walking distance of the site first had to travel to Brooklyn, arriving hours before their shifts to be processed, before they boarded the buses that took them back to Manhattan. On their way to the Trade Center, they drove by barricaded streets where hundreds of people walked in silence. Each time a truck full of workers went by, "people applauded and held big signs" and then the silence set in again. "People were keeping vigil," one said, "and that was as close as they could get." Before entering the Respite Centers, therapists had to pass through military checkpoints that marked "the frontlines of the war." The site was divided into four quadrants, each of which had been assigned to a particular construction company. One therapist was reminded of other war zones she had seen; for a moment, she thought she was back in Bosnia, "where the Norwegian tanks are staring down at you from this sector, and the Russian tanks are staring down at you from that sector." Other therapists broke down when they arrived at the site. Some were so disoriented that they "couldn't take it in; it was in some ways like watching a movie."

One therapist was asked to visit the site for the specific purpose of urging police officers who were stationed there, and who were under considerable stress, to utilize the Respite Center's free psychological services. Donning a hardhat and a respirator, she waded through a "devastating battlefield" that was full of "things of fire." As she handed out pamphlets on mental health, and told every police officer she encountered that "it's OK to have PTSD, and it's OK to come and talk about it," the therapist was asking herself, "Is this dust on me human remains?" In spite of her efforts, most police officers acted "all macho about it," or refused to speak with "an outsider." Even those who had lost friends in the attack quickly turned away from her. "I'm not looking up," one said. "I'm going to keep working." Yet while this therapist was encouraging others to get help, she was preoccupied by a loss of her own. A patient of hers who worked near the Trade Center had been killed on 9/11. As she looked into the pile she wondered, "Is my patient down there? Are they going to find him?"

Another therapist who volunteered at Ground Zero worked from four in the afternoon until midnight in a Respite Center that was set in a condemned hotel. To guard against contaminants, the walls were lined with radiation detectors and "everything was covered with plastic – the walls, the floors, everything." On one floor of the hotel was a ballroom that had been converted into a dining room with a buffet. Although workers left their equipment outside, when they ate "all the dust and soot all over these people" was "dropping into their food."

On the next floor was a room with televisions, massage tables, booths with clean socks, reclining chairs, a nurse's station, clergy, and mental health professionals. As this therapist sat in the room, the overpowering "smell of death" gave her the sense of "being in this biological stew." She spent much of her time "trying not to vomit," or "going to the bathroom to wash my hands and wash out my nose." Her eight-hour shifts were punctuated by "Catholic priests rushing in and throwing on Red Cross jackets and rushing out," which meant that "they'd found a body or body parts."

The Red Cross had instructed therapists "to just sit down and talk" with people in the Respite Center, and some posted themselves in the dining area where workers took their breaks. One therapist observed that the different groups of workers rarely mixed; she compared them to tribes with distinctive costumes and habits. Firefighters sat at tables in huge packs, replicating the seating arrangements of their firehouse kitchens. In contrast, HAZMAT workers wearing "moon suits" sat as far away from everyone else as possible. Despite their protective uniforms, or perhaps because they were most aware of the hazardous materials at the site, they seemed to fear being contaminated by others.

Many rescue and recovery workers who did double shifts at the site labored around the clock, clearing away debris one bucketful at a time while searching for the bodies of their friends. After five or six days in a row on the pile, they spent their days off attending multiple funerals. Therapists noted that many of them were exhausted and in shock. One said that,

"All you had to do was look at the faces of any firefighter or recovery worker who was there for more than a couple of days and you saw that this was a population absolutely gripped with the despair of not finding anyone alive."

Some of them were "losing it"; they were sobbing or shaking, looking glazed and unresponsive, and "self-medicating like nobody's business." To avoid thinking about what they had found in the pile, some workers "were just going, going, going, driving themselves." Others were driving themselves because they had sustained dozens of losses. They refused to quit working until they had recovered all of their friends' remains. One therapist remarked that,

"All of the firefighters I dealt with, they had lost anywhere from two very close friends to 20 very close friends ... Some of them knew 100 people who were dead. ... The most common thing that they were willing to talk about, and you could tell that they were constantly talking about it with one another, is that you never leave anybody behind."

Another therapist realized the extent to which recovery workers were "on the edge" only when he invited a group of them to stay in his nearby apartment. One worker declined, explaining that, "we smell of death." "If we sleep here," he said, "you'll never get the smell of death out of your house." But as this therapist remarked, the worker's perceptions were distorted, because "he didn't smell of death. He just thought he did." This therapist also reported that rescue and recovery workers had broken into a diner near the Trade Center, where they went to drink after their shifts. The police refused to shut it down because they thought that the workers needed it. "That's what they were doing," the therapist said, "instead of thinking about what they were in the middle of."

Although mental health professionals at the Respite Centers were well aware of workers' anguish, they were equally aware that their help might be unwanted. They were unsure "how much to push" or how to intervene "so you didn't become a pain in the neck on the one hand, and on the other hand you were available if somebody needed you."[14] They found firefighters especially avoidant; therapists learned "never to approach a table of firemen," because "they looked real closed." One therapist who was familiar with this population stated that, even before 9/11, firefighters had not been receptive to psychological treatment, preferring to "take care of their own" by using their "very close-knit, very closed support system." "These people are rescuers," she said, who are "trained to respond to other peoples' problems." They "don't think in terms of stress," and admitting to emotional difficulties, even in the line of duty, was commonly seen as "weak." In consequence, while some rescue and recovery workers did interact with therapists, the majority of them insisted that they were fine. One therapist concluded that they simply could not afford to connect with mental health professionals about their experiences at the site. "The only way for them to survive was not to talk about it," because as soon as their breaks were over, they had to go back out to the pile.

When therapists finished their shifts, some were formally debriefed. That is, they logged their encounters with rescue and recovery workers, and were questioned by Red Cross staff members as to which interactions were the most and least difficult for them, and which interventions seemed the most and least useful to the workers. Some therapists considered the debriefings an essential "catharsis" that helped them "get rid of" some of the horrible stories they heard. Without them, they remained "full of the experience" and weren't able to "contain it and make sense of it" for themselves. One therapist learned this the hard way; certain that she could handle her volunteer work on her own, she had avoided debriefings until she unexpectedly started to weep while delivering a professional lecture. Others who skipped formal debriefings, but who processed their experiences at Ground Zero with colleagues, stopped doing so once they realized that they might be traumatizing fellow therapists. Not only did members of the Red Cross regularly debrief mental health professionals, but therapists occasionally debriefed relief workers who broke down at various sites. One therapist described a relief worker who had come to the United States as a refugee, and who during his shift at the FAC had "flashbacks of running from his country as a child, desperate and terrified that he would lose grip of his mother's hand." She advised him that if he continued to work at the FAC, he was likely to reexperience traumatic events from his past.

After being debriefed, with fires burning in the distance "in this world that's perpetually light," therapists walked through the "absolute muck" of the site and arrived at the wash stations, where they tried to clean off their shoes.[15] The absurdity of the situation was apparent to one therapist, who said,

"I'm thinking, I've just walked through toxic material. Are we both going to participate in this fiction that my shoes have just been made clean with water from a hose?"

Some mental health professionals worked long shifts at Ground Zero at night, and returned to their usual jobs during the day. A therapist who shuttled between the Trade Center site downtown and her private practice uptown said that if she planned it right, when her shift was over,

"I could get back here and get a couple of hours of sleep before I sort of tumbled into the next day . . . throw water on my face, and not look, or smell, like I had just come from there."

Other therapists also experienced difficulties when they returned to the rest of their lives. Those who worked long shifts at the FAC noticed that the despair that pervaded the place followed them when they went home. One recalled being so exhausted after days at her regular job and nights at Pier 94 that when she arrived at her office one morning, she turned out the lights and went to sleep under her desk. Another had trouble containing the graphic stories he heard every day at the pier. He repeated them to his friends until they asked him to be quiet. "It was very difficult for me to realize that not everyone wanted to hear it," he said. Therapists who worked in Respite Centers tried, with mixed results, to get the dust and the smell of Ground Zero off of their bodies, out of their clothes, and out of their apartments. They also tried to erase the scenes of Ground Zero from their memories, but at unexpected moments, "those guys would pop into my mind."

Many therapists found that the faces of rescue and recovery workers, and of the injured, the displaced, and the bereaved, as well as fragments of their conversations, remained in their minds. Years later, some therapists still worried about the people they had spoken with, if only for a few minutes, in states of profound shock, desperation, anguish, and fatigue, and had never seen again.

CHAPTER 3

"Get Me Counselors!"

෴

PSYCHOLOGICAL FIRST AID

WHILE THOUSANDS OF mental health professionals sought volunteer assignments through the Red Cross, numerous metropolitan area therapists realized that they could not rely on traditional relief organizations to find them places to volunteer. Whether they were put off by the disorganization of the initial mental health response, or whether they lacked the necessary state licenses to be accepted as Red Cross volunteers, they sought other ways to provide psychological assistance after the World Trade Center attack.[1] Without an overarching plan to guide them, therapists had no choice but to improvise. Many struck out on their own, manifesting an open, inclusive, and entrepreneurial spirit notably different in tone from their customary privacy and exclusivity. A few therapists set up tables on the sidewalks of their Brooklyn neighborhood, handing out literature on trauma and referring passersby in need to psychological treatment. A psychoanalytic institute that, like many others in the city, normally hid itself from view, its small sign barely visible from the street, opened its doors to the public; its free group therapy sessions were advertised on television. Some therapists were revitalized when they reached out in unconventional ways – it took them back to their professional roots. One felt as if "it was 1890, and you were a charitable organization social worker, and you had to go door to door ... we were out there."

While therapists were searching for ways to help, the demand for their services grew.[2] The demand came not only from persons seeking individual treatment but also from all kinds of organizations. Firms that were located near the Trade Center – whose employees had seen people on fire, been trapped in clouds of dust, climbed over bodies as they fled, walked miles in states of terror, or lost colleagues or close friends – hired therapists to help those who were too numb, too disoriented, or too terrified to go back to work.[3] Therapists were expected to be available immediately, sometimes without pay, and to provide large-scale relief instantaneously. All over town, from corporate boardrooms to university classrooms, people were shouting, "Get me counselors!"

To meet the increasing demand, therapists' professional organizations, academic institutions, and psychoanalytic institutes acted like clearinghouses, compiling lists of mental health professionals who wished to donate their services and matching them with places searching for assistance. But the number of requests for mental health professionals with expertise in trauma far exceeded the number of therapists available. In response, trauma specialists quickly developed a range of training programs to teach their colleagues rudimentary skills. The director of the Disaster Trauma Working Group of the New York City chapter of the National Association of Social Workers organized a five-session course to train therapists in the treatment of trauma. Other mental health professionals offered volunteers one-hour trainings before they left for their assignments. Clinical directors hired experts from Israel or Oklahoma City to teach their staff how to treat the psychological consequences of terrorism. Given that these courses covered no more than the basics of trauma treatment, it is not surprising that therapists doubted that they were sufficient. Some who received a "one shot deal" or "a couple of group workshops" felt they had not been adequately prepared and that they required more intensive training. Other therapists stayed away from these programs, worried that instead of teaching skills, they might traumatize those who took them.

Whether they were properly trained or not, therapists soon were placed in various extremely challenging settings. One trauma specialist was asked to aid a corporation whose downtown offices had been located in the north tower on the floors where the airplane hit. Hundreds of its employees were missing and feared dead. More than a thousand others who survived the attack were transferred to the corporation's midtown offices. When the trauma specialist arrived, she encountered mass "hysteria"; in her estimation, there were more than 3,000 people with acute stress disorder. On September 11, scores of employees in midtown had watched through windows facing south while the towers, which contained their families and friends, burned and then disintegrated. Human resource managers had long lists of employees who refused to come to work, some of whom were suicidal after having directly experienced the attack. Other employees came to work but were unable "to take their heads off their desks" or were "breaking down." These managers also had to handle the families of the missing, who were calling them to ask where they could pick up the bodies of their relatives, or who were appearing unannounced to pick up their final paychecks.

Hoping to quell the chaos, help the staff, and get employees back to work so that the business would survive, one manager in that corporation demanded that the trauma specialist immediately provide "29 therapists on the 29 floors of our building prepared to give counseling 12 hours a day for a month." She quickly recruited a hundred volunteers who took time off from their private practices, trained them in the fundamental principles of trauma treatment, and assigned them to specific locations in the corporation's offices. The volunteer therapists agreed to provide help for a week, giving human resource managers time to develop long-range plans for employees' mental health care.

Another therapist ended up at the same corporation, though, unlike the trauma specialist, he had no prior training in trauma, had only been licensed for several months, and had not seen patients in years. He along with a number of other mental health professionals – "by the end of the week there were 40 of us" – were assigned to work with the families of employees who had been lost since the attack. He spent most of his days sitting around a big conference table with a dozen other therapists, waiting for "someone to bring me a grieving family." "Nobody in the company really knew how to deal with them," he said, "so they would just pawn everybody off on us." Although his original assignment did not include assisting the corporation's staff, many employees sought him out as well since they were "falling apart"; "they were working crazy hours, they'd lost ten friends, they were trying to do what they could, and they were having a rough time." Despite their grim desperation, the company "was doing everything it could to keep hope alive," even when such optimism became "unrealistic." The therapist suspected that this was because its benefits officers were not ready to deal with the paperwork that was necessary to process each employee's demise.

Other corporations also invited therapists to come in and work with their employees. A therapist who was born in Japan, but who resided in New York City and had been trained in the United States, received a call from a Japanese bank with offices in the financial district. Although everyone in the firm survived the attack, many had run for their lives, a few had been hospitalized due to injuries, and many had lost colleagues at other firms downtown; some felt guilty about being alive. At first the therapist was concerned that, because mental health treatment was largely stigmatized in Japan, "certain protocols which are very much unspoken" might prevent employees from openly discussing what they had experienced. Contrary to her expectations, the director of the firm's head office in Japan, who wanted to ensure that his employees were taken care of, strongly supported her work. She wondered whether the

American media's explicit discussions of the importance of seeking professional help to deal with the psychological consequences of the attack had found their way to Japan, making mental health interventions "totally acceptable." This therapist later was asked to meet with Japanese women whose husbands had worked for multinational corporations near the World Trade Center, and who were widowed on 9/11. Some women were immediately called back to Japan, to communities that understood neither their experiences of the disaster nor the nature of their families' losses. Others remained near New York City until their spouses' remains were found, and then returned to Japan to bury them. Most of them felt isolated; their husbands had been their principal ties to the corporations, which also constituted their primary communities. Although the companies provided them with concrete assistance – by signing them up for victims' compensation, organizing their business affairs, and making arrangements for funeral services – they did not address the families' grief. In this therapist's view, few of the widows and their children had received adequate emotional support while they were still in the United States, and they were less likely to receive it once they returned to Japan.

The rising demand for psychological services in the wake of the attack meant that even therapists who remained in their usual clinical settings saw their roles and responsibilities change. A psychological consultant to an elementary school located a few blocks from the Trade Center had had an "arm's length relationship" with the school before 9/11; his schedule at that school quickly grew from 3 hours a week to 30. He became intensely involved with this "seriously traumatized" community where "everyone had run at some point in that hour and a half on the 11th." Parents and children who had been on their way to school when they saw an airplane fly down the street in front of them and drive itself into the north tower had turned on their heels and fled. Parents who had already dropped off their children had rushed back to collect them "in various states of hysteria," and teachers and children who had evacuated the school after the north tower collapsed had raced to escape the hurricane of debris. While most children's psychological symptoms proved shortlived, the psychological consultant estimated that almost one-third needed either extra time outside of class to discuss 9/11 or intensive mental health treatment.

In the following weeks, teachers who no longer felt capable of teaching, administrators who were unable to make decisions, and parents whose children either refused to speak of the attack or spoke of nothing else began to rely on him. When the consultant ran a group for parents shortly after the attack, more than 300 people attended. They requested his presence at every meeting, and when the school moved to safer quarters, he was expected to greet teachers and children at the door. Parents regularly told him what they had witnessed on the morning of the attack; they confided their heightened anxieties when an airplane crashed in Queens, and when anthrax was discovered in midtown. As part of his day-to-day work, the consultant educated parents about PTSD symptoms, referred children to outside therapists, rallied the staff, and negotiated disagreements within and among these groups. He also had to answer to the school board, which wanted him to determine when the community would be emotionally ready to return to its original building. Some parents did not think that their children would ever be ready. Since police officers and firefighters had used the school building as a staging area during rescue and recovery operations, they worried that it was physically as well as emotionally toxic. Under pressure from the school board for the community to come back in December, the consultant had to psychologically prepare reluctant children, teachers, and parents – many of whom, in his estimation, required more time – for their imminent return.

A therapist who directed the student counseling center of a university near the Trade Center also saw the demands on him radically increase. After the attack, he suddenly felt responsible for the well-being not only of students but also of the entire university community. From the moment he heard the plane hit the north tower he had gone into "action mode," first gathering and evacuating his staff, and then helping vacate classrooms, residence halls, and offices. Later, when the north tower crashed and the streets filled with smoke and debris, he shepherded everyone into a gymnasium where they waited for the air to clear. He organized therapy groups for faculty and staff, as well as special debriefings for students who had witnessed the attack from their dorm rooms, run into the streets to give firefighters water, or seen victims' charred bodies arriving at local hospitals. This director also was involved in relocating students whose dorms were no longer inhabitable, in sending international students home, and in informing students that their classmates had died in the attack. As he carried out these new duties, he continued to run the student counseling center, which treated an unusually high number of new patients in the months after 9/11.

While therapists' overtime efforts and outreach strategies often proceeded smoothly and were gratefully received, they reported a number of instances where their interventions were not appreciated. A few days after 9/11 one therapist walked into her neighborhood fire department, which had been among the first responders to the attack, determined to offer her help. Finding "a lot of guys that were in shock, a lot of PTSD . . . they were crying, they were numb, they were flashing back," she spontaneously conducted a group therapy session. One firefighter admitted that on the morning of the attack, as he drove the rig from Brooklyn to the World Trade Center with a clear view of the towers in flames, he knew that the situation was well beyond what the fire department could handle. This firefighter was so certain that he was "driving to his death" that he "wanted to take the rig and drive it into the wall." Since then, he had frequently been inclined to "put his head under a gallon of vodka." In the view of the therapist running the group, he "was in no position to drive a rig." Nor did she think that the other firefighters in the group were fit for active duty – as she put it, "I wouldn't want them responding to *my* fire" – and she counseled them to take time off to recover. But the firehouse lieutenant angrily rejected her advice, telling her, "You don't understand. We can't put them on leave, we don't have anybody here. They have to go back."

Other therapists may have been just as surprised when their offers to help were rejected, sometimes by fellow mental health professionals. As an example, the psychological consultant to the elementary school near the Trade Center spoke privately with renowned trauma specialists, but rebuffed the scores of therapists who were eager to take charge of the school community's emotional recovery. The community itself was in conflict. Some parents and teachers wanted to hire a team of trauma experts to help them cope with the attack, but most of them were dead set against it, in part because they were wary of their children being diagnosed with psychiatric disorders. In addition, they had heard disheartening stories about another nearby school, which had engaged several outside mental health professionals after numerous students' parents were killed on 9/11. Instead of uniting the community, these therapists' for-mulaic psychological debriefings and structured PTSD treatments, some of which encouraged parents and teachers to relive their experiences of the attack, had inflicted emotional damage. Moreover, therapists' offers to help "didn't inspire a lot of confidence," because they wanted "to move in with their own agenda" instead of familiarizing themselves with the community and its particular needs. In the school consultant's view, asking people to "sit down with a professional to talk about the things that were the most difficult to talk about" simply was "out of touch with what people seemed to need." Rather than relying on outside experts, the members of the school community wanted "something much more personal," and they also "wanted to feel part of a group." For them, the most "therapeutic" post-9/11 activity was setting up the new school building, which was "like a Tribeca barn-raising on 13th Street," and which created "a kind of euphoria" about what they had been able to accomplish.

While most mental health professionals chose to volunteer, some who staffed social service agencies and academic institutions felt "mandated" to serve. When their regular workday was over, they were pressed to provide psycho-logical services wherever their employers assigned them. Even mental health professionals who were policy specialists or researchers rather than clinicians "were forced to be therapists at a time when maybe they didn't want to be therapists." Some suffered substantial financial losses. For one therapist whose husband had recently lost his job, doing pro bono work in the evenings, at her employer's behest, deprived the family of sorely needed income from her private practice. It also required her to deliver services she was not trained to provide, night after night, to one traumatized group after another. Although "nobody had even had one course on debriefing," and "disaster was not something anybody had ever been taught,"

"It was, 'you're doing debriefing on Monday, and you're doing debriefing on Wednesday...and can you also do debriefing here, and can you do debriefing there?'"[4]

Without coordination among the numerous charitable organizations, city agencies, and private institutions that hastily dispatched mental health professionals, services were frequently redundant and disorganized. One therapist who was sent to a city hospital where several mental health professionals already had been placed found "too many therapists competing" to help; on her arrival, the other volunteers exclaimed, "What are you doing here? We're the therapists here!" No one showed up for her debriefings "because there was no need for more debriefings." Further, the services that volunteers were instructed to provide sometimes were inappropriate for the populations they targeted. When this therapist was assigned to a shelter for the homeless mentally ill, who recently had been removed from their usual places in subway tunnels and under bridges, they showed no interest in her help:

"They didn't know what was happening. They just wanted to go back to their place – they didn't want to talk to you...So why am I here? What is my function at this moment? And I'm slotted to be here for four hours...I could be with my family!"

In other agency and institutional settings below 14th Street, staff therapists had little reprieve. Unlike colleagues who worked uptown, and who "could draw this cocoon around them," those with downtown offices walked streets that were eerily closed to traffic and breathed air that was fouled by smoke from the site. Therapists who worked in the World Trade Center area constantly had to confront the "hole in the city" (Kolbert 2002:71). Some worked in offices where new machines filtered toxins from the air; others had windows facing the site, where the destruction was in full view and the recovery of bodies was in progress. In such highly stressful environments, they were expected to work longer hours treating numerous individuals destabilized by the attack, but without being given additional training, supervision, compensation, or support. Many felt resentful and "used" when they continued to receive their usual wages while outside crisis consultants, who were hired especially for the occasion, were paid at much higher rates. In some organizational settings, the combination of extraordinary demands, blatant financial inequities, and lack of gratitude for their contributions exacerbated unresolved grievances, and staff therapists promptly resigned.

In midtown, the trauma specialist who had recruited, trained, and managed more than a hundred therapists was agonized to discover that the corporation she had served did not appreciate her efforts. Although she was satisfied that the therapists she supplied "were as helpful as anyone can be," she became the target of a manager's rage when the volunteers, as previously planned, terminated their services after a week. Deeply shocked by his reaction, she was unable to eat or sleep. The work itself took a toll on the therapists she had trained. When she debriefed them after their shifts, she found them "overwhelmed by the degree of anguish they were witnessing." At the end of every day, "we had an additional 15 therapists with acute stress disorder."

The other therapist who worked with families at the same corporation also saw his initial satisfaction with his placement turn into frustration. At first, he had been gratified by the "camaraderie" among volunteer therapists, by his work with several families, and by the chance to provide psychological services without the intrusion of supervisors. But the situation soon changed. The delivery of mental health services grew into a virtual industry; so many therapists were on hand that the office came to resemble "a chaotic, busy clinic." Some therapists began to impose standard clinical procedures, agreeing to meet with bereaved families who were in crisis and in shock only in their designated spaces and only by appointment, rather than wherever and whenever they needed to be seen. Other mental health professionals "were starting to capitalize on the opportunities"; they were conducting psychological studies on traumatized employees, passing their business cards around, and promoting their private practices. "It became a feeding frenzy," he said, and "therapists were beginning to pick at the carcass."

THE UNDERSERVED

Several therapists remarked that, in the wake of the World Trade Center attack, New York City and the nation experienced a "honeymoon phase of everyone pulling together." They interpreted the astonishing amounts of money and goods that began to flow into Manhattan for victims, families, and rescue and recovery workers as a sign of national solidarity. Indeed, monetary donations were in the billions, and so many work boots, blankets, flashlights, gloves, and other supplies were contributed for the ongoing work at Ground Zero that the city had to set up a trucking operation to cart the excess away (Langewiesche 2002). Yet if the attack caused many people to feel that they belonged to a unified community, it made others face the extent to which they felt like, and were perceived as, outsiders. Some therapists referred to the "classic American xenophobia" that intensified after the attack. Immigrants and refugees, especially those who were assumed to be of Arab descent or Muslim, were suddenly considered threats to national security, and rapidly became the targets of both government and individual reprisals (Clark 2002). These and other minority communities were less likely to reap the benefits of the supposed honeymoon phase. Instead, they grew increasingly estranged as the attack worsened existing social divisions, disparities, and biases.

Such disparities and divisions inevitably were reflected in the delivery of mental health services following 9/11. In spite of the vast mobilization of mental health professionals, and their aggressive outreach strategies, there are mixed reports as to their success in extending sufficient support to many of New York City's least protected residents. Disaster specialists claim that large-scale catastrophes disproportionately damage communities that are socially and economically vulnerable, and that lack strong support systems (Oliver-Smith 1996).[5] According to this perspective, New Yorkers who were poor and unemployed, who endured discrimination, and who lived in unsafe neighborhoods were at greater psychological risk than those with social power and economic security; consequently, they required supplementary resources and care.

Yet mental health initiatives, including those sponsored by Project Liberty, often were unavailable to, or culturally inappropriate for, various populations at risk (Garfinkel, Kaushal, Teitler, & Garcia 2005). One therapist asserted that Project Liberty utterly failed to reach out to minority communities, so that people "never knew what their rights were" and had no idea "where to go to do what they needed to do." Another therapist commented that services for immigrants and refugees "were extremely limited," and that most of them "were not getting anything."

Such assessments of Project Liberty's performance are at odds with its intent to attract "non-white, non-English-speaking groups at rates proportional to their representation in the general population of the disaster area" (Felton 2002:432). To achieve this goal, Project Liberty put considerable effort into training bilingual and bicultural mental health workers and developing innovative psychological programs that were linguistically and culturally accessible. These programs were delivered in at least 37 languages, and included outreach to various minority communities (Gurvitch 2005; Naturale 2005; Waizer, Dorin, Stoller, & Laird 2005).[6] However, it took so long to recruit and train these workers, and to design and fund these programs, that by the time the services were up and running, Project Liberty was being phased out. As a result, Project Liberty's services, like many other post-9/11 mental health programs, were "vastly underutilized by immigrants" (Gurvitch 2005:547). Underserved groups included Muslims and persons of Arab descent, who became targets of hate crimes, deportations, and arrests; illegal immigrants and undocumented workers, who worried they would be deported if they used Project Liberty and other mental health services; and Latinos, whose responses to the attack were exacerbated by economic difficulties, ongoing discrimination, and the November 2001 crash of an airplane en route to the Dominican Republic. Also in this category were the elderly, some of whom were afraid to leave their apartments after the attack, and African Americans, who feared that if they took advantage of available services and benefits they would be perceived as "want[ing] handouts."

There were additional obstacles to providing adequate help to communities at risk. A mental health professional who directed a nonprofit organization that provided services to survivors of trauma tried to assess the needs of immigrants, refugees, and asylum seekers who lost family members on 9/11, who escaped from the Trade Center vicinity, or who subsequently were subjected to racial profiling, raids, or detention. When he met with members of local Pakistani, Afghani, and Indian communities, he realized the dire consequences of the attack for both its direct and indirect victims. Thousands of immigrant families, where "the only moneymakers" had been killed, detained, or expelled, were "in total, absolute poverty." Refugees who had survived genocide or torture at home, and who had fled to the United States seeking shelter, lost their sense of safety; this event "stimulated the old trauma," engendering "a lot of emotional problems, a lot of family problems, and an increase in domestic violence." Despite his organization's efforts, it reached only a small fraction of immigrants and refugees at risk. "Seeking services is already not in their repertoire," this therapist remarked, "but now on top of that they are scared, they are suspicious, and they don't trust you, so it's very hard to reach them." Many who feared retaliation either went into seclusion or obliterated signs of their identities, effectively cutting themselves off from potential community support. But he also was critical of therapists who assumed they were "the only ones who can help them if they have emotional problems." In his estimation, people "are really creative, and they find other ways to cope." Further, the people he met with needed legal and financial assistance just as urgently as they required psychological services.

Also among the underserved were undocumented workers, who have been called the "invisible victims" of 9/11 (Louie 2001). Individuals who were missing and presumed deceased after the attack were from 115 different countries (Boss 2004); some of them were in the United States illegally. Large numbers of undocumented workers were among the low-wage employees of hotels, restaurants, and small businesses near the Trade Center. Although many of those who survived lost their jobs because of the attack, they were ineligible for FEMA assistance and unemployment compensation, and often were denied emergency relief funds for food and shelter because they lacked pay stubs or other evidence of employment. Families of undocumented workers who were killed on 9/11 – including families of missing workers who had borrowed other peoples' papers for the purposes of employment, and thus could not be accurately identified – were afraid of being sent home if they made financial claims or used psychological services (Louie 2001).

Psychological services were not utilized for other reasons as well. The kinds of services that typically were provided after the attack were infused with mainstream American notions of mental wellness, individualism, emotion, and loss (Seeley 2000). They were a poor fit for persons from minority communities who did not privilege a psychological interior, who felt their anguish as bodily pains, who did not view their distress as an illness requiring professional intervention, who could not separate their needs from those of their families, who had divergent conceptions of death and mourning, who saw mental health treatment as exclusively for the insane, who did not believe in the curative powers of speaking with strangers about life's difficulties, and who were more concerned with their social and economic well-being than with their emotional health. Nor did such individuals have reason to trust that American mental health professionals, who were predominantly white and middle class, who did not speak their languages or share their lives, and who were outsiders to their communities, would understand their views, protect them, or take their side.[7]

Even therapists with the necessary language skills and cultural knowledge, and with similar ethnic backgrounds, could feel challenged by their work with minority communities. A Latina mental health professional who was trained in the United States felt "torn between cultural views" when a Dominican social service agency asked her to work with families who were devastated by 9/11. Many of these families' relatives had worked at "Windows of the World," the restaurant on the 105th floor of the north tower, and had been killed in the attack. The therapist found it impossible to reconcile standard crisis intervention models, which stressed brief contact, short-term assistance, and empowerment, with the kinds of interventions the Dominican agency's staff employed. Typically, they would "go to a family's house, have coffee with them and dinner, do therapy, eat a little bit more, and sit there for four hours if they have to." After a full day of visiting family members at home, they accompanied them to the morgue to identify bodies; later, they attended "every funeral." In spite of her affiliation with this community, the therapist's formal training in American models of mental health caused her to see the agency's approach as counterproductive. She said,

> *"I don't think that you actually have to hold a person's hand for that long to help them with relief. And if you hold it too long, you're telling them that they actually need you for that long . . . and then people cling longer and mourn longer than they should."*

On a personal level, implementing this approach was less than optimal for her. Already pushed to her limit by the combined demands of her full-time job, other volunteer commitments, and her family, these lengthy therapeutic encounters, which she squeezed into the weekends, left her without time to recoup. Yet she continued to use this approach, because "when you work with the Latino community, you're expected to participate in the rituals, and if you don't that's a problem."[8]

Another therapist who volunteered had answered phones for Red Cross hotlines, and had assisted the employees of a company that sustained hundreds of casualties. But her most difficult work involved running a group for gays and lesbians who lost partners in the attack. The weeks following 9/11 were particularly trying for this community. Although there were numerous gay firefighters, police officers, and construction workers on the rescue and recovery crews, the gay community's contributions were never publicly recognized. Surviving partners in gay relationships were ineligible for government benefits, and frequently were shut out of the formal mourning ceremonies arranged by their partners' families. Those who had been in the closet, and who came out after the attack, sometimes were poorly received. One member of the group came out after the man he had lived with for several years was killed on 9/11. He introduced himself to his partner's parents, who "didn't know their son was gay, and weren't dying to acknowledge this guy." On the first anniversary of the attack, he planned to go to the official ceremony for families at Ground Zero, where the name of each victim was to be read aloud, but his partner's parents were so uncomfortable with the idea that he decided not to attend. This and similar incidents gave the therapist who ran the group a keen appreciation of the gay community's invisibility. She recalled a session where the group had looked at the obituary of one of its members' partners, which was published in the *New York Times*.[9] The couple had been together for 20 years, but as the obituary was read aloud,

> *"We all thought we would die, cause it said something to the effect of, he was so busy with his work, he wasn't interested in having a relationship."*

Several therapists noted that the social hierarchy was reproduced after the Trade Center attack, complete with its glaring disparities. Groups who were marginalized and devalued before 9/11 remained "at the bottom of the totem pole." In contrast, the families of survivors and victims – who were the first set of individuals affected by a terrorist attack to receive generous government compensation – were the "number one priority." Residents of impoverished neighborhoods, "where picking your way across either the bodies of drugged-out crack addicts or the bodies of murder victims en route to school or work is not a particularly unusual occurrence," often resented the enormous sums that were rapidly raised and allocated.[10] The September 11 Victim Compensation Fund, which was established by a law passed on September 22, 2001, gave more than $7 billion in federal monies, tax free, to families of the deceased and to persons wounded in the attack. Mayor Giuliani created a fund for families of the city's uniformed services personnel and the Port Authority Police Department, which received $216 million in donations (Dwyer & Flynn 2005). An additional $2.7 billion was donated to charitable organizations (Feinberg 2005). While monies were being funneled into World Trade Center assistance, other New York City services, including those that aided vulnerable communities, suffered from lack of funds (Rosner & Markowitz 2006).

Individuals in dire financial need who qualified for various kinds of 9/11 aid could not always negotiate the complexities of disaster relief systems. As the therapist whose business and apartment were severely damaged in the attack remarked, dealing with social service agencies was "a full-time job." Even completing the necessary forms was daunting; he had to fill out more than 10 applications, including a FEMA application dozens of pages long. This therapist also noted that the distribution of relief seemed inequitable, so that certain people obtained relief more easily than others. While some individuals barely succeeded in obtaining vouchers that covered their basic necessities, others were doubly or triply compensated, receiving monies from various funds and federal grants as well as from charitable organizations. He found it difficult to understand "why some people were just immediately given whatever resources were there and others were denied them," especially when "often the ones who were given the money were ones who seemed to be very affluent." He offered his case as an example. Although he had incurred hundreds of thousands of dollars in expenses to repair his damaged apartment, restore his ailing business, relocate multiple times, pay his daughter's tuition, cover his family's medical bills, and take time off from work, through a combination of federal grants for small businesses and Red Cross funds that were "forced on them," his costs were reimbursed "and then some."

If certain kinds of survivors of the attack, along with victims' families, were privileged recipients of vast quantities of public and private monies, then even among those who were given such funds, some were more privileged than others. The special master of the September 11 Victim Compensation Fund aimed to "narrow the gap" between its wealthiest and most impoverished beneficiaries by putting a cap on the awards they received. However, because the relevant statute directed him to base the amount of each family's award on the specific victim's projected lifetime earning power, the Fund "created a scale of victimhood" (Feinberg 2005:155) that reinforced the status quo. Moreover, according to the therapist who was perhaps too generously reimbursed for his expenses, due to the way calculations were made and funds were dispersed, "just purely economically, many, many, many people are better off now than they were before."

Many therapists worked overtime to serve those who were disenfranchised before 9/11, and who were certainly more marginalized afterward. Some reached out to underserved groups who were severely affected by the attack but were ineligible for official disaster relief, or who slipped through the cracks of government systems. On top of their usual professional responsibilities and volunteer work, they labored to locate bilingual therapists, design culturally accessible services, supply free legal aid to undocumented workers and detainees, set up alternative supports for illegal immigrants, and establish collaborative relationships with community and religious organizations.

AMBIGUOUS LOSS

The lethality of the attack on the World Trade Center now seems obvious, and the official death toll has been tabulated. However, in the days and weeks immediately following September 11 it was far from clear how many people had successfully evacuated the towers, whether people who were close to the points of the airplanes' impact could have survived the crash and the fires, and whether hundreds of individuals eventually would be rescued from the mountainous rubble at the site.[11] Only 18 people were found alive after 9/11, all within two days of the attack (Langeweische 2002). Yet many families held onto hope much longer, sure that their relatives soon would be found in sections of the structure that had held, or in cavities of the ruins where they had been protected from the collapse. "It really was such a hurdle to decide whether the person was alive or not, to accept that they were dead, and then to begin the grief process," one therapist said.

Such hurdles seemed especially insurmountable given that so many people vanished without leaving a physical trace. Most families provided the Medical Examiner's Office with the DNA samples necessary to identify relatives' remains. Volunteers traveled as far Guatemala and El Salvador to collect DNA samples from relatives of the missing (Louie 2001). But tens of thousands of human fragments that were discovered at the site, which were stored in a dozen refrigerated tractor-trailers, were too degraded by force or by fire to yield the genetic material necessary for positive identification. In the spring of 2005, the Medical Examiner's Office announced the completion of work costing $80 million and employing the latest DNA identification technologies.[12] Still, only 58% of the attack's 2,749 victims had been identified, so that 1,157 families had not received their relatives' remains (Lipton 2005).[13]

Mental health professionals with expertise in treating bereaved individuals claim that mourning is most intractable in cases where family members do not have a body to bury. Lacking conclusive evidence of a friend's or a relative's demise, people have little incentive to fully relinquish hope. These situations of "ambiguous loss," where it is impossible to be entirely certain whether a person is dead or alive, tend to delay mourning, complicate grief, rupture family ties, and engender chronic strain (Boss, Beaulieu, Weiling, Turner, & LaCruz 2003). In some societies, family members who do not have a body to bury are prohibited from participating in traditional funeral rituals that provide comfort and support, and that encourage psychological resolution (Boss 2004).

Toward the end of September 2001, when families still lacked evidence that their kin were alive, many began to lose hope. Some reluctantly concluded that their relatives were lost when a new Web site that allowed individuals who had not yet been heard from to post information "that will let loved ones know they are safe" did not include their messages (American Red Cross in Greater New York, 2004a). Others came to the same conclusion when relatives' names did not appear on updated lists of World Trade Center survivors, or when exhaustive searches of local hospitals proved fruitless. For many, the turning point was an article in the *New York Times* that showed exactly where each airplane had hit the towers and listed the companies located on nearby floors. A therapist who met with the same families week after week witnessed their optimism fade over time. "It was horrifying to watch that hopefulness turn to hopelessness," he said. Therapists encountered tensions between couples and among siblings in cases where family members disagreed whether their relatives were lost. Some family members "were incredibly hopeful beyond all logic," while others wanted to start notifying friends and arranging memorial services. Once family members agreed that their relative had perished, therapists' activities changed, and their crisis counseling turned into grief counseling. Families without bodies or remains to bury searched for alternative ways to honor their relatives' lives and to formally bid them farewell. Some held funeral services where they buried empty coffins; others buried coffins holding the possessions of the deceased, including photographs, musical instruments, and bowling balls (Boss 2004).

While each family struggled privately to come to terms with its loss, the residents of New York City also had to face the fact that thousands of lives had been lost, and that additional survivors would not be found. To manage New Yorkers' emotional recovery, Mayor Giuliani established a commission, which included several mental health professionals with expertise in bereavement or trauma, and asked its members to design, initiate, and orchestrate public expressions of grief in the most sensitive manner possible (Cohen 2005). One bereavement specialist who consulted with this commission recalled that its members recognized the need for "an acknowledgment that people were dead, so that the mourning could start." This acknowledgment entailed a formal public announcement by Mayor Giuliani stating that the mission of Ground Zero workers had officially been changed from one of rescue – with the objective of discovering people who were alive – to one of recovery, which focused on the retrieval of human remains. Commission members tried "to gauge the emotional status of the city" to determine when residents would be ready to take in such an announcement. The Mayor "wanted to do the right thing" by not moving ahead too quickly. But at the same time, given that sections of the financial district were closed and that numerous businesses throughout the city had been destroyed by the attack, he felt pressured to balance concerns for the city's emotional health with concerns for its economic well-being.

In addition to making plans for the city's emotional recovery, the commission was in charge of facilitating the mourning of families whose relatives were killed on 9/11. The bereavement specialist was aware that mental health professionals lacked sophisticated understandings of traumatic mourning,[14] and she was skeptical of their ability to handle it. Yet the commission quickly created a set of procedures to help families acknowledge their losses and express their grief. Families were issued official death certificates so that they might more easily accept the death of their relatives, even when no remains had been found. Those who chose to receive these certificates were permitted to visit Ground

Zero, where they could "say goodbye" and "leave something" for their kin. Families were taken to the World Trade Center site on boats with numerous other passengers, including clergy, emergency medical workers, therapy dogs, and mental health professionals; there were also military escorts with machine guns. Members of the commission had debated whether going to the site would be traumatic for the families, but had failed to consider its impact on the mental health professionals who accompanied them. The trip apparently was traumatizing for therapists as well. The bereavement specialist, who was on the first boat to the site, felt "like it was happening to somebody else." She couldn't believe that Ground Zero was real – "it felt like this place was screaming anguish." That night, she woke up screaming from a nightmare about the Holocaust.

The commission also was responsible for developing funeral rituals for families who had neither a body nor remains to inter. Mental health professionals who had worked with victims' families in the wake of previous atrocities had learned that, in the absence of relatives' bodies, family members benefited from receiving some sort of substance or object that was drawn from the place of their death, that symbolized their life, and that could be passed down through the generations (Lori 2005). Commission members decided that every family that signed a death certificate but had nothing concrete to bury would receive a container holding dust from Ground Zero, which was blessed by a chaplain at the site (Sturken 2004). In trying to select an appropriate container for the dust, they first considered a brass cube engraved with the image of the World Trade Center, which, in the opinion of the bereavement specialist, "looked like a souvenir that you get when you go visit the Empire State Building." They settled instead on wooden urns made of polished cherry, so that families would have "something small and organic that you could hold." The commission then designed a memorial ceremony in which each family would be formally presented with an urn, which was placed inside a blue velvet bag that was put into a box (Yaeger 2003).[15]

During one of her volunteer shifts in a service center as a "floating mental health professional," a therapist who specialized in trauma was pulled from the floor and sent to a private room. Once inside, she witnessed a series of memorial ceremonies that were held for friends and relatives of the dead. She watched as two young women who were aides to the Mayor read a brief text while they somberly handed urns to family members.

"They had this little urn, and they had an American flag folded in that very special way on the urn. They had to stand up – the urns were all stacked up behind flags – somehow put a hand on their heart, and hold

this thing. And then they had to recite something, several paragraphs, about 'we're giving this to you to honor your beloved who perished during the terrorist attacks of 9/11, with the thanks of the Mayor of the City of New York.'"

But the Mayor's aides, who had been working long hours in this highly charged environment performing "the most terrifying of all tasks," were themselves utterly distraught. They had not been properly prepared either for their own emotional reactions or for those of the families. According to this trauma specialist, a few of the families who came to collect the urns had chosen to believe that they actually contained the remains of their relatives, and they were grateful to receive them. Some didn't care how the urns were presented to them, but simply "needed the ashes." Others were "enormously angry and just needed to vent." They said, "All they found was this piece of my husband; did I need to hear this?"[16] The young women who were conducting the ceremonies appeared to be quite frightened by what they had seen at Ground Zero, by what they were doing with the urns, and by the intensity of family members' emotions. Their fear made it difficult for them to read the required text, and they stumbled over the words. When they handed out each urn, they cried and embraced the person who was taking it, "whether the person wanted to be embraced or not." The trauma specialist realized that the aides desperately needed her support to carry out their task.

Crises and disasters commonly are thought to produce a "predictable series of events" that follow a regular timetable (Mirabito & Rosenthal 2002:45). According to this timetable, an initial phase of extreme emergency and hazard is addressed by rescue and repair operations, and by an array of services for victims, that quickly return the affected community to its predisaster state. However, due to the scale and gravity of the World Trade Center attack, the initial phase of emergency and hazard, rather than winding down, persisted. One therapist wondered how long the initial period of crisis would continue: "As long as the fires were going? As long as the site was open? As long as the DNA identification was going on?" Such questions made it more difficult to predict when individuals who were psychologically wounded – or when New York City itself – might fully recover from the attack. Moreover, as such questions seemed to suggest, not all metropolitan area residents were equally affected by 9/11. For thousands of New Yorkers, the crisis continued unabated as they waited for relatives to appear, for injuries to heal, for apartments to be repaired, for family members to be released from detention, for offices to reopen, or for new jobs to be found. In contrast, for New Yorkers who were comparatively unscathed, the official public acknowledgment that thousands of persons were lost, that additional rescues were unlikely, and that the ruins of the World Trade Center would rapidly be removed marked the end of the disaster's first phase.

For many New York City therapists, the end of the crisis phase of the disaster was marked by shifts in the delivery of mental health services. As previously noted, Project Liberty, like the Red Cross and other disaster relief organizations, generally provided the psychologically wounded with short-term mental health treatments, and referred those who needed more care to intensive, long-term therapies. In consequence, when mental professionals completed their volunteer assignments and returned to their regular clinical work, World Trade Center survivors, friends and relatives of the deceased, and rescue and recovery workers were among their new patients. So were numerous city inhabitants who, though less directly harmed by the attack, felt unsettled and disturbed by its disruption of their lives, by the traumatic memories it triggered, or by the ominous, ubiquitous shadings of what was referred to as "the new normal." In their private offices and in other clinical settings, therapists began to provide patients who were variously affected by the terrorist attack with ongoing mental health care. They would continue to treat some of them for months and years to come.

CHAPTER 4

The Psychological Treatment of Trauma

の

Lᴵᴷᴱ ᴛʜᴇɪʀ ᴄᴏʟʟᴇᴀɢᴜᴇs who confronted extraordinary demands when they volunteered after the attack, New York City mental health professionals who worked in private practices, or in hospitals, social service agencies, or educational institutions, faced substantial clinical challenges following the events of 9/11. No matter how extensive their experience, many were taken aback by the ways this unexpected act of mass violence penetrated individuals' bodies and disrupted the workings of their minds. Without the formal training that might have helped prepare them for patients' widely variant reactions, many therapists turned to the clinical literature for direction. Yet they found it largely silent on topics of urgent importance. Because this literature did not adequately address the treatment of patients who were abruptly bereaved by a terrorist attack, whose grief was compounded by trauma, whose losses could be counted in the dozens, who had to mourn in the public eye, or whose suffering seemed interminable, there was little for therapists to draw on as they embarked on the most difficult work of their professional careers.

Mental health professionals who were involved in the immediate disaster response frequently were impressed by the unconventional, and sometimes nonverbal, therapeutic interventions that were delivered after the attack. One thought that the most effective relief workers were those "giving out the cookies and the coffee," because "they're the ones who are truly touching people. They create an environment where people will talk." Several noted the psychological benefits of the therapy dogs that were stationed at many sites serving the relatives of the deceased (cf. Therapy Dogs International n.d.). Unlike their human counterparts, they did not ask intrusive questions and were available for physical contact. Although family members might refuse to discuss their emotional states with mental health professionals, "You can pet a dog, and you're relating."

Although mental health professionals appreciated such innovations, when they returned to their offices, many felt most comfortable employing their customary therapeutic methods. They hoped that, as in more ordinary clinical encounters, after 9/11, psychological healing would occur by virtue of "being there with another person, and helping them to understand their experience and reframe their experience . . . in some way that moves them forward." Accordingly, psychoanalysts found value in long-term, in-depth treatments, and in interpreting the unconscious meanings of traumatic experiences that surfaced in fantasies, symbols, and dreams. Psychodynamically oriented therapists helped patients grasp the links between recent external events and their internal psychic worlds, and between prior and current calamities. Supportive therapists counted on the benefits of listening empathically to patients, even when their stories "were really hard to hear," and of "mobiliz[ing] the hope of a future even when things were really grim." Those who emphasized psychoeducation taught the individuals they worked with the physiology of traumatic stress reactions, and normalized their responses to the attack. The therapist who consulted for the elementary school favored a community-based approach that rallied the strengths of the group, utilized its own resources, and allowed it to "round up the wagons, pull together, and take care of ourselves." Many others relied on fundamental clinical skills. As one therapist said, although he didn't know much about trauma, he knew how to "sit in a small room with a family that's just lost their father."

VIOLENT EMOTIONS

In the interest of delivering treatments that were as beneficial as possible, therapists also tried to predict which of their preexisting patients, and which new 9/11-related patients, would be seriously psychologically destabilized. Many therapists assumed that those who had been closest to the attack were most likely to be traumatized or to develop debilitating mental disorders. Yet patients' psychological responses often contradicted their expectations. Some individuals who had waded through thick smoke and debris as they evacuated the towers seemed to regain their bearings rapidly, while others who were exposed less directly became dangerously self-destructive. Some were eager to recount their experiences of the attack immediately, perhaps to rid themselves of unbearable memories, while others still were unable to speak of the devastation they had witnessed more than a year later. One therapist who sought to explain such variation from patient to patient claimed that persons' specific reactions to 9/11 were shaped not by their proximity to the attack, but by their individual psychological histories:

"External experiences resonate internally with each person in unique ways and that's where the work is: to understand how the reality of what we all know is going on dredged up old feelings of being unsafe or old feelings of being vulnerable."

In support of this view, therapists observed surprisingly strong reactions among patients who lacked firsthand exposure to the events of 9/11. Because the attack was a clear demonstration that people could not be trusted, that the environment was dangerous, that loved ones disappeared, and that murderous violence was possible, it was especially disturbing to patients who already were preoccupied by these fears. They began to have dreams about collisions, floods, airplane disasters, and entire cities in flames. With the future itself called into question, some also began to behave more recklessly. In the fall of 2002, a year after the attack, the director of the university counseling center near the Trade Center site noticed a marked increase in assault, alcohol abuse, and sexual violence among the student population.

Other therapists anticipated that patients with significant histories of trauma, whether due to physical abuse, sexual assault, or to experiences of political terror, would be retraumatized by the attack, and would develop a rash of psychological symptoms. Given that trauma may be transmitted from one generation to the next, and handed down from parents to children (Danieli 1998; Epstein 1979), therapists also expected that patients whose parents had been subjected to genocide, interpersonal violence, or war similarly would experience a marked psychological decline. To some extent, their predictions were accurate. In the following weeks and months, some trauma survivors were in a "more hyperaroused state." Many had flashbacks to earlier traumas; one therapist observed so much dissociation in her patients that "I had to help them come back into their bodies."[1] Survivors of torture were particularly susceptible to retraumatization after 9/11; they found it nearly impossible to reestablish a sense of security when what they had considered to be a safe haven turned out to be full of danger. Vietnam veterans also were at risk. A therapist who worked at a veteran's hospital noticed a "gradual swell" of veterans who had been symptom-free for years, but for whom PTSD once again was "rearing its ugly head." Patients from Europe and Japan whose cities had been bombed during World War II, and patients from China who had grown up hearing the screams of neighbors being tortured during the Cultural Revolution, were flooded with intensely vivid memories of atrocities that had earlier threatened their families and their lives. For patients who had been abused in their youth, the attack frequently reactivated childhood and adolescent traumas. One therapist noted that patients reacted most strongly to the particular features of 9/11 that most closely mirrored their early histories. Those who had been violated as children were disturbed by intense feelings of invasion, while others were more distressed by the government's failure to prevent the attack, which suggested that "nobody was protecting them," just as they had been unprotected from abuse in the past.

But some therapists were surprised to discover that patients who had suffered from prior traumas envied individuals who were harmed on 9/11. Patients who had hidden their traumatic histories from everyone in their lives, and had remained alone with their pain, often envied those whose injuries were readily acknowledged by others, either because they were public and "out in the open," or because they were shared by communities of fellow sufferers. Some of them were most upset by the extensive emotional and financial support that was extended to the families of 9/11 victims. One patient complained that no one had diverted traffic, brought cookies to her house, set up a memorial, or mourned alongside her when her mother had died. Others were gratified to see that millions of New Yorkers were stricken with anguish and grief. They felt that others finally understood, and shared in, their everyday experiences of misery. As one patient told her therapist, "Someone is finally talking about what it's like to be me."

Therapists observed that the attack had significant psychic repercussions for patients without histories of trauma as well. Having seen one part of the world do violence to another in this supremely destructive attack inflamed patients' latent aggression, in some cases inciting "the wish to be violent themselves." One therapist said that 9/11 gave rise to the "mass wish that there should be a war, because there's mass violence and the opportunity to engage in it." Patients who otherwise seemed mild-mannered exhibited a fury that rose to a fever pitch. Enraged by the attack, they wanted to "go in and bomb the hell out of the whole area," or to "nuke every one of them." Those who normally succeeded in encapsulating their anger grew uncontrollably explosive, like one patient who resembled "a dynamite keg"; his therapist worried that he was perilously close to losing control and murdering someone. Other patients whose rage was inflamed by the attack became focused on destroying themselves. The chaos at the World Trade Center had made them fear that their thoughts and feelings were dangerously chaotic, and that their emotional center would no longer hold. In one therapist's view, the attack, where "all sorts of boundaries were broken, buildings were collapsing, and eruptions were taking place externally," caused patients to fear that "their internal structures would collapse as well."

Therapists noticed that an increasing number of patients were making suicide plans, whether due to concerns about psychological breakdowns, or to worries about further terrorist strikes – saying, for example, that "they would kill themselves if a nuclear blast went off." One patient who had lost dozens of friends and colleagues directly involved his therapist in his plan to end his life. Early one morning several months after the attack, he phoned his therapist to say that he was standing on an overpass and wanted to leap to his death. He then requested her help in convincing him not to jump.

While some patients experienced new impulses to kill, others grew anxious about being the victims of violent assaults. The events of 9/11, in which "one part of the world was attacking another," confirmed patients' fears that violence lurked beneath the surface of all human relationships, and evoked worries about being its target. Some developed paranoid anxieties that were blatantly racist in character; one feared that the South Asian man at the corner newsstand would attack him, and another was certain that he would be poisoned by the Middle Eastern owners of his local diner.

In addition, the fabulous scale of the violence that was unleashed on 9/11 challenged some patients' capacities to separate fantasy from reality, especially in cases where the line between them was already indistinct. Those whose emotions or imaginations tended toward the violent were terribly unnerved to find that their most incendiary fantasies had come true, or that the enormous devastation they previously had envisioned had actually come to pass. Some began to worry that their feelings and fantasies were dangerous. One therapist remarked,

> "It made people worry that if they'd ever been enraged, if they'd ever had the fantasy of killing somebody, if they'd ever had the thought of blowing something up, that somehow they were a part of this."

Some patients felt responsible for the attack. Those who previously had imagined murdering their parents worried that they were in league with the terrorists, in part because the twin towers represented "mother-father symbols." Patients who had heard about terrorists' plans to fly airplanes into the twin towers, or who had predicted similar kinds of attacks, were concerned that they had precipitated the destruction of the World Trade Center.

For therapists who were inclined to analyze the unconscious, the meticulously planned and wildly violent assault on the World Trade Center offered an interpretive bonanza; it was "like we were living in a dream" where nothing was rational or real. In one psychoanalyst's view, the attack represented "a breaking of our boundaries," and was "a metaphor for the collapse of structure." The destruction of the towers symbolized not only the defeat of the parents and the impotence of the nation but also was tied to the crash of the stock market, the loss of faith in corporations, and the total demise of authority. Thus it offered proof that the world was completely chaotic, and that people were fundamentally helpless. When notions of this kind infiltrated patients' intrapsychic worlds, they "stirred up some very powerful stuff," including desperate fears of brutal violation, hidden wishes for utter bedlam, and buried desires for unfettered aggression.

Unlike patients whose psychic worlds were upended by the attack, therapists found that "there were some people for whom this was really not at the top of their list in terms of what was on their minds." Persons who were inured to catastrophe often felt at home with this massive assault, as it reinforced their sense that the world was a terrible and perilous place. Children from areas filled with violence, who were "living in a war zone all the time," seemed unfazed by the vast destruction. Residents of miserable, impoverished neighborhoods observed that "we've already been living in hell." Some patients of color saw the attack as a well-deserved strike against the structures of American power that systematically marginalized and oppressed them, and they felt little sympathy for its victims. Others who failed to react to the attack were those who had been so brutally abused in their earlier years that they "had been basically living with terrorists in their families." The events of 9/11 "paled in comparison to what they had been through" – they were "just a blip" on a lengthy resume of trauma.

When therapists met with patients who failed to react to the attack, and who would "come into sessions and speak to me like they were going to discuss the latest movie," they sometimes found their capacity for empathy considerably diminished. Although they realized that, in some cases, patients focused on trifling personal problems to protect themselves from more terrifying and less controllable threats, they recalled listening to "the same old, same old," and finding it "so moronic." One admitted that she had "very little patience for people for whom the story of 9/11 was over two weeks later," because "their self-involvement was more than I could bear." In contrast, a therapist who specialized in bereavement, and who worked closely with several families whose relatives died in the attack, looked forward to bickering couples and to other "superficial therapy cases." After listening to so many painful stories of devastation and death, she found their comparatively minor concerns "refreshing."

Therapists also discovered unexpected pockets of resilience. They observed that a few patients with histories of trauma weathered 9/11 well. Individuals who had previously been in psychological treatment, and had worked through their original traumas, had learned how to manage their responses to catastrophic events. Persons who had grown up in countries with long histories of political terror could be especially resilient, because they had not been socialized into "the American illusion that we're all safe." Moreover, contrary to therapists' expectations, some patients felt healed by a massive act of horror that normalized a personal history of violence, or that trivialized a private misery.[2] Some made use of the crisis to leave unsatisfying jobs and relationships, and to change their lives for the better.

TRAUMATIC TRANSFERENCES

While contemporary notions of transference are too variable and complex to be thoroughly addressed in this chapter (cf. Aron 1996; Mitchell 1997), these notions generally refer to patients' active, idiosyncratic constructions of the intentions, identities, and personal characteristics of their therapists. Such constructions, which significantly shape clinical relationships, inevitably are colored not only by therapists' actual qualities but also by the indelible residues of patients' primary emotional relationships, which they unknowingly reenact in treatment. For the purposes of this chapter, transference broadly signifies the distinctive ways in which patients constructed and reconstructed their therapists after 9/11.

Therapists who specialize in trauma claim that the transferences of patients with violent histories replay prior instances of victimization. Such patients alternately experience their therapists as omnipotent protectors, abject victims, and malignant perpetrators as they relive scenes of trespass and abuse in clinical sessions (Herman 1997). Many therapists observed that, after the attack, patients' transferences contained similar themes of rescue, threat, and desolation. For patients with histories of abandonment and loss, 9/11 produced the understanding that their therapists were vulnerable. They feared that their therapists would disappear, that a tragedy would befall them, or that they might die at any time. Newly afraid that therapists sometimes took unnecessary risks – which after the attack, included traveling – several patients went into a panic. Some whose therapists were out of town on the day of the attack, or who canceled standing appointments to work as volunteers, felt that they had been utterly deserted.

Moreover, many patients' transferences were suffused with anxiety and rage. Displaying the spike in aggression commonly incited by the enormous assault, patients grew concerned that they would somehow injure their therapists. Those who had informed their therapists of the attack in the early morning of September 11 feared having caused them unbearable pain, or having so totally contaminated the clinical relationship that the entire therapeutic project would crash. Other patients were concerned that their gruesome accounts of 9/11, violent fantasies of retaliation, or explicit desires for military revenge would cause their therapists harm, or would open rifts between them; some were frightened that their therapists would punish them for expressing opposing political views. One therapist spoke of patients who alternately wished to murder him and dreaded his demise.

Because, for many individuals, the attack engendered a crisis of faith, many patients yearned for someone they could thoroughly believe in and trust. Some of them turned to their therapists. Several therapists observed that patients wanted to see them as invincible after the attack. One noted that patients needed to see that their therapists "could continue to think, function, and not collapse psychologically like the World Trade towers." A second thought that many of her patients came to view her as "a symbol of life or a symbol of hope." Such idealizing transferences could be ephemeral, and were vulnerable to sudden shifts. The psychological consultant to the elementary school near the Trade Center said that immediately after the attack his steady presence became essential to the community, because "I represent understanding, I represent support, I represent being there." For community members who had confided their horrifying experiences in him, and who relied on him to soothe their suffering, he symbolized "all the good." The more they connected him with the attack, however, the more he acquired its taint. Rather than being seen as a savior, he became a constant reminder of what they had endured, arousing disturbing memories of events they preferred to forget. He also became a symbol of dire news. "When I walk into a situation, I've now got the association to that experience," he said. "If people see me early in the morning or at the end of the school day, that's crisis mode; that means something is afoot."

Transferences necessarily are cultural as well as psychological. Patients attribute specific cultural identities and social positions to their therapists, and may view them through the lenses of prevalent ethnic and racial stereotypes (Seeley 2000). After the Trade Center attack, patients' cultural transferences were altered, so that some saw their therapists through new eyes. Public suspicions of Arabs and Muslims extended, at least temporarily, to mental health professionals. In consequence, the identities of therapists of color, therapists from countries other than the United States, and therapists who spoke English as a second language abruptly entered the clinical foreground. Patients' desires for their therapists to comfort and protect them inevitably were thwarted when they imagined them as the other or, in some cases, as the enemy.

Two therapists stated that a few of their patients began to worry about their ancestry and allegiances. The first therapist, who was from the Middle East, noticed that new patients "were a little bit cautious in the first few sessions." The second therapist remarked that some of his patients had begun to discuss "untrustworthy foreigners" in sessions; he interpreted such comments as expressions of their anxieties about him:

"People can suspect that I could be from some other part of the world. Could I be like these hated fanatics? Am I one of them? And am I safe? Who am I?"

The suspicions of newly fearful patients also materialized in the stories they told their therapists:

"The patient started to talk about the fact that the other day some U-Haul trucks were stolen by some unknown Arabs, and they were dangerously running around the country with explosives, and there might be attacks. And I could see that in many ways there are concerns about me – that can I be trusted or am I one of these dangerous Arabs with powerful explosives running around in the street?"

Though these therapists were concerned that such negative cultural transferences would intensify, as a rule they did not get out of hand, and most of their patients remained in treatment with them.

A South American patient who had grown up in a country with a long history of state terror experienced a different kind of negative cultural transference after the attack. Upset that her therapist was uninformed about the psychological consequences of terrorism, and was unfamiliar with political terror in other countries, including hers, she began to doubt her therapist's capacity to understand her.

EMOTIONAL PROFITEERING

Although mental health professionals see it as their job to cultivate conversations about every facet of human experience, the American "taboo" prohibiting frank discussions of money affects all levels of clinical practice (Trachtman 1999:275). Students training to be mental health professionals receive little or no instruction in setting and collecting fees, and colleagues who freely consult with each other about the most intimate details of patients' lives may refuse to reveal how much they charge them for sessions. The clinical literature on the meanings of money is comparatively thin. Published work tends to endorse the ideas of Freud (1908/1961), who famously drew parallels between money and feces, and who stated that patients' feelings about money symbolized deep-seated psychological conflicts (Beltsiou n.d.). Contemporary mental health professionals have explored patients' fury at being charged for treatment, their refusal to pay their bills, and their tendency to bounce checks (Altman 1995). However, they have been less inclined to examine their own views about the place of money in their professional activities, whether pertaining to their feelings about collecting fees for their services, or to the potential for personal financial gain. Therapists' silence on these subjects may derive from a reluctance to acknowledge their economic dependence on their patients, without whom they "would be out of a job" (Holmes 1998:125). Alternatively, they may be loath to admit that their intimate and benevolent therapeutic endeavors, which some view as "a manifestation of love" (Lear 1990:28), are also transactions involving cold cash.

Though it is not widely discussed within the mental health field, therapists, like other highly trained professionals, must create a demand for their services, secure a loyal clientele, diversify their offerings, market their expertise, and make a steady profit in order to sustain their livelihoods. Over the past few decades, mental health professionals have sought to do so, in part, by carving out salaried, staff positions in schools, corporations, universities, hospitals, the military, and other institutions. Further, by labeling more and more behaviors as pathological, and by identifying new psychiatric syndromes, they have expanded the territory of mental illness, at once broadening their sphere of authority and creating larger pools of potential patients. Such activities have become critical to mental health professionals' survival at a time when managed care corporations and other market forces have increasingly chipped away at their earnings.

The therapy-friendly climate following 9/11 offered mental health professionals momentary relief from dominant trends that seemed to promise reduced financial returns. When the abject suffering and violent emotions inflamed by the attack were framed as mental disorders, therapists stood to benefit. Though generally publicity-shy, after the attack therapists proved adept at marketing their services, and at extending professional relief to those who were in misery. By offering to help persons harmed in the attack, therapists gained new kinds of influence, a more favorable public profile, and uncounted numbers of incoming patients. In these endeavors, they received unusual backing. Mental health services were publicly recommended, and were paid for by charitable organizations as well as by state and local governments. Although many therapists suffered financial losses after the attack – either they couldn't get to their offices in the "frozen zone" below 14th Street, or they scaled down their practices to volunteer their services, or their patients from other boroughs and the suburbs were too frightened to come to Manhattan – those who specialized in trauma or bereavement were flooded with referrals. Even those who lacked such skills realized that they were handed a rare economic opportunity. In New

York City, where millions of individuals were destabilized by the attack, and where a number of third parties were willing to pay for their treatment, there was money to be made. Some organizations reaped remarkable profits; one large counseling firm that provided assistance to nearly 200 companies billed $4 million in psychological services (Sommers & Satel 2005).

But such opportunities aroused conflicts for several mental health professionals treating individuals who were devastated by the attack. After 9/11, many therapists in private practice questioned the morality of benefiting financially from a devastating national catastrophe. In their view, taking money for ministering to victims' suffering seemed like emotional profiteering; it poisoned their sense of contributing selflessly to the city's psychological recovery. In response, some continued to display the generous volunteerism characteristic of therapists' early reactions to the attack. Citing the duty "to be available after 9/11 for whomever I needed to be available for," they gave regular patients extra sessions without charge, or offered free therapy to those who couldn't afford it. Others refused to accept Red Cross reimbursements for the mental health services they provided, because they felt that it "sullied" their work.

In contrast were mental health professionals who saw their colleagues' altruism and sacrifice as misguided or ill conceived. They were wary of setting dangerous precedents by offering psychological treatment for free, and by making their specialized, professional services seem no more valuable than those provided by less skilled volunteers. Instead, they sought to use 9/11 to publicly boost the worth of their expertise, and to demand that they be fairly compensated for it. One therapist found it "irrational" that her colleagues would elect not to profit from the attack, stating that "there's no reason in the world why . . . I shouldn't accept the money and do with it what I want." She noted,

"It's really no different in principle from benefiting from any disaster. You could say my entire work life is based on benefiting – earning my living anyway – on the basis of other peoples' troubles."

This therapist described a professional meeting shortly after 9/11 where one of her colleagues urged the audience "not to do too much pro bono work because there was going to be a fair amount of money involved."

"And of course she was absolutely right, but nobody wanted to hear it then. We all wanted to make sacrifices then. Nobody wanted to hear that this was going to be treated professionally eventually."

SUDDEN DEATH

As New York City mental health professionals grappled with new ethical questions concerning the financial dimensions of their practices, they also confronted new kinds of patients who were entirely desolated by the shocking and sudden deaths of loved ones in a terrorist attack. For many mental health professionals, the most wrenching therapeutic encounters involved individuals whose friends or relatives had perished on 9/11. Even therapists who specialized in bereavement, and whose long careers in cancer wards or hospices had made them all too familiar with death, believed that conventional models of mourning did not apply to this population, and that they had entered uncharted clinical terrain. Therapists who considered the attack a flagrant act of war also found themselves at a loss. Only a minority of New York City mental health professionals had had personal experiences of war, or had been trained to treat the surviving relatives of civilian casualties after a surprise attack on home soil. As a result, one therapist remarked, "We had no idea what was really helpful."

Many therapists encountered particular difficulties in their work with patients whose losses were entirely unexpected, and occurred with "no preparation, no process, and no good-bye" (M. Miller 2003:13). In the case of 9/11, the utter suddenness of death inevitably was exacerbated by the catastrophic circumstances surrounding it. Some therapists invoked the notion of traumatic loss to characterize patients whose grief and disorientation at the deaths of family members or friends were significantly compounded by the incomprehensible assault that caused them. Because many patients were too shocked to fully digest the events that had irrevocably shattered their lives, their ability to acknowledge their loss, and to mourn it, decreased. One therapist explained that, for patients whose losses occurred in a manner that was traumatic, the usual psychological approaches to bereavement were less likely to be helpful.

> *"Before you can get to bereavement, you've got to deal with the trauma. And it can take a person a year to be in a position where they're ready to deal with the loss because of the trauma."*

A second therapist observed that individuals "can walk around knowing that something happened, but it doesn't translate into your heart, you don't feel it for a long time." Many patients she worked with in the first year after the attack "were walking around like zombies." Their psychological treatments were narrowly focused on practical necessities, such as getting their children to school, determining the status of their finances, and processing insurance forms and other paperwork related to the attack. "The real suffering part" did not begin until more than a year later. At that time, rather than beginning to recover,

"People are really starting to feel their sadness. They're really processing that 'He's not coming back,' or 'She's not coming back,' or 'I'm never going to see him again.'"

Another therapist found treating the families of 9/11 victims especially difficult because existing psychological models did not apply to them, and because "there is no category to put them in." In his view, to treat this population it was imperative for mental health professionals to "suspend what you think you know and learn a different paradigm." A central feature of this new paradigm was that these family members were "suffering differently" because their relatives had been killed by an act that they found utterly unfathomable. For family members, the events of 9/11, unlike familiar and expectable causes of death, simply "don't make sense . . . that people fly planes into buildings doesn't happen." Because their relatives were killed by an event they found literally unbelievable, individuals were less able to process it psychologically, or to integrate it into the rest of their lives.

Moreover, many patients were "suffering differently" because they had sustained an inconceivable number of losses in the attack. In some cases, the losses were so staggering that they amounted to the "total destruction of a relational world." Therapists treated traders who lost dozens of close friends in the towers, police officers who lost everyone in their unit, firefighters who "knew 100 people who were dead," and former employees of "Windows of the World" who had skipped work the day of the attack, with the result that "everyone they know is dead." In many cases, clinical work with people who were multiply bereaved, and with persons whose family members died in the attack, was complicated by an uncompromising and "ugly anger." A bereavement therapist observed,

"An awful lot of the people feel a huge amount of anger, toward the government, God, the FBI, Clinton, that maybe somebody could have stopped this; that somebody was asleep at the switch."

When patients considered their friends' and relatives' deaths "an insult," their grief was especially intractable.

The profound grief, shock, and anger of some families of 9/11 victims further escalated when they learned of the financial awards that were available to them. The September 11th Victim Compensation Fund was established to provide economic security to families who sustained losses in the attack. But initially, many families wanted nothing to do with it. In their eyes, the Fund's money was "guilt money" or "bad money," and it was intended to purchase their silence, to put a price on the relatives they lost, or to replace what was irreplaceable.[3] Some families who had lost children in the attack, and who were likely to receive millions of dollars after submitting the Fund's lengthy claim form, "felt dirty, as if they were compromising something," and were "in total conflict about what to do." However, while some family members expressed deep misgivings about accepting the awards, others appealed for greater compensation. They sought private hearings with the Fund's special master at which they testified about their relatives' exceptional qualities, or about their critical economic contributions to the family, in order to increase the amount they received. Although 97% of the families eventually accepted these awards, this did not put an end to conflicts surrounding the Fund. The Fund's administrators strictly followed state laws in determining which particular relatives of World Trade Center victims were legally entitled to the generous monies it disbursed. Yet its decisions were sometimes bitterly contested. Lengthy battles over which relatives received the money erupted between individuals who were widowed in the attack and the parents of the dead, between those who were engaged to the deceased and the persons who would have been their in-laws, and between family members of those who perished and their long-term gay partners, who lacked the legal rights of spouses. They fought over who among them were the rightful – if not legal – recipients of the awards, and whether those who received payments would share them with others who made moral and emotional claims on them (cf. Feinberg 2005).

If patients' bereavement was exacerbated by multiple losses, by trauma and feelings of anger, by the unfathomable nature of the act that produced it, or by disputes pertaining to sizable financial awards, then it also was made extraordinarily agonizing by the various meanings that were attached to these deaths. It has been said that the bodies of the dead go on to have "political lives" (Verdery 1999), and the bodies of those who died in the World Trade Center attack were no exception. Rather, these bodies were used to advance a variety of contradictory agendas, and were turned into symbols that reverberated locally, nationally, and internationally.

The bodies of fallen firefighters had exceptionally robust political lives. In the New York metropolitan area, their physical remains served a variety of ends. For one, the fire department invoked them in its bitter competition with the New York City police department for authority in future catastrophes. These bodies and remains also provided economic gain. When visitors from far and near engaged in disaster tourism, visiting New York City firehouses and buying so many t-shirts and baseball caps with the fire department logo that sales at the Fire Zone store averaged $25,000 a day, the fire department hired a professional marketer to manage the branding of its name (Corry 2002). More important, the city invoked their bodies to discourage violent acts of retribution, channeling individuals' inchoate rage at the attack into a solemn veneration of deceased firefighters. Indeed, the bodies and remains of firefighters led active political lives as heroes. Following an attack that outsmarted the United States, and that resulted in global advertisements of American vulnerability, the dead bodies of New York City firefighters symbolized brute courage and strength. Though the acres of ashes at Ground Zero contained little that could be celebrated, stories of firefighters' remarkable valor rapidly proliferated in the media, fortifying national myths of limitless goodness and power.[4]

These heroic narratives were employed not only to rehabilitate the city and the nation but also to restore the reputation of the New York City fire department. They did so by overshadowing considerably bleaker stories of the department's missteps and deficiencies in responding to the attack. As one firefighter later stated, "We were doing nothing. Nothing. What's the plan? Nobody had a plan" (Dwyer & Flynn 2005:222). Some have claimed that the fire department's disorganization, insubordination, and lack of preparation actually may have contributed to the deaths of civilians and of uniformed services personnel. Firefighters' inferior radio equipment made it impossible for them to deliver a coordinated disaster response, to advise persons of the grave dangers of remaining in the towers, to insist on their immediate evacuation, and to specify the stairways by which they could safely escape. Approximately two hundred firefighters remained in the north tower when its stability was known to be precarious simply because no one was able to contact them and order them to leave.

In a similar fashion, such heroic narratives remade the deaths of hundreds of individual firefighters, turning the demise of those who had failed to tame enormous fires, to move unwieldy debris, to rescue scores of screaming civilians, and to overcome fatigue after carrying 56 pounds of equipment up dozens of smoke-filled flights of stairs, into honorable and acceptable "good deaths" (Verdery 1999:42). Tales of extraordinary heroism were frequently recounted at their funerals; because they considered each other brothers, every death was the death of kin, and each funeral was widely attended by surviving firefighters. When Mayor Giuliani, who spoke at a number of funerals, lauded deceased firefighters for saving some 50,000 people in the "'greatest rescue ever recorded'" (Dwyer & Flynn 2005:248), he sought to transform a catastrophic tragedy, and a highly public show of professional ineffectiveness, into a spectacular triumph. Though some families were distressed by the inaccuracies of such portrayals, turning firefighters into heroes lent comfort to many of their relatives and bestowed honor on their colleagues.

If firefighters' bodies lived full lives as local and national heroes, then those of the thousands of civilians who were killed in the attack were less easily redeemed. In contrast with widespread accounts of valiant firefighters, and in spite of the fact that approximately 15,000 civilians succeeding in escaping the towers by digging their way out of elevators, vaulting over piles of rubble, or sprinting down hundreds of stairs, sometimes carrying those who were weaker on their backs, they commonly were depicted as helpless victims who passively awaited their rescue from the towers (Dwyer & Flynn 2005). Some families of civilians who died in the attack complained that the public cared less about their relatives' deaths than about the deaths of those who were hailed as heroes. In their view, nothing better illustrated the disregard for their dead than the treatment of tiny fragments of tissue and bone that were discovered during the cleanup at Ground Zero. These fragments were not returned to family members, but were transported with other incinerated debris, which included tons of dust full of human remains, to Fresh Kills landfill in Staten Island – otherwise known as the largest garbage dump in the world. There, they were mixed in with ordinary household waste. Despite the pleas of more than 1,100 families whose relatives' remains were unceremoniously consigned to the landfill, Mayor Michael Bloomberg, Mayor Giuliani's successor, declared that it was too expensive to retrieve and then rebury them (Baird 2004; Davies 2004).

Yet the bodies and remains of civilians proved to have resonant political lives as well. This resonance was largely derived from the fact that unlike other deaths in the United States, which commonly are hidden away, these deaths were exceptionally public. Because they were the result of an attack on the nation, the names of the dead were widely publicized, the deceased were mourned all over the country, and ceremonies for those who were killed in the attack were broadcast on national television. Unfortunately, for the families who were bereaved by the attack, and whose relatives' bodies led political lives as symbols of national innocence, having to mourn in the public eye, and being denied a sense of privacy, further complicated their suffering.[5] One therapist said that,

> *"When people lost somebody just the ordinary way, sometimes they feel like, why doesn't the world stop? The bottom has just fallen out of my world, why don't they acknowledge it? But the 9/11 people are saying, 'I want people to stop paying attention to us for a little while so I can just be alone and do this my own way.'"*

Not only did the families of those who were killed on 9/11 feel that their mourning was uncomfortably public, but the public appropriations of their relatives' deaths disturbed them in other ways as well. Immediately after the attack, when family members traveled from one hospital to another holding posters of those who were missing, they retained full possession of their relatives, carrying their likenesses in their hands and defining them down to their nicknames, hair color, and height. However, as mounting evidence suggested that the missing would not return, their families seemed to lose control over them. The deceased no longer belonged solely to them, but had to be shared with a general public so eager to partake in their passing that the Trade Center site, which contained their remains, became a place of frequent pilgrimage and a popular tourist attraction.[6]

Given the national fascination with all varieties of celebrity, perhaps it is not surprising that those who died on 9/11 achieved a kind of renown. The desires of average Americans to identify with them as victims, to honor them as casualties of war, or simply to get to know them as distinguished individuals may have been sated by the "Portraits of Grief" that were published in the *New York Times*. These Portraits, to which families contributed, guaranteed that unlike those who were struck down by previous atrocities and remained part of an undifferentiated mass, or who were so degraded and dehumanized by tragedy that identifying with them was impossible (Alexander 2002), the victims of September 11 were personally identified and described. This "series of miniature profiles" provided a moving and efficient way to grasp the "individual humanity swallowed in the dehumanizing vastness of the toll" (Scott 2003:ix). In contrast to conventional obituaries that flatly stated basic facts about the life of the deceased, the Portraits were sentimental, and even uplifting, "snapshots of lives interrupted as they were being actively lived." They celebrated "the subtle nobility of everyday existence" (Raines 2003:vii) by conveying individuals' distinctive personalities, intriguing hobbies, and endearing quirks.[7]

Far worse for many families than the public's appropriation of their relatives was the federal government's cynical abuse of their dead bodies to justify the invasion of Afghanistan and the coming war in Iraq. Some families were enraged with the government because, as one therapist reported,

"They felt they were being used, that the event was being used. It was bad enough that their relatives had died, but they were now being used to push this so-called war on terrorism."

To defend themselves against such misappropriations, some family members actively reclaimed their relatives' identities. If their bodies and remains were fated to have continuing political lives, then they grew determined to repossess them to promote the particular projects that they deemed important. Defining themselves as the sole individuals with the authority to speak on their relatives' behalf, sometimes attending political meetings with photographs of them pinned to their chests, they spoke in the names of civilians who were killed in an attack on the United States. Family members formed a number of organizations that vigorously lobbied for various social and political causes. They used the new leverage that was attached to the bodies of the deceased to establish an official investigation into the attack, to protest the war in Iraq, to increase the safety of skyscrapers, to create a memorial at Ground Zero, and to demand that the Fresh Kills landfill not become the final resting place of their relatives (Baird 2004; Davies 2004).

Long-Distance Runners

A final factor that contributed to the clinical challenges therapists faced in treating individuals whose relatives were killed on 9/11 was that many patients seemed to be incapable of dislodging themselves from, or moving beyond, the moment of the assault. They remained there, in part, due to the countless reminders of the attack that constantly surrounded them. Because discussions, analyses, and reports of 9/11 were everywhere, "the chances of them going a day without 9/11 being mentioned are nil." Other therapists thought that for these families, "the passage of time is experienced much differently" in the sense that "time hasn't moved." Family members were in "suspended animation" as if it was always September 11 and they were forever trapped in the instant of the attack. One therapist said that more than a year later,

"I have people who come into my office and sit down, and I say, 'How are you doing?' And they say, 'Well, you asked me that on November 1 [2001], and that's how I'm doing. I'm still right there where I was. I'm still watching the plane on television hit my son.'"

The passage of time was further complicated for the hundreds of families whose relatives' bodies were returned to them in pieces. Another therapist recalled working with one patient who had recently received her relative's right hand, and another who had gotten a pelvis. Some who were given remains were strongly advised not to look at them because they were so terribly lacerated, degraded, or burned. When the DNA tests that identified human tissue and bone were set up to continue for several years, families who had received small fragments of bodies were promised that "more fragments are yet to come."

This news made family members uncertain how long they should wait before burying the remains on hand, and how to handle the receipt of additional body parts.

"The word is out among the family members that you will get more of your son, of your daughter. And the families say, 'What are we going to do? Have another memorial service? Are we going to dig up what we buried?'"

Such uncertainties inevitably delayed the usual rituals of mourning. One family whose relative's remains were among the last to be identified did not hold a funeral service until June 2005, nearly four years after the attack (Kilgannon 2005).[8]

Families' profound anguish was exacerbated when various parties urged them to recover their bearings rapidly. The same public that initially had desired to grieve alongside them soon lost patience with their continuing pain, and wanted their mourning to come to an end. Friends and relatives pressured them to go back to work, and to resume their normal routines, hoping that this would return them to the lives they had led before the attack. The special master of the September 11 Victim Compensation Fund, who sought to "lance the emotional intensity" (Feinberg 2005:112) of his meetings with numerous families, was surprised to discover that they "could not get past their loss"; he sometimes suspected their grief had been "staged" to procure more sizable awards (Feinberg 2005:113).

Even therapists could find it difficult to bear patients' unrelenting sorrow, in part because it made them feel incompetent and ineffective. When patients failed to show improvement, or to fully resolve questions surrounding their relatives' deaths, therapists sometimes pushed them to work faster, rather than helping them come to terms with their losses at their own pace. Some patients were acutely aware of the frustration they induced in others, and worried that they had become burdensome. Others blamed themselves for being "defective," concerned that "everybody moved on, but I'm stuck here. Am I crazy? What's wrong with me?" While the notion of closure frequently surfaced in discussions of 9/11, many families considered it a "deadening word." To them, closure implied that their "loved ones didn't exist," that their "hearts and lives were dead to that person," or that "the person is over." Instead, what they most desired was to "live constantly in the moment of the loss and in the memory of the loss."

Some therapists were surprised to find that more than a year after the attack, both new and existing patients remained so firmly in its grip that the events of 9/11 were all they wanted to talk about. One therapist observed,

"You think it's going to end, or think other issues are going to come up . . . that clients are going to come in for other things. But that's not what happens."

Treatments not only seemed to be endless but they also acquired a new, intermittent quality as patients who terminated therapy returned again and again for more psychological help. "Where in the past you finish with someone," one therapist said, "people keep coming back." People regularly returned to treatment during holidays, birthdays, and anniversaries, when they were flooded with memories of the ones they had lost and their grief was especially keen. As one therapist noted, "Each landmark brings another ripple. Each holiday brings up more memories and more side effects."

Therapists also saw the attack's emotional impact widen over time. When waves of crews at Ground Zero finished their jobs, including Verizon workers who repaired damaged electrical lines, mechanics who fixed city elevators, and police officers who bagged body parts in the landfill, they trickled into treatment. Moreover, one therapist remarked that following catastrophic events of this scale, "you're not just talking about the persons to whom this happened, you're talking about anybody whose lives these people touch." A year later, many began to see a "second tier" of patients composed of victims' and survivors' more distant relatives and acquaintances. This second tier also was composed of the spouses of recovery workers who had "brought the trauma home, either by talking about it or by not talking about it." Spouses who stayed at home, and who saw the hellish pit where their husbands worked on television, feared that toxic particles from the disaster, which stuck to their bodies and garments, would invade and contaminate their homes. One spouse worried that her husband's work clothes would bring "all the chemicals and the poisons and the jet fuel fumes in the house and poison the baby."

If the report of a therapist who treated a woman injured in the 1993 bombing of the twin towers is any indication, the suffering of those who were harmed in the attack, and of their closest friends and relatives, will continue for years to come. Like many 2001 World Trade Center survivors, this patient's psychological trauma was exacerbated by the physical harm she suffered while escaping from the towers. During her seven-year psychotherapy, the therapist witnessed her patient's life "disintegrate." Too traumatized to return to work at the World Trade Center – indeed, too physically injured to return to work at all – her personal identity was shattered. Her marriage deteriorated, and "her husband became an old man." The patient's psychological treatment, which began shortly after the bombing, ended only with her death from complications of her injuries.

Anticipating agonizing and protracted psychotherapies with patients profoundly damaged on September 11, therapists realized that they were in it "for the long haul," and tried to pace themselves. One said that his task was to help patients see that they were in "a suffering place," and to stay there with them indefinitely. A second therapist agreed, stating,

"I feel like I've got to be a long-distance runner here. I feel like I'm going to be best for them if I can be the slow and steady and predictable and permanent presence for as long as they choose to be here."

CHAPTER 5

The Trauma of Psychological Treatment

✌

As in their routine, pre-9/11 therapeutic encounters, in their clinical work following the attack, mental health professionals focused squarely on their patients, inquiring into what they had experienced and offering them solace and support. Before long, however, the inordinate demands of working with individuals in varying states of fury, shock, and anguish began to unsettle and deplete them. Therapists abruptly were thrown into unimagined professional circumstances in which cases that were technically daunting, and unusually emotionally disturbing, incessantly came their way. When their long work-days with scores of grieving and traumatized patients finally were over, they had nowhere to turn for shelter. Instead, they repaired to a world that seemed scarred beyond recognition. The horrific stories they heard at work were compounded by the terrors that gripped their families, the losses of friends and relatives, and by the sudden shattering of their city's vivacity and its hard-won sense of security. As these circumstances accumulated, many mental health professionals grew progressively unhinged. It soon became painfully clear that the World Trade Center attack had damaged not only the patients who received psychological services but also the therapists who delivered them.

Reeling from multiple blows, many therapists who dedicated themselves to their clinical work in the aftermath of 9/11 did so at their own expense. Several metropolitan area mental health professionals found that the year after the attack was the most agonizing by far of their long professional careers. Some felt that they were infected by patients' inconsolable sorrow or by their persistent and runaway fears. Others with personal histories of trauma unexpectedly were retraumatized by patients' gruesome accounts of their experiences on 9/11. Indeed, as they treated individuals who had narrowly survived the attack, as well as the relatives of those it had killed, therapists encountered a variety of novel occupational hazards that had unanticipated consequences for them.

EMOTIONAL CONTAGION

Contrary to conventional American conceptions of emotions as essences that are firmly contained inside the physical boundaries of individual bodies (Geertz 1973), sentiments are known to spread from one person to another (Brennan 2004). Those that are produced by traumatic incidents are considered especially contagious (Herman 1997). As discussed in Chapter 1, mental health professionals have coined terms such as "vicarious trauma" and "secondary trauma" to describe the transmission of trauma-related affects from patients to their therapists. The contagion of these and other emotions is exacerbated by the unusual intimacies of clinical relationships. Therapists who are finely and empathically attuned to their patients are more vulnerable to penetration by their affective and cognitive states. Moreover, the enclosed and intensely charged atmospheres of clinical consulting rooms, where mental health professionals repeatedly are exposed to patients' vivid accounts of every sort of violation, provide exceptionally fertile breeding grounds for the spread of virulent affects.

Therapists frequently reported experiences of emotional contagion after the events of 9/11. The affects and responses in circulation included those that are characteristic of trauma, as well as other sentiments that were evoked by the attack's volatile emotional mix of shock, disorientation, and despair. In post-9/11 clinical encounters, such affects were commonly passed from troubled patients to their therapists. Many therapists had never felt so susceptible to their patients' subjective states. As one remarked, "If I'm treating an alcoholic, I'm not going to start drinking." But their work after 9/11 was different, so that, "There wasn't one of us that wasn't hearing it and taking it on."

Therapists' heightened susceptibility to the emotional states of their patients was partly due to the fact that, after the attack, they were not always able to implement the standard rules of clinical engagement. These rules, which generally stipulate the optimal distance between themselves and their patients, lay the groundwork for clinical relationships that permit heightened degrees of both transparency and privacy. They make it safe for patients to reveal the most intimate details of their lives to their therapists, and they allow therapists to be highly attuned to them. But at the same time, they place many aspects of therapists' personal identities, states of mind, and opinions outside of the clinical frame, so that they are off-limits to their patients.

Despite recent moves toward greater mutuality in psychological treatments, and toward greater openness and self-disclosure on the part of mental health professionals (Aron 1996, Mitchell 1997), therapeutic relationships are hardly reciprocal. Rather, they remain out of balance by design, and are intentionally skewed to shed the maximum light on patients' interior and relational worlds. As is discussed later in this chapter, even when therapists elect to share their personal thoughts and feelings with patients in order to deepen the work, or to help them arrive at new insights, they maintain an emotional reserve. The clinical distance that results is believed to benefit patients, in that it provides the necessary space for psychological analysis and intervention. Without it, therapists would be less capable of viewing patients' concerns from different angles, asking them questions that expand their understanding, lending them their egos, and extending them their hope.

However, the events of 9/11 suggest that this distance is advantageous for both members of the clinical dyad. It defends therapists against being so permeable to patients' affective states that they fully take them on, and it buffers them against the frightening material and elevated emotions that they face in long days of back-to-back sessions, or during lengthy clinical careers. Additional factors reinforce mental health professionals' protection against the onslaught of emotions. Some therapists restrict their practices to the kinds of patients with whom they feel safest and most effective, with whom they feel the greatest kinship, or whom they find most interesting. To avoid becoming overwhelmed, and to guard against vicarious trauma, they may cultivate a stance of detachment or neutrality, and may limit the number of patients they see who are severely traumatized, disturbed, or depressed (Zimering, Munroe, & Gulliver 2005).

Moreover, therapists strictly regulate the amount of time they spend in each session, and design their clinical spaces with their personal comfort in mind. These factors help therapists manage the feelings their patients induce in them, which are known as countertransferences, while enhancing their sense of control. One therapist acknowledged these benefits, saying,

"It's my place, my time, it's forty-five minutes. I know what the boundaries are. If I feel a countertransferential buildup I can distance myself from it."

After 9/11, however, he felt that he lost control over sessions. In contrast with the predictable, measured pace of his usual clinical work, "this thing was going at 90 miles per hour." In addition,

"The intensity was up a hundredfold, and it was all there in the room. You could not hide behind any neutrality, or curiosity about 'what does that mean?'"

Many other therapists similarly experienced a diminished sense of protection and control. At the same time, their receptivity to patients' subjective states and affects grew. One therapist explained that doing psychotherapy requires therapists to enter each patient's subjective world:

"I was taught that you can't really understand what your patient is feeling unless you allow yourself to be drawn into that subjectivity. And then the work of the therapy is really to pull yourself back and come out, and look at it in a much more objective way."

Yet many therapists discovered a peculiar inability to pull themselves out of patients' subjectivities after 9/11.

Therapists' heightened vulnerabilities to the sentiments of their patients also were linked to their strong identifications with those who were injured or bereaved by the attack. It has been suggested that therapists are drawn to stories about the extremes of human experience because hearing these tragic accounts allows them to take their own psychic measure, reflect on their personal conflicts, and revisit their early histories. In the view of a psychoanalyst,

"Every analytic career is always a lengthy self-analysis. So I'm always discovering parts of myself. By listening to other people I can find something I've missed, something that I've shut out . . . There's something I'm going to hear that will help me if I listen well enough."

Moreover, as therapists listen to their patients, they imagine themselves being subjected to the specific catastrophes that are described before disavowing such identifications and recovering their sense of self (Thomas 2002).

But in listening to patients after 9/11, therapists encountered a range of iden-tifications, both with their patients and with the victims they discussed, that were much too close for comfort. Some were unable to fully shake these identi-fications due to eerie similarities between themselves and fellow New Yorkers who perished in the attack. To them, the photographs of the deceased that were on missing persons flyers all over town, and in the *New York Times* every day, "all looked vaguely familiar." One therapist had the upsetting realization that "it could be me":

"I remember seeing a flyer of a woman who was missing, and she was exactly my age, born on my birthday, same year, and I knew of course she must be dead. And I thought, why her? Why not me?"

Some therapists found it so difficult to differentiate themselves from their patients that "when they tell me these things, I'm living it." When patients spoke of what they had experienced as they made their way out of the twin towers on the morning of September 11, one imagined that she was in their place, so that,

> "*I am knocked to the fucking floor. And I am stuck in the elevator, and I am choking down the stairs and tripping over something and losing my briefcase. It's all very vivid, and it was a lot to carry around.*"

For some therapists, continual immersion in such disturbing material seemed to produce a direct transfer of affect and information, so that patients' violent emotions and experiences were indelibly inscribed in their minds. When therapists listened to patients' accounts, they "recorded" everything that was said. One therapist remarked,

> "*There are times as I listen to people – when I know that I'm with someone and really hearing it – when everything that they say can always be played like a tape in my mind. It has been recorded, it has been seared into my memory as it's seared into theirs.*"

Because many therapists were in the habit of creating detailed mental pictures of the stories they were told, these "tapes" contained not only the sounds of patients' voices recounting the "most abject horror stories" they had ever heard but also explicit visual images and highly charged emotions. Some therapists described vivid, internalized "videotapes" that portrayed the specific events patients had witnessed during the attack, and that they endlessly replayed. They felt emotionally battered after visualizing patients' graphic depictions of "stepping over heads" as they ran from the towers, watching the expressions of "somebody holding hands with a co-worker jumping out of the 90th floor of a building," finding fragments of a friend's body as they sifted through the debris, or standing next to someone who had escaped the tower only to be killed by a falling body. Their difficulties digesting such grotesque and surreal images no doubt contributed to their inability to pull themselves out of their patients' subjectivities, and increased their susceptibility to patients' contagious emotions.

Infected by patients' mental states, therapists reproduced specific aspects of their responses to the attack, by coping the same ways they coped or by feeling similar feelings. A therapist who worked with firefighters noticed unmistakable parallels between her reactions and theirs. Just as they no longer wanted to go home to be with families who couldn't fully understand what they had endured, she grew reluctant to leave her office, and to spend time with family and friends, because "it was important to be sitting in a room with people who know exactly what you're going through, versus sitting with people who have no idea." A second therapist had the same nightmares as those her patients described. A third shared the terrible guilt of patients who survived the attack when so many of their colleagues had died, or who felt responsible for the death of a spouse, saying, "If only I didn't drive him to the train, or if only I was late that morning." She also took on their preoccupations, especially where patients needed to know exactly how their relatives had died. Like them, she kept repeating, "I think he would be one of the ones who jumped, I bet he jumped, I bet he jumped, I think he jumped."

Some therapists suffered most from their new acquaintance with the dead. As a specialist in bereavement explained, "When you work with grief, in a way, you become introduced to the dead person"; she compared it to "reading a novel and having a character grow for you." Through her work with numerous families of the deceased after 9/11, she was "getting to know the people who died extremely well through the people who are talking about them." As a result, the dead began to "inhabit" her. She started to wonder the same kinds of things that their families were wondering:

> *"Did you suffer? Were you panicking? What was it like for you in the last few minutes? Did you know what was happening?"*

When the *New York Times* published the "Portraits of Grief," she found herself "looking for the pictures of the people I know through the people I'm working with," and thinking, "Oh, so that's what you look like."

Therapists took on patients' anguish, and their horrifying fears as well. Although many attempted to manage their own anxieties by turning off the television and throwing away the newspapers, they were unable to completely stanch the flow of information, thanks in part to patients who regularly conveyed the latest news and rumors. Patients also routinely confided their most terrifying fantasies, including specific cataclysms that their therapists had never imagined. One therapist said,

> *"I found myself becoming much more anxious when I had certain patients coming in talking about their theories, and talking about how they would only ride on the front of the train or the back of the train, because a bomber wouldn't go to those cars. Or how they would kill themselves if a nuclear blast went off, because they didn't want to die of radiation poisoning."*

Therapists described clinical sessions in which they felt immobilized by patients' panic:

"Someone would be sitting there crying and talking about how terrified she was . . . and I could not analyze it, I could not move; we would just sit together."

Sometimes, patients' frightening material was so overpowering that it challenged not only their personal reactions to the attack but also their usual worldviews, which suddenly seemed to be based on an "irrational sense of safety":

"I had a few patients coming in with their suicide plan, or how they were going to escape the city, or maybe they shouldn't stay here. And I remember sitting there feeling like . . . should I be leaving?"

Some of the reactions that therapists took in were saturated with trauma's characteristic taint. Just as time had stopped for patients who had lost family members or friends in the attack, it also stopped for them, so that they were "stuck in that intense, crazy time." Unlike other people they knew, who no longer were entirely preoccupied with 9/11, their continuing treatment of patients who constantly relived the attack meant that they were perpetually "looking backwards" to it. In addition, like survivors of trauma who experience an "altered relationship to the rest of humankind" (Erikson 1995:186), therapists felt marked and estranged. Some withdrew from their usual social circles because they couldn't "conjure up anything to give," or because they could no longer tolerate being with friends who focused on "petty things." Everything else seemed insignificant compared to the anguished stories they heard every day.

The contagion of virulent emotions was further intensified by the fact that following September 11, therapists abandoned their usual practice of restricting the number of patients who had suffered traumatic losses. The therapist who specialized in bereavement, and who had worked in hospital cancer wards for years, generally limited the number of "horror cases" she worked with at any one time to "stay sane." But after 9/11, she felt it was her "duty" to be available. As a result, a few months after the attack, she was treating several women who had lost their husbands, a woman who had lost both of her sisters, a few couples who had lost children, two women who had lost their fiancés, and a man who had lost more than 50 colleagues, as well as several people who had worked in the towers and had managed to evacuate in time. As a result, for this therapist, every day was "death and destruction and grief and abject pain; it's like hours every day."

A number of therapists, including those who before the attack had been uncertain how much tragedy they could cope with, felt pushed beyond their capacities. Unable to distance themselves from the horror, or to take refuge in the "protective coma" (Didion 2003:54) that shielded so many others, they struggled to remain emotionally present several hours a day, for weeks and months on end, to patients whose stories were impossibly painful and gruesome. They felt dazed, exhausted, and numb; after spending long days listening to patients, they spent nights at home in tears.

Desperate to restore some kind of protective buffer that might shield them from such virulent sentiments, some therapists withdrew from their patients. Although the talking cure may more accurately be called a listening cure, in that patients derive great psychological relief from being heard in clinical sessions (Seeley 2005a), many therapists could no longer listen attentively to the stories their patients told. In this respect, their behavior resembled that of therapists who treated victims of previous atrocities or of violent abuse (Lori 2005). As noted in Chapter 1, mental health professionals who worked with Holocaust survivors found dozens of ways to avoid listening to patients' detailed accounts of their suffering and losses during World War II (Danieli 1984). Similarly, a therapist who treated Vietnam veterans tended to seal herself off from such patients due to her "reluctance to have any knowledge of these atrocities" (Boulanger 2005:27). After 9/11, several therapists found it impossible to be constantly emotionally available to comparatively large numbers of "very highly traumatized people." To ward off their disturbing feelings, they cut themselves off or shut themselves down, refusing to fully acknowledge patients' devastation and grief. Others struggled to regulate their emotional states, so that they were neither distanced and dissociated nor submerged in patients' despair. One therapist commented that in working with catastrophic trauma,

"There is this place between feeling too much and feeling too little. You feel too much, and you can't do it. You feel too little, and you're not really there with the kind of empathy that's needed. . . . You have to be able to ask the questions that open up something painful, but not be so aware that you can't do the next session or you don't sleep the next night."

No matter how grueling their clinical encounters or how contagious the emotions they contained, many therapists felt compelled to carry on with their task. Their patients needed someone to bear witness to the devastation they had suffered, and therapists wanted to be that witness. As one said, "What kind of a therapist would I be if I said to a client, 'Stop, I can't hear anymore, I'm too upset!'" Another echoed this sentiment. Although she "was having a hard time being fully present" when she met with her most desolated patients, and longed to "run away and escape," she asked herself, "If I can't listen to that, if he can't process that here, what good am I to him?"

SIMULTANEOUS TRAUMA

While the contagion of virulent emotions complicated the psychological treatments therapists conducted in the aftermath of the attack, it did not completely account for the difficulties they encountered in their work. Rather, such difficulties also derived from the fact that the World Trade Center attack produced an extremely rare clinical situation in which therapists were deeply shaken by the same catastrophic events that injured the patients they were treating. If 9/11 was an attack on American society, then it was also an attack on them, with clear and potent impacts on their families, their city, and their lives. As one therapist noted, "We were as much victims as anyone else. It wasn't vicarious traumatization, it was firsthand." Indeed, the attack resulted in what may be conceptualized as the simultaneous trauma of therapists and their patients.[1]

Reports of specific traumatic stressors that are psychologically disturbing to both members of the clinical dyad rarely appear in the mental health literature. Published articles on this topic tend to address national calamities, particularly those involving the death or assassination of political leaders (cf. Somer & Saadon 1997). However, these articles focus primarily on patients' reactions to national catastrophes, and fail to elaborate how therapists are affected both personally and professionally. They thus are of limited utility in understanding the simultaneous trauma of 9/11, in which New York City patients and therapists shared visceral experiences of terror pursuant to an attack on civilians. In contrast, an article by Israeli mental health professionals (Kretsch, Benyakar, Baruch, & Roth 1997:29, 32) examines how local therapists responded when they and other civilians were simultaneously exposed to an imminent missile attack during the first Gulf War. According to this article, after the sounding of the National Defense Alert siren that warned them of the attack, therapists were models of stability and calm. Although they were fearful as they sat in sealed rooms alongside evacuees, "gas masks on their faces, experiencing an identical threat," they remained competent and in control, and were able to employ the "shared reality as a useful clinical tool rather than as a confusing impediment to therapy."[2]

In all likelihood, at the time of the attack, most New York City mental health professionals were less familiar than their Israeli counterparts with situations of simultaneous trauma. The therapist who treated traumatized veterans of the war in Vietnam distinguished her postattack clinical work from all that had preceded it:

"The guys I saw as Vietnam vets, it was in their past. It was distant. It was in a far away place. They would talk about atrocities, and they would

have flashbacks, but I was separated from it. It didn't affect me. I had never witnessed a trauma like that, or been part of it. This one, I was in it. I didn't know if walking through Manhattan I was going to be bombed or killed or if I had to take my kid and run for shelter. And it was my land, my home, that they were bombing. It was very personal. "

Nor had these therapists been professionally prepared to manage situations of simultaneous trauma. One who was trained to treat crime victims observed that, "Nobody ever said, 'now remember, this could happen to you too. And you might have to deal with it at the same time that you're helping somebody else.'"

The concept of simultaneous trauma does not necessarily imply that therapists' psychological injuries were as grave as those of their patients. As in every collective catastrophe, New Yorkers experienced different kinds of losses on 9/11, and were wounded to varying degrees. Some therapists, including those who witnessed the attack at close range, lost relatives, friends, and – in some cases – patients, suffered damage to their apartments or offices, or fled for their lives, were affected more directly. Yet even therapists who did not experience the attack firsthand, and who did not incur such immediate personal damage, inhabited a city that had sustained a painfully high number of casualties, and whose environment had been physically scarred. In some cases, therapists felt that injuries to the city were also injuries to the self; one therapist who identified himself "more as a New Yorker than as an American" took his city's agony and its grotesque disfigurement as devastating personal blows. For those who viewed the attack as an act of war, and who had been reassured as children that "You don't have to worry, we don't have war in America. Nobody bombs us," there was shock at the insecurity of their homeland, and at the loss of cherished assumptions of national invulnerability. Having survived "the death of their world as [they] had known it," therapists, along with their patients, had to find new ways to "reinhabit the world" (Das 2000:223): to ready themselves for what might happen next, to master a new vocabulary of disaster, and to adapt to the atmosphere of menace.

Also like their patients, therapists developed reactions that were characteristic of trauma. One therapist became startled whenever he heard airplanes overhead. When the subway stopped between stations he worried, "Is this going to be just a momentary thing, or is this the start of something awful?" Another avoided the phone booth from which he had watched the airplanes fly into the towers, because it filled him with horrible memories. A third had "my own flashbacks" when her patients discussed what they experienced in the attack. Others feared that city bridges and tunnels would explode in the course of their daily commute.

Just as the attack on the World Trade Center entailed the breaking of national boundaries, it ruptured clinical boundaries as well, shattering the usual barrier between the worlds inside and outside the consulting room. Therapists could no longer depend on firm boundaries between their work and the rest of their lives, because the attack was fully present "not only in this room, but when I walk outside, it's all over." More important, because therapists and their patients had been stricken by the same catastrophic event, the usual distinction between them – doubtless the most essential distinction in psychological treatment – no longer fully held.[3] Unlike typical clinical dyads where there are clear and significant differences between the troubled patients who are in need of help and the comparatively intact and steady therapists who provide it, many city therapists were as frightened and as fragile as their patients. As one therapist remarked, "If you're my patient and you've been through this, and I've been through it, and I'm calling you sick, then I'm sick too." Another therapist added, "We crossed a line, because there was no line anymore. We were in it with everyone else."

This situation of simultaneous trauma had a variety of repercussions for clinical encounters after the attack. Therapists who attempted to heal their patients while their own wounds and fears were still raw noted how difficult it was "to absorb everyone else's pain" when they were overwhelmed by their own:

> *"It's easy to underestimate what it's like to listen to other people process-ing something. And when you have both people processing the same thing, over and over, each in their own way, some with more anxiety than others, it's a lot to digest."*

Several found that the combination of their injuries and those of their patients upset their emotional balance; they were "rocked more" by the material they heard. The more they identified with patients' devastation, the less they felt capable of performing therapeutic functions that were critical in treating sur-vivors of catastrophic trauma. Rather than receiving patients' disclosures and returning them in less toxic forms (Boulanger 2005), they may have added to their potency, as evidenced by the therapist who stated, "If someone said 'I feel helpless,' I could say, 'Yeah, me too! Tell me helpless, I'll tell you helpless!'" Conversely, some therapists felt soothed and comforted when their patients expressed thoughts and feelings that they shared. One therapist said, "So many times I've been in session, and I want to say, 'Me too! Me too!'"

Many therapists grew so distressed that they could no longer muster any hope for the individuals they were treating. Sharing their patients' bleak views of the future, one said, "It was very hard for me to reassure people, which is my job." Another supported this view, saying,

"I had to do my own emotional, spiritual homework all the time to keep myself in a decent place. Because if I sink into despair, or if I become overwhelmed, or if I don't take care of myself, or if I get so depressed that I don't have the energy for this, then I'm not a help to anyone."

Therapists also experienced uncomfortable feelings of uncertainty concerning how to intervene. One stated that unlike her regular clinical cases, where "I usually felt that I had some semblance of knowing what I'm doing," she felt at a loss after 9/11. When patients told her they were too frightened to take the subway, she was unsure how to respond:

"I didn't know if I should say, 'I have the same feelings,' or 'It's hard not to know,' or 'If you don't want to go on the train, don't go on the train until you're ready to go on the fucking train!'"

Further, the situation of simultaneous trauma violated a central principle of clinical practice, which discouraged therapists from assuming that their experiences were the same as those of their patients. A therapist explained that under normal clinical circumstances, when a patient asked if she had seen a particular movie,

"Whether I saw it or not, the answer is, 'Tell me about it.' Because even if I did see it, I didn't have the experience that she had, and she has to bring in what's important to her, and I can't infect it with my stuff."

Similarly, if a patient said, 'I felt terrified,'" the therapist was supposed to say, "'Tell me more. What do you mean by that?' Because I don't know what that means." In the aftermath of the attack, however, some therapists believed that they and their patients "were all in the same world in a way that we hadn't been." As a result,

"When a patient would say to me, 'That smoke, the smell of that smoke' – I smelled it, it was in my lungs. We couldn't pretend that she had to tell me what that was."

This novel sense of having shared an external experience posed unfamiliar clinical hazards. Suddenly inhabiting the same world as their patients gave some therapists the false impression that they knew exactly what their patients were talking about, how they felt, and what they required. Therapists were deprived of the clinical distance that allowed them to have perspectives that were distinct from those of their patients. Moreover, therapists who assumed that they already knew the precise nature of patients' suffering were less likely to invite them to describe their particular experiences and reactions. As one therapist remarked,

"You have to let them tell their story, even if you think you know it, or even if you don't think you can stand to listen to it."

Therapists who felt they inhabited the same world as the individuals they were treating also found it increasingly difficult to distinguish their own lives from those of their patients. They continually had to remind themselves, "This is your life. Your husband isn't dead. Your kids aren't dead. You're okay." One therapist said that after working for several months with families who had lost children, and who had repeated their final words to them, whenever she saw her son,

"If he said goodbye in a particular way, I'd be going, 'Oh jeez, the way he said that! Something is surely going to happen! That was significant, that was different than the way he usually said that!'"

Many therapists noted the irony of providing mental health treatment to others when they themselves felt sorely in need of it. Some felt so fearful, helpless, or anguished that they reentered psychological treatment, while others contemplated giving up their professional roles:

"You don't want to be the therapist, the one who couldn't cry, who had to know what to do. What happens if I couldn't cope? I didn't want everybody depending on me."

TRAUMATIC MEMORIES

The experience of simultaneous trauma was exacerbated for therapists with histories of trauma, who after 9/11 were flooded with traumatic memories.[4] Therapists' retraumatization seemed to take them by surprise. Although they expected that the attack would retraumatize patients who previously had been subjected to violence or abuse, and trigger their most disturbing memories, many were unprepared for the pieces of their past that came back to life for them.

Like a number of their patients with prior experiences of trauma, therapists felt upended not only by the violent assault on their city, and by the pervasive atmosphere of threat, but by vivid, intrusive memories of violation and disaster. In general, therapists with traumatic histories who listen repeatedly to patients' stories of violence are more likely to develop secondary trauma (Zimering et al. 2005). In this case, their constant exposure to detailed narratives of the attack stimulated personal traumatic memories. Many therapists were caught off guard when this public and collective trauma uncovered aspects of private calamities that had formerly been inaccessible to them.[5]

Several kinds of traumatic memories were reevoked by the events of 9/11, and were intensified by therapists' work with psychologically injured patients. One therapist recalled a life-threatening accident that he had sustained as a very small child. Shortly after the attack, he began to see vague images of extremely red skin, and to dream about a body that was severely disfigured by burns. He soon realized that these dreams and images portrayed his own body, which had been seriously burned when he was a year and a half old. He had been in a coma for a couple of weeks, and for the next several months, his family had had tremendous anxiety about whether or not he would live. These memories had failed to emerge during his lengthy psychoanalysis; but they surfaced with a vengeance after 9/11, perhaps due to specific parallels between his accident and the attack. Like the individuals who were wounded on 9/11, the therapist had been struck by a sudden calamity that instantaneously moved him from a state of health and security to one of injury and peril. In both cases, there was the sense that the events could have been prevented had the persons in authority paid sufficient attention and protected those for whom they were responsible. In addition, the panic that had engulfed his family after his accident resembled the climate of catastrophe surrounding the World Trade Center attack. This similar emotional atmosphere gave rise to traumatic memories with which he had been out of touch.

Two mental health professionals relived traumatic experiences that occurred during World War II. The first, a Jewish psychoanalyst, had been indirectly traumatized by the atrocities his parents had suffered in the course of the war. His mother, who was a pogrom survivor, had lost most of her family in the Holocaust. Although the psychoanalyst grew up in New York City, her trauma had been transmitted to him, and he had internalized the family history of systematic extermination. The events of 9/11 reawakened this intergenerational trauma. At the same time, they aroused memories of his mother that previously had been inaccessible, so that he had to mourn her all over again. The second therapist, who grew up in Japan, had lived with her family in a sizable city that was devastated by Allied air raids. One of her earliest memories was of "my whole city burning." The war destroyed her city, and because it produced "an entire country in dislocation" it also destroyed her family. Her father had remained in the city while the rest of the family was evacuated to the countryside, and they never were reunited. These "deeply buried" memories of her life during World War II returned with a "strong emotional force" in the year after 9/11. In her work with Japanese women whose husbands had offices near the World Trade Center, and who had been widowed by the attack, she often accompanied them and their children to the funerals of their spouses. These activities caused her to reexperience the separation of her family and the loss of her father. In addition, on the morning of September 11, she had stood on the sidewalk in front of her Greenwich Village office. As she stared down lower Fifth Avenue, watching the towers burn and dissolve, she began to have vivid recollections of "a beautiful orange sky, and things falling from the sky." Only later did she realize that early memories of the bombing of her city in Japan were stimulated when she witnessed the World Trade Center on fire.

For another mental health professional, the attack on the World Trade Center and its political repercussions brought back a traumatic history of living in the Republic of Ireland during the decades of the Troubles. Because her parents belonged to the Irish Republican Army, her family was a frequent target of state terror and abuse. When she was a child, the police had conducted unannounced house raids, bringing search dogs into her bedroom early in the morning "solely with the intent to harass." Close relatives and friends were also subjected to state violence, and some had been taken as political prisoners. After 9/11, she began to be afraid that her son, who lived in New York City, was going to be arrested and taken away. Moreover, in the course of more than 20 years of bombings in Ireland, the political climate had become repressive and civil liberties had been stripped away. When the Trade Center attack engendered restrictions on civil rights in the United States, the feelings of liberty and security that this therapist had previously enjoyed thoroughly disappeared. The attack shattered her belief that "I could speak more freely, I could live my life more anonymously here." Instead, as she relived prior incidents of state violation in Ireland, she worried that if she stayed in the United States, "my days are going to end up in the same manner, not knowing if there's going to be a house search." The destruction of "the illusion that I had found a safe place for myself in the world" was so complete that she considered leaving New York and moving back to Ireland.

In addition to traumatic memories of nearly fatal injury, of wartime separations and atrocities, and of organized state terror, two therapists of color revisited prior racial traumas, including experiences of repression and discrimination, after September 11. The first remarked that immediately after the attack, when her supervisors placed mental health professionals in various volunteer settings, they invariably sent her to sites with much lower visibility than those to which they assigned her white colleagues. For example, while she was dispatched to work with the homeless, they were sent to work at "prestigious" corporations. The second therapist also observed that therapists of color were given less responsibility, and that Project Liberty excluded minority mental health professionals from positions of authority. In the "command station" that was established to connect her social service agency with government offices and other mental health organizations, "There was not one, one, one person of color ever in the room to do the work." The fact that "none of the blacks got the chance to be in high positions" caused her to feel so "denigrated" and "alienated" that she reexperienced previous instances of racial discrimination. The attack "reawakened all the other experiences of looking at things with that color lens on," and brought back "the pain of really being repressed in many ways, in terms of being an African American woman." In the weeks after 9/11, when newly installed security guards asked her for identification, she wondered, 'Do you do this to other people, or is it just because I'm a black African American woman?"

The combination of therapists' retraumatization, the new experience of simultaneous trauma, and the erasure of clinical boundaries made some therapists uncertain as to whether, or to what extent, to share their personal experiences of the events of 9/11 with their patients. At the time of the attack, issues regarding therapists' self-disclosure were under debate in the mental health field. Some practitioners, in keeping with Freudian psychoanalysis, believed that therapists should remain anonymous and neutral, and should keep their private lives and views out of clinical encounters (Mitchell 1997). They meticulously refrained from revealing personal information, opinions, and emotions to their patients. In their view, those who made such revelations in the course of clinical discussions obstructed the analytic project by inhibiting patients' reactions, undermining their transferences, overriding their concerns, usurping their space, and invading their intrapsychic worlds. Alternatively, proponents of self-disclosure contended that anonymity and neutrality were impossible. They further claimed that therapists' carefully considered and well-timed references to their subjective impressions and states, especially those that directly pertained to the material at hand, could be clinically advantageous by showing their honest reactions to the stuff of patients' lives (Aron 1996).

In the face of such disagreements, mental health professionals proposed a number of clinical guidelines on self-disclosure. The guidelines recommended that therapists restrict such disclosures to thoughts and feelings regarding patients' experiences; that they refrain from discussing their private lives and from volunteering unsolicited personal information; that they self-disclose to serve patients' emotional needs rather than their own; and above all, that they use self-disclosure solely to further therapeutic exploration. These guidelines expressly discouraged therapists from disclosing their sentiments and views unless they had previously thought through them. Rather than self-disclosing in response to the emotional press of the moment, therapists were to carefully evaluate how such information would affect each patient, clinical relationship, and treatment (Aron 1996).

To be sure, these guidelines were not created with a devastating attack like 9/11 in mind. As a result, therapists were uncertain how to handle self-disclosures following a shocking act of mass violence that produced a community disaster and a national political crisis in addition to countless psychological injuries. In particular, they found it impossible to predict whether disclosing their personal reactions would advance or impede clinical exploration in each specific case. With some patients becoming increasingly volatile and others dangerously on edge, therapists could not be sure whether discussing their own responses to the attack would soothe them, destabilize them, or unleash uncontrollable rage. They were equally uncertain how patients would receive their expressions of vulnerability. Though such expressions were intended to acknowledge a shared humanity and a frightening external reality, it was possible that patients would take them as shameful displays of weakness, as fuel for their own anxieties, or as the frustration of needs to be rescued by paragons of strength after their world had been shaken to its core.

Further, existing guidelines on self-disclosure had not been designed for situations of simultaneous trauma that may have temporarily compromised therapists' clinical judgment. Therapists who were terrified or aggrieved by 9/11 lacked sufficient time to plumb the depths of their despair, or to assess the extent of their fears, before they returned to work.[6] The fact that many therapists over-identified with their patients, and had difficulties distinguishing patients' emotions and needs from their own, suggests that they may have been unaware of their motives for disclosing personal experiences and feelings after the attack.

Therapists held a wide range of views about self-disclosure after 9/11. For those who were already at work that morning, the inclination to self-disclose was strengthened by the fact that they had learned of the attack, in increments, from their patients. In some cases, therapists' 9:00 A.M. patients told them that an airplane had crashed into the north tower, their 10:00 A.M. patients told them that a second airplane had hit the south tower, and their 11:00 A.M. patients told them that the towers had collapsed. As a result, they had the unusual sense that they and their patients had experienced these disastrous events together. Some therapists concluded that it was pointless and disingenuous to maintain their customary stance of clinical neutrality and detachment. They thought it was "only human" to voice their sorrow and bewilderment, and to reassure their patients that their families were safe. Some felt obliged to disclose personal information in response to patients who asked, "Were you there? Were you involved? Do you have kids? My son was there; do you have a son?" Other therapists who longed to be closer to their patients, or to let their patients know more about them, finally had a legitimate reason to indulge their "desire for exposure," and to reveal facets of their lives that they usually kept under wraps. One realized only later that she had told her patients about her volunteer work because she wanted them to "idealize" her.

But others were vehemently opposed to discussing the specific ways the attack had affected them. One therapist who sought to be as anonymous as possible was discomfited by the fact that her patients suddenly were privy to personal information about her, simply because they assumed that she had been touched by 9/11. She found it difficult to bear "a level of exposure that I've never had to tolerate." Others maintained that therapists' self-disclosures concerning their reactions to the attack had no place in the treatments they provided because "it's not the issue whether I'm okay or not." They worried that patients who were told of their therapists' wounds would fear reinjuring them, or would feel the need to take care of them – in either case inhibiting their freedom to fully examine their reactions to 9/11. While these therapists believed that they should use their personal responses to the attack to inform their clinical work, they drew clear distinctions between applying what they had learned and revealing what they had experienced. As one said,

> *"I don't think they need my story. I think they need my compassion and my love, and my attention, and my frailty, and my humanity, but I don't think they need my story."*

Therapists struggled to determine not only how much personal information to disclose to their patients but also what kinds of emotional reactions to show them. Several therapists said that after 9/11 they had wept in front of patients for the first time. One unapologetically stated that some of her patients had been "dismayed by the tears in my eyes." Another said that she simply had responded naturally to patients' misery:

> *"Especially at the beginning, when you sit with someone who's telling you how they were climbing over legs and feet and body parts and looking for their friends, and they're crying, you cry too. It was just so immediate."*

But other therapists were horrified to learn of colleagues who, whether in private practice or as volunteers, had deliberately shown such emotions, or who had failed to control them, while meeting with their patients. One therapist described her patient's distress when a Red Cross worker broke down after hearing his story:

> *"All he kept saying [was], 'I made the Red Cross lady cry, I made the Red Cross lady cry. I must be really bad because I made the Red Cross lady cry.' I wanted to find this Red Cross lady – her crying traumatized this guy."*

A second therapist who had worked extensively with Vietnam veterans maintained that it was imperative for therapists to maintain their composure, no matter how harrowing or sorrowful the stories their patients recounted. In her view, what was most important in working with victims of catastrophic trauma was,

> *"To look somebody right in the eye and let them tell you about the atrocities or the devastation and not flinch . . . cause if they would see you backing down, they weren't going to tell you. They weren't going to show their pain."*

THE FLORENCE NIGHTINGALES OF THE WORLD

As therapists served individuals who were profoundly wounded by the attack, they themselves had little relief. More than a year later, many therapists remained so fully immersed in the work of helping others that they still had not had taken the time to come to terms with these events. Nor had they taken sufficient care of themselves; it was as if they were "stymied" when it came to addressing their personal emotional needs (Twemlow 2004:715). The therapist who worked with firefighters typified this pattern. She said that in the days and weeks following the attack,

> *"The rest of the country was gathering with family and friends and going to vigils and grieving this whole thing, and we were just here working."*

One evening, she was in the office when she and a co-worker heard noise from the street. They looked out the window,

> *"And the whole street was filled with people holding candles. And it was like, it's nice that everybody's doing this, but we have a department to take care of. You worry about yourself later."*

Some mental health professionals considered themselves so well trained, well analyzed, and clinically experienced that they were sure of their ability to handle every case that came their way. But after more than a year of constantly bearing witness to scores of patients' raw accounts of their horrifying experiences, these witnesses also required witnesses, or "some forum in which to process" the attack. When they couldn't get out of bed, or broke down while speaking to colleagues, or woke up screaming from nightmares, it was "a real eye opener about how vulnerable we all are." Many therapists who had previously worked with severely disturbed or traumatized patients recognized the importance of safeguarding their emotional well-being; if their work began to overwhelm them, they knew how to pull back. In the past, such strategies as taking time off from work, taking on patients with less pressing concerns, and reinforcing the safety of the clinical consulting room decreased their susceptibility to patients' brutal accounts, and to developing secondary trauma (Zimering et al. 2005). But such strategies were nearly impossible to implement in this instance of simultaneous trauma. With New York City seemingly under siege, there was no safe place to which therapists might retreat. It was impossible for them to ensure that their clinical spaces were safe, and difficult to limit their contact with deeply troubled patients who made increasing demands on their time. In addition, therapists who had volunteered at service centers and Respite Centers had not been encouraged to take proper care of themselves. Indeed, one therapist who worked at Ground Zero recalled disincentives to self-care, noting that the mental health professionals who worked the longest hours received paid positions and rewards, including badges permitting entry to the pit that were "the equivalent of winning the lottery." In contrast, those who took time off were assigned less appealing tasks (Garrison 2005:269). Such pressures to push themselves and to disregard their emotional well-being may have carried over to their regular practices.

Moreover, a central feature of therapists' self-care involves establishing nurturing relationships with other mental health professionals (M. Miller 2003). After the attack, some therapists found colleagues they could turn to for comfort and advice, and they "did a lot of lunch." The Latina therapist was grateful for the meetings that took place before her volunteer shifts at the Dominican agency, where the director "would order food, and we would talk, and we would cry, and we would talk, and then we would go to work." However, many never found fellow therapists whom they could rely on for professional support, or for help in coming to grips with the emotional fallout of their work. Numerous therapists worked independently in isolated private practices, disconnected from communities of other mental health professionals. Those who normally enjoyed close collegial relationships felt that it was important to exercise caution when discussing 9/11 patients' terrifying material, because "you end up putting other people in distress." They commonly withheld the most disturbing aspects of such accounts, explaining that "my colleagues don't want to hear all of the gory details. I protect them from the gory details, and they protect me." Exposing friends, family, and other nonclinicians to the gruesome stories they heard in the office every day was also out of the question; as one therapist said, "You're doing work that you can't really share at the dinner table."

Therapists' difficulties finding colleagues with whom they could sort through the emotional repercussions of their work were worsened by the fact that, in this situation of simultaneous trauma, those to whom they usually turned for support were also fending off their reactions to the catastrophe. One therapist remarked that several of her colleagues "were in a manic state," accelerating the pace of their clinical activities and becoming overly involved with their patients to avoid confronting the attack's effects on them. Another therapist belatedly recognized that, by immersing himself in his work, he had become "like the firemen who won't quit digging, because if you quit then you've got to deal with what's going on." Some therapists felt so drained after a full day of work that they were in no condition to help their colleagues. After spending the day with patients,

"I couldn't listen to anything else. I didn't want anybody else stressing me out. I could not listen to other people's problems. I just wanted to do my patients and listen to the families who were going through this trauma. And that's what I did for a year."

As a result, while therapists were taking care of the city, no one was taking care of the city's therapists. One said that, "It was almost like we didn't count. We were just the Florence Nightingales of the world." Without proper care, many therapists suffered. Several described periods during which they were unable to eat or sleep, became irrationally enraged, had persistent flashbacks of the attack, or were utterly exhausted. Some "had never been so tired in my whole life." One recalled,

"I would leave work, and I would barely be able to walk home. I felt like I was keeping it all together a lot of the time, trying to be stronger than I felt. I was just exhausted by the end of the day. In some ways, my whole self wasn't really in operation."

Many became so numb and depressed, or so irritable and withdrawn, that their suffering affected their work. They vacillated between feeling that they were "superhuman," and could emotionally rescue their patients by undoing whatever damage they had sustained, and feeling that they were ineffective, and that the treatments they provided were useless. They grew frustrated with patients who had been wounded on 9/11, whose problems seemed intractable, and who showed no signs of recovery, and they became intolerant of patients who seemed entirely untouched by the attack. Many had difficulty leaving their work behind when they went home. Some felt so overwhelmed that they isolated themselves from others, or shut down the rest of their lives, because, as one said,

> "I just need time, I just need to be home, I just need not to do anything, like not to have a list of things to do, not to have chores . . . where whatever I want to do I can do, just paying attention to me."

A few therapists worried that patients' disclosures had overexposed them to the "poisonous knowledge" (Das 2000:205) that acts of mass violence were real possibilities, thus radically altering their previous views of a world that was predictable and benign. They also were concerned that their continual exposure to such stories had inflicted long-term psychological harm. The therapist who treated scores of ravaged firefighters feared that, in the years to come, she would be "curled up in a ball somewhere, unable to go to work." A therapist who was pregnant on September 11 worried that her constant crying after a full day of hearing her patients' miserable stories would seriously damage her baby.

Lacking reliable systems of support, therapists took care of themselves by going to bed early, cooking their favorite foods, and seeing fewer patients in a day. Some went back into psychotherapy to understand how the attack had affected them, both as individuals and as providers of mental health care. Others sought refuge in their art, or developed new spiritual practices.[7] One began to do art projects in her office in which she staged whimsical scenes between patients and therapists. It was "my own adult play therapy," and she used it to "externalize what was going on inside so I could work through it." A second therapist created private rituals not only "to clear my mind" in between her patients but also to purify herself of the toxins she felt herself absorbing as she listened to their stories. Needing to find new ways to "empty myself out," she imagined herself as a "lightning rod," or as "a tree with roots in Mother Earth." She then "asked Mother Earth to take out everything that the last patient put in and contain it," and to "give me energy for the next person." Many therapists responded more practically by preparing themselves for the future. They took every course they could find on trauma and disaster, or organized professional conferences on terrorism. One gathered her family's passports, put her financial affairs in order, and made plans to escape the country in the event of another attack.

Having experienced simultaneous trauma for the first time in the wake of 9/11, therapists considered its effects on their clinical work after the attack, and on their broader professional capacities. The therapist who consulted with the elementary school a few blocks from the World Trade Center thought that it had been helpful to his community that he had not been in the school at the moment of the attack. Despite the fact that he had heard the airplanes fly overhead, and had watched both towers collapse from his apartment in Greenwich Village a mile or so away, compared to most families in the school, he had experienced the attack from a safe distance. He said,

"I didn't see the plane fly down Greenwich Street, which many of our parents did see. I didn't have the graphic, visceral experience that people had here, and I didn't spend an hour and a half in the building uncertain about what was happening next, or experience parents running into the building in various states of hysteria and taking their children out of school. And I wasn't there when the last group of students and teachers evacuated the building just as the north tower collapsed and they were completely engulfed in that cloud of debris and the complete darkness."

In his view, although he and the school community had suffered from the same catastrophic event, his less direct exposure to it, and his lack of a "graphic, visceral experience" of it, made him significantly less "disabled." Accordingly, he felt more capable of providing students, faculty, parents, and staff with the necessary psychological assistance.

In contrast, some mental health professionals thought that the simultaneous trauma they and their patients had experienced had made them better therapists, because it allowed them to more fully comprehend another dimension of human experience. One therapist considered himself better able to recognize the myriad ways in which traumatic incidents affect individuals. He used his personal experience of the attack to normalize their plight by subtly conveying to them that, "We're all in this together. I've been affected as well as you, so let's try and get through it." Therapists who were reeling not only from 9/11 but also from the previous traumas it had reactivated sometimes felt that reliving catastrophic experiences made them more attuned to patients who were injured in the attack. Such firsthand knowledge of trauma made them "acutely aware of what [patients] were going through" and enhanced their "empathic connectedness." In some cases it also made them feel that they understood precisely what patients needed. The therapist who had felt like an outcast until he found a community of fellow sufferers in line at a social service center applied this newfound knowledge in his practice. He urged families whose relatives had died on 9/11, and who felt apart from the rest of society, to find other families with similar losses, "because otherwise they feel like outsiders and burdens and unwanted people in this world." Similarly, the therapist who had lived through World War II as a child in Japan used her traumatic history to inform her clinical work. Her experience had taught her that after an act of mass violence, people needed not only to grieve but also to "connect to a surviving force." This understanding allowed her to "identify it, encourage it, work with it, and articulate it" with patients after the attack; indeed, she felt that "I was meant to be there for them."

Other therapists found that their personal experiences of the attack had caused them to reconceptualize the world they inhabited, as well as their places in it, in ways that were useful to share with their patients. The attack's sudden and irreversible consequences had forced them into a new relationship with the present because "We really are going to die, and this isn't a dress rehearsal." For one therapist, the events of September 11 underscored life's inherent fragility:

"On September 10, we were in essence as vulnerable as on September 11. So it becomes a focal point for something that is a constant part of being a human being, which is being aware that life is finite, and that we're all at risk, and anything could happen at any moment. We don't have control over some things."

Another therapist put in more bluntly. "So this is the world we live in," he said. "You'd better well face it, and find ways of dealing with it."

CHAPTER 6

Diagnosing Posttraumatic Stress Disorder

ぷ

A S THERAPISTS STRUGGLED TO manage a variety of novel occupational haz-ards after 9/11, they also grappled with the practical challenges of classify-ing the psychological injuries of individuals who were wounded in the attack. This chapter examines the practice of diagnosis after 9/11. It begins by consid-ering varying perspectives on psychiatric diagnosis in general before looking at the diagnostic category of posttraumatic stress disorder (PTSD) in particular. It then takes a closer look at the multiple factors that affected mental health professionals' diagnoses of patients after the attack.

PSYCHIATRIC DIAGNOSIS

Like physicians in medical encounters, mental health professionals must diag-nose their patients before they can determine the proper treatments to admin-ister. Yet diagnosis has long been a problematic activity in the field of mental health. Perhaps because mental disorders have proven more mysterious and unknowable than physical disorders – because the brain, consciousness, and the processes of thinking and feeling remain less visible, and less comprehen-sible, than the workings of kidneys and spleens – there has been markedly less agreement in the identification and classification of their malfunctions. It has not been uncommon for various practitioners to diagnose the same patients dif-ferently, or for patients with similar symptoms to receive dissimilar diagnoses. In previous decades, diagnostic consensus has occurred with remarkable infre-quency. According to one extensive study, mental health professionals agreed on diagnoses of particular patients in as few as four of ten clinical cases (Beck 1962).

Widespread diagnostic disagreements greatly trouble mental health professionals who seek to enhance the authority and prestige of their field by representing their practices as true medical endeavors. For their field to progress in this direction, it must meet various scientific standards of objectivity, including inter-rater reliability. When applied to scientific research, inter-rater reliability means that experiments must be reproducible regardless of which scientist conducts them. With regards to mental health practice, it holds that the same patients must be evaluated as having the same disorders no matter which clinician diagnoses them.

To increase inter-rater reliability, mental health professionals who designed the third edition of the *Diagnostic and Statistical Manual of Mental Disorders* (DSM) (American Psychiatric Association 1980) completely revamped its diagnostic system. In contrast with previous editions of the DSM, which were rooted in classical psychoanalytic theory and which categorized mental disorders according to the specific unconscious conflicts thought to have caused them, the DSM-III's new diagnostic system was portrayed as theoretically neutral (Maser, Kaelber, & Weise 1991; Widiger, Frances, Pincus, Davis, & First 1991). This new system no longer based diagnosis on invisible and hypothetical intrapsychic processes, or on a single metapsychological theory, but on observable behavioral symptoms that were considered characteristic of particular psychiatric disorders. The DSM clearly described these symptoms, and neatly displayed them on checklists, to make them apparent to all practitioners regardless of professional training and theoretical orientation. In doing so, it was designed to eliminate, or at least to significantly reduce, diagnostic disagreements. The DSM-IV-TR, which was published in 2000, intended to advance these aims, "striving for brevity of criteria sets, clarity of language, and explicit statements of the constructs embodied in the diagnostic criteria" (American Psychiatric Association 2000:xxiii). However, despite these efforts, diagnostic agreement among mental health professionals has remained frustratingly elusive (Thakker & Ward 1998).

Failures to produce diagnostic consensus result in part from the fact that diagnosis is not an objective, scientific, atheoretical activity, as some mental health professionals claim, but rather is an act of interpretation, "a thoroughly semiotic activity" that depends on the translation and decoding of signs (Kleinman 1988:16). Practitioners may read bodily and behavioral signs in a number of contrasting ways, suggesting divergent disorders. Pains in the head, for example, may signify a headache, a heartache, a toothache, or a tumor. For mental health professionals to make sense of such signs, and to choose among possible diagnoses, they must scan patients' mental and physical states for evidence of disorder, convert this evidence into known symptoms, identify symptoms that cluster together, and then match these clusters to the DSM category that best contains and explains them (Seeley 2005c). The fact that formal diagnosis is based on the *Diagnostic and Statistical Manual* contributes an additional level of interpretation. No matter how concrete and explicit this handbook's diagnostic scheme, the DSM, like all texts, is open to multiple readings, making the elimination of diagnostic disagreement extremely unlikely.

This view of diagnosis is in clear opposition to the original therapeutic project. Notions of the practitioner's objectivity were central to Freudian psychoanalysis; over the course of the twentieth century, they trickled down to psychotherapists of less classical persuasions. Freud claimed that psychoanalysis was a science, and likened analysts to surgeons not only in the precision of their methods but also in their lack of bias. To promote their objectivity – and to deter them from being swayed by theoretical preconceptions – he instructed them to listen to patients with "evenly hovering attention" (Freud 1912). However reasonable as theory, listening with evenly hovering attention is virtually impossible in practice. Instead, clinical listening, like all other kinds of listening, is active and selective. Therapists pay most attention to the particular kinds of material that their theoretical formulations deem psychically significant (Aron 1996; Seeley 2005a). Classical psychoanalysts listen selectively for material that suggests unconscious conflicts, while family therapists are alert to signs of counterproductive interpersonal patterns. Moreover, because the material patients disclose is "fundamentally ambiguous" (Mitchell 1993:56), therapists must organize and interpret it. Therapists' theoretical assumptions shape the ways they make sense of ambiguities and give order to patients' stories (Schafer 1983). The contemporary profusion of psychological theories and models of treatment, each of which differently explains and acts to alleviate mental suffering, increases the possibility that therapists of dissimilar professional formations will variously interpret the same material, and will produce contrasting diagnoses.

Just as diagnosis is contingent on therapists' theoretical orientations, it also involves sensibilities and skills that are inherently subjective. Many mental health professionals grow adept at sensing patients' emotional states, and at detecting isolated behaviors that suggest specific disorders. Rather than systematically scrutinizing DSM categories to determine the correct diagnosis, they may skip this process entirely, arriving at diagnoses on the basis of their "clinical intuition" (Luhrmann 2000:33). They also base diagnoses on the particular feeling states their patients induce in them. For example, patients who arouse feelings of hopelessness, lethargy, or sadness in their therapists are likely to be diagnosed with depression (Rhodes 1991). For mental health professionals who are capable of intuiting or sensing psychiatric disorders, diagnosis is less a technical process of matching symptoms to diagnostic criteria and "'more of a feel'" (Luhrmann 2000:40). The subjective features of diagnosis extend to the ways therapists' individual characteristics and social experiences shape their assessments of patients. Despite the Freudian claim that they are unaffected by personal biases, "everything that the analyst knows about the patient is mediated through the analyst's own experience" (Mitchell 1993:60). In other words, therapists' internal fantasies, psychological conflicts, relational patterns, social locations, and cultural histories significantly inform their interactions with, and evaluations of, patients (Aron 1996; Hoffman 1992; Renick 1993; Seeley 2001; Stolorow & Brandchaft 1994).

Moreover, although diagnosis generally is represented as taking place in hermetic consulting rooms, which like scientific laboratories have been cleansed of external contaminants, diagnosis is significantly shaped by the social, material, and political contexts in which it occurs. Numerous external factors impinge on diagnostic decisions. In highly pressured clinical settings that are short on resources, staff, and time, overworked mental health professionals may deploy diagnoses for "strategic rather than medical purposes" (Rhodes 1991:93), selecting the diagnostic label that requires the least amount of chart writing, secures third-party payments, commits patients who are violent, or releases those who have been stabilized so that incoming patients can have their beds (Barrett 1988; Rhodes 1991). Their diagnoses also may be influenced by new and faster acting pharmaceuticals, which typically turn the specific disorders they target into "'major growth industr[ies]'" (Good 1992:188). For example, after the introduction of lithium, diagnoses of manic depression increased dramatically, just as the development of improved antianxiety drugs produced a rise in diagnoses of panic disorder (Good 1992; Rhodes 1991). In addition, since the advent of the asylum, psychiatric diagnosis has served political ends. Diagnosing mental disorders in unproductive, nonconforming, or otherwise undesirable members of society justified their incarceration and continuous surveillance (Foucault 1965/1998). In more recent decades, mental health professionals in the United States and the United Kingdom have assigned the most severe diagnoses to immigrants and minorities, resulting in lengthy institutional confinement or sedating pharmaceutical treatments (Lindsay & Gordon, 1989; Littlewood & Lipsedge 1989). Patients also play active roles in diagnosis, manufacturing the specific symptoms that are required to receive desired diagnostic labels (Barrett 1988). To cite one well-known case, when the federal government offered disability benefits to Vietnam War veterans with posttraumatic stress disorder, some fabricated brutal combat histories, or performed flashbacks and other key symptoms of trauma, in order to qualify for such assistance (McNally 2003).

Many of these factors played a part in making psychiatric diagnosis a highly contested activity after 9/11. In many respects, the diagnostic category of PTSD, although originally created for soldiers who were wounded in a foreign war, seemed tailor-made for civilians injured by a terrorist attack at home. The unprecedented nature of the World Trade Center attack, and the extraordinary destruction it wrought, satisfied the most stringent definitions of traumatic stressors; there was no question that the events of September 11 posed actual threats to individuals' lives or were well outside the range of usual experience. However, although mental health professionals were largely in agreement concerning the traumatic properties of the attack, they failed to reach a consensus as to how to diagnose the people it injured – and in particular, whether to diagnose them with PTSD.

The following sections closely examine the makings of diagnostic disagreement after 9/11. They discuss the ways therapists' divergent conceptions of trauma, varying levels of experience treating the traumatized, and personal involvement in the attack affected their assessments of patients' disordered states, and resulted in contrasting diagnostic formulations. These sections also consider how therapists' readings – and in some cases, misreadings – of PTSD criteria led them to opposite conclusions as to whether individuals who had been harmed on 9/11 qualified for this diagnosis. The DSM itself provided little guidance, as it failed to reduce the ambiguities of specific diagnostic criteria, or to resolve therapists' conflicting interpretations of their relevance to the attack.

DIAGNOSIS AFTER 9/11

When therapists evaluated patients for PTSD after 9/11, one of the first elements they had to address was the "post" in posttraumatic stress disorder. The DSM IV-TR, which was current at the time of the attack, specified a time frame for this disorder; criterion E states that the disturbance – the necessary PTSD symptoms – must persist for "more than 1 month" for PTSD to be diagnosed (American Psychiatric Association 2000:468). Accordingly, individuals who were injured on September 11 should not have been diagnosed with PTSD before October 12, 2001. However, in the atmosphere of crisis that followed the attack, many mental health professionals misunderstood, overlooked, or ignored this criterion, and immediately diagnosed numerous patients with PTSD. Some selected this diagnosis simply because, in their view, the attack clearly constituted a catastrophic trauma, and PTSD was the only diagnostic category "that's got that key word in it: traumatic." Diagnosing PTSD in the heat of the attack was "kind of a knee-jerk response." Consequently,

> *"It took a little while for everyone to realize, oh, it's post-traumatic stress disorder. . . . There is that month lapse."*

While some therapists overlooked the "post" in PTSD, others emphasized it to an extent that precluded this diagnosis. They maintained that this category was inappropriate for individuals who were emotionally injured on 9/11 because it conceptualized catastrophic stressors as finite, delimited, and discrete. In contrast, after the World Trade Center attack a succession of menacing incidents, including bomb scares, additional terrorist threats, an airplane crash, anthrax attacks, and talk of foreign invasions, kept the original disaster in the present, so that people "were constantly being traumatized and retraumatized." The persistence of traumatic conditions meant that "there was nothing 'post' about it," and that the diagnosis of PTSD did not apply. Still other therapists were equally concerned about the "post" in PTSD, but for different reasons; they were unsure exactly how "post" PTSD could be. The DSM-IV-TR explicitly acknowledges that catastrophic events can be so difficult for the mind to integrate that the onset of PTSD may be delayed six months or more after the traumatic incident occurs (American Psychiatric Association 2000). Although it accounts for such delays, the DSM does not specify a time limit within which PTSD symptoms must emerge. Yet some therapists who first met with patients more than a year and a half after 9/11 thought that it was too late for them to qualify for PTSD, and assigned other diagnoses.

A second source of diagnostic disagreement after 9/11 concerned therapists' varying assumptions about the "trauma" that is central to PTSD. As discussed in Chapter 1, contemporary mental health professionals are divided as to the kinds of events that are traumatic and the kinds of individuals who can be traumatized. Moreover, before the attack occurred, only a minority of therapists had worked extensively with traumatized patients. Disparities in their conceptions of, and familiarity with, both traumatic stressors and traumatic reactions contributed to varying patient assessments. Some insight-oriented therapists were reluctant to diagnose new patients with PTSD, preferring to create more intricate portraits of their emotional wounds. Assuming that traumatic reactions to the attack were informed by, and layered on top of, existing psychic structures, they tried to understand how previous experiences of trauma influenced current responses. Trauma specialists sometimes expressed similar views, stating that "people have layers of trauma, layers of loss, layers of disruption, and other psychosocial issues that compound the picture." They worried that Project Liberty's publicity campaigns conveyed simplistic conceptions of trauma by suggesting that individuals' reactions to the attack were best understood as discrete symptoms that could be separated from, and treated independently of, complex psychological patterns and histories. They were further concerned that this publicity falsely promised formulaic "quick fixes" for difficulties that invariably were idiosyncratic and entrenched. Above all, they strongly objected to the checklists of PTSD symptoms that were posted all over the city.

"It's never appropriate to simply give people a list of symptoms, a diagnosis, and say, 'This is what you can expect in the next several weeks. Have plenty of rest, eat well, and have some exercise. Stay close to your family.'. . . . People need to be able to talk about it. And sometimes they don't feel ready. And it's too easy to shut them up like that."

Therapists' prior conceptions of trauma also predisposed them to discover PTSD in certain individuals while ruling it out in others. Therapists who believed that PTSD only afflicted adults who previously had been traumatized did not assign this diagnosis to persons without such histories. Similarly, therapists who believed that PTSD only emerged in individuals who had suffered from annihilation anxiety during traumatic events restricted this diagnosis to those who had feared that their lives were in imminent danger. On the other hand, therapists who held more flexible notions of trauma saw no reason not to diagnose PTSD in individuals who lacked traumatic histories and who had not felt mortally threatened by the attack. Focusing on the destructive power inherent in particular stressors, and convinced that people could be traumatized to varying degrees, they maintained that the devastating terrorist attack had traumatized every New Yorker "to some extent." Accordingly, they applied this diagnosis broadly.

Additional diagnostic disagreements resulted from therapists' contrasting interpretations of PTSD's criterion A. This criterion requires that "the person has been exposed to a traumatic event where the person experienced, witnessed, or was confronted by an event or events that involved actual or threatened death or serious injury, or a threat to the physical integrity or self or others," and that "the person's response involved intense fear, helplessness, or horror" (American Psychiatric Association 2000:467). Although the criterion seems straightforward, mental health professionals variously interpreted the meaning of exposure. One therapist disregarded DSM provisions for indirect exposure, refusing to diagnose patients with PTSD unless they had experienced the attack firsthand. As he stated,

"You can't have PTSD if you're sitting in your house in Kansas City watching it on TV. That doesn't make one physically threatened. . . . People who were in the tower, people who were nearby, could have PTSD. But somebody who's uptown, who's not exposed, can't have PTSD."

A second therapist contested this strict interpretation of criterion A, stating that most patients he diagnosed with PTSD had been nowhere near the towers at the time of the attack. He defended his diagnoses in cases where patients had developed the requisite symptoms, including irritability, hypervigilance, and difficulties sleeping and concentrating, to qualify for PTSD. He explained,

> "*Even though they weren't there, they heard something's at the towers, and, 'Oh my God! My wife is there!' Or 'Oh my God! My uncle's there!' So they were having the physiological arousal symptoms even though they weren't there.*"

Other therapists interpreted the notion of exposure even more broadly. They maintained that "the exposure that began on September 11 didn't stop for a very long time" and that, after the attack, multiple kinds of ongoing exposures made city residents continue to feel both physically and emotionally threatened. For one, millions saw the burning towers, as they were visible from more than 20 miles away (Susser, Herman, & Aaron 2002). According to a trauma specialist, these exposures included "the smell of burning embers that permeated our consciousness," and that led people to ask, "What am I breathing in, what is this really?"[1a] In her view, exposures also included a general awareness of the damaging impacts of 9/11, such as

> "*being exposed to the enormity of the situation, the numbers of those that had perished, the numbers of those that had close contact to people who were lost, the numbers of people that lost homes [and] neighborhood schools.*"

Many mentioned the incessant exposure provided by the media, which repeatedly broadcast disturbing footage of the airplanes crashing into the towers and reported elevations in color-coded terror alerts. Exposure to the media stimulated such high levels of anxiety that, according to some therapists, even persons who watched reruns of the attack on television from the safety of their homes felt that their lives were at risk. Given the variety of ongoing exposures, they expected individuals' psychological difficulties to persist.

Diagnostic disagreements were further exacerbated when therapists found it difficult to distinguish between PTSD and other mental disorders. The most recent edition of the DSM states that diagnostic categories are not distinct entities with "absolute boundaries" that separate them from other categories of disorder. Rather, it acknowledges that mental disorders share symptoms and overlap, and that "boundary cases will be difficult to diagnose" (American

Psychiatric Association 2000:xxxi). This difficulty extends to PTSD, which shares symptoms with many other disorders. Decreased interest in everyday activities, and difficulties sleeping and concentrating, which are symptoms of PTSD, also characterize depressive disorders, while increased irritability, which is among the criteria for PTSD, is also a symptom of anxiety disorders. Due to this overlap, one therapist admitted that, after 9/11, he had found it difficult "to sift out what is general anxiety disorder, and what is a posttraumatic stress reaction." Only after having diagnosed numerous patients with PTSD did he realize that patients who were highly agitated following the attack did not necessarily have this disorder. Moreover, diagnostic ambiguities resulted from the fact that plural mental disorders frequently co-occur (Young 2001); recent research suggests that, when it comes to PTSD, "single-disorder presentations are the exception rather than the rule" (Westen, Novotny, & Thompson-Brenner 2004:635). Accordingly, after 9/11, therapists struggled to differentiate between diagnostic formulations with shared symptoms, to distinguish primary from secondary disorders, and to identify co-morbid disorders. As the above therapist said,

"A lot of people had dystonia, a lot of people were very shocked, there was bereavement, there were all these things that shouldn't necessarily be clumped into PTSD. "

Another therapist maintained that the correct diagnosis in the attack's immediate aftermath was not PTSD but ASD, or acute stress disorder. The diagnostic criteria for ASD closely resemble those for PTSD. Both categories are contingent on exposure to stressful external events, and both produce debilitating symptoms of intrusion, constriction, and hyperarousal. The key difference between these two categories has to do with time. ASD refers to stress reactions that emerge rapidly after catastrophic incidents and last a maximum of four weeks, whereas PTSD involves those that are present a month after the stressor is experienced and are of unlimited duration (American Psychiatric Association 2000). Such clear stipulations regarding the onset of these disorders should have led mental health professionals to rule out PTSD in the first few days and weeks after the attack. Yet as noted above, many diagnosed it nonetheless, suggesting either that they were unfamiliar with the contrasting temporal features of ASD and PTSD, or that they considered the attack so devastating that they overrode mere technical concerns.

Finally, therapists held differing views of the "disorder" in posttraumatic stress disorder. Some doubted that individuals who were destabilized by the events of 9/11 were suffering from mental disorders at all. Unlike colleagues who were quick to identify psychological injuries, and to offer formal diagnoses – thereby medicalizing the attack – these therapists refrained from labeling persons' reactions as psychiatric illnesses. Rather, they normalized such reactions as expectable and transient responses to exceptionally abnormal events. Yet making sharp distinctions between normal and pathological responses, and avoiding medicalized languages of mental disorder, were not simple matters. Like notions of physical health and illness, notions of psychological normality and abnormality are mutually constitutive. As a result, many therapists employed the language of psychiatric symptoms and mental illnesses even as they normalized individuals' reactions to 9/11.[2]

The considerable overlap between normalizing and medicalizing perspectives was clearly displayed in numerous flyers that saturated the New York City area following the attack (September 11 Digital Archive n.d.). Distributed by the American Red Cross and other nongovernmental agencies; by the National Institute of Mental Health, FEMA, and other federal organizations as well as by Columbia University, the Center for Modern Psychoanalytic Studies, and other private academic and training institutions, these flyers were designed to raise public awareness about psychological responses to 9/11. They also were meant to distinguish reactions that were normal from those that were pathological. However, they often blurred rather than clarified these differences. Instead of providing a distinctive language of coping, resilience, and strength to describe normal reactions to the attack, the flyers employed identical vocabularies of psychic injury for both normal reactions and those common to PTSD and other mental illnesses.

A Red Cross flyer entitled, "Your Mental Health Survival: Coping After a Disaster," typified this approach, identifying central symptoms of PTSD, such as nightmares, sleep disturbances, numbness, and startle reactions, as "normal reactions" to 9/11. Similarly, the Center for Modern Psychoanalytic Studies distributed a flyer listing trouble sleeping, nightmares, loss of appetite, forgetfulness, increased heart rate, irritability, and depressed mood as "normal stress reaction[s] to the Trade Center disaster." A flyer disseminated by the Department of Veterans Affairs in the National Center for Post-Traumatic Stress Disorder exemplified the difficulties involved in separating normal and pathological reactions. It stated that "changes after a trauma are normal," but also that most people who directly experienced major traumas had "severe problems in the immediate aftermath." In describing these severe problems, it presented a detailed description of PTSD symptoms. Other flyers – especially those addressed to war veterans – cautioned that "people who have previously survived traumatic events" might be "particularly sensitive to effects of later traumatic events." As a second Department of Veterans Affairs flyer warned, even "normal" reactions to 9/11 could be cause for alarm, as the effects of terrorist acts could range from "general distress to an increase in PTSD symptoms." As a protective measure, veterans with histories of combat-related trauma were advised to "anticipate and prepare for the worst, so that they are not retraumatized by a subsequent shock."

While some flyers instructed individuals to pay attention to their own emotional responses, additional flyers encouraged them to be alert to reactions in others. A FEMA flyer titled "How Are You Doing?" asked if "you or someone you know" was having "normal reactions," including feeling anxious or depressed, getting "jumpy from loud noises," being afraid to leave home or to take public transportation, or having vivid flashbacks. Because such reactions were not restricted to adults but could "happen to anyone at any age," several flyers strongly urged parents to look for signs of distress in their children. A flyer circulated by LifeNet, a 24-hour telephone service providing psychological referrals, explained that "children react differently to stress than adults," that their reactions "may be hard to detect," and that extra vigilance was required. After noticing changes in children's behavior, parents were not to "wait for them to come to you," but to ask them if they were having troubles or were "feeling less safe than before." Such flyers appeared to be aimed at reassuring parents that children's post-9/11 nightmares, anger, sadness, guilt, and fear could be traced to the attack, and were "normal reactions to traumatic events." Yet a flyer put out by the American Academy of Child & Adolescent Psychiatry cautioned that "a child or adolescent who experiences a catastrophic event may develop ongoing difficulties known as posttraumatic stress disorder" – which, as this Academy stated in a second flyer, "may last from several months to many years."

Other flyers, like the one disseminated by the National Institute of Mental Health, sought to more explicitly differentiate "severe symptoms of stress in the days and weeks following the event" – which were "normal" – from full-blown PTSD, which was "a real illness that needs to be treated." Some flyers drew such distinctions by referring to the duration of distress, and by specifying when reactions that originally were normal turned into serious disorders. Flyers disseminated by the New York State Psychiatric Institute stated that physical and emotional symptoms, which were "normal in every way," could "become dangerous to a person's health" when they were "prolonged." But exactly how long was prolonged? An American Red Cross flyer advised people to "see a mental health counselor" if their symptoms lasted longer than one month. In contrast, a flyer for the Department of Veterans Affairs in the National Center for Post-Traumatic Stress Disorder sketched a hazier time frame, saying that while many people would feel better within three months, others would recover "more slowly." The National Institute of Mental Health was even less precise. Its flyer stated that if symptoms that emerged "in the days and weeks following the event" failed to "decrease over time and then disappear," some persons would "go on to develop PTSD."

Contradictory and ambiguous messages extended to flyers' suggestions regarding psychological help. Most flyers recommended professional mental health treatment; even individuals experiencing "normal reactions" were encouraged to obtain such support. Yet they failed to consistently advise which kinds of remedies to seek. The National Institute of Mental Health, which might have been expected to offer detailed advice about treatments, advocated "talk[ing] to a professional" and "working with a therapist," but did not elaborate further. Similarly, while the Department of Veterans Affairs stated that "as you process these experiences during treatment, the symptoms should become less distressing," it failed to identify the particular kinds of treatments that might facilitate such processing. Some flyers seemed to recommend supportive psychological services. Flyers from the Parent Child Center of the New York Psychoanalytic Society noted that "practitioners who have learned the art of listening are most helpful to people in times of stress and crisis," and Columbia University's flyer mentioned that it had expanded its counseling services "to support students during this challenging time." Other flyers advertised group therapy in addition to, or perhaps instead of, individual treatment. The Jewish Board of Family and Children's Services offered free "drop-in centers" for New Yorkers "to come in and talk with mental health professionals in groups or on an individual level," while a Project Liberty program called "The Bridge" offered free individual counseling in addition to "group rap sessions" and "education groups on trauma." Neither explained the relative benefits of group and individual treatment. In addition, several organizations offered crisis debriefing. While the Center for Modern Psychoanalytic Studies claimed that debriefing groups "reduce[d] your stress and anxiety," the New York State Psychiatric Institute went a step further, crediting such groups with "reduc[ing] the probability of post-traumatic stress symptoms and other psychological and physical complications." Flyers also alluded to mental health treatments involving medication. The PTSD Community Outreach Program flyer publicized a public educational forum called "Moving Past Trauma." Because the forum was co-sponsored by Pfizer – the pharmaceutical corporation that manufactures medications that are commonly used to treat PTSD – most likely, attendees were advised that one effective way to move past trauma entailed taking psychiatric medicines.

Moreover, flyers alerting parents to the attack's psychological consequences for their offspring recommended mental health treatment for children.

LifeNet's flyers stated unambiguously that "free, specialized treatment and support services" were available for children, and that "they work." Flyers urged parents to "act quickly," and to seek professional help if they were worried about their children's behavior. An American Academy of Child and Adolescent Psychiatry's flyer warned against waiting to seek treatment, because "early intervention is essential." Its flyer claimed that "child and adolescent psychiatrists can be very helpful in diagnosing and treating children with PTSD." It identified psychotherapy as "helpful" and medication as potentially "useful."

Attempts to normalize PTSD employed other strategies as well. Flyers sought to dismiss the view that PTSD was "a sign of weakness," characterizing it as a "real illness" that "can happen to anyone who has experienced, witnessed, or learned about a traumatic event." Some normalized PTSD by pointing to statistics. The Bridge's flyer claimed that "25% to 30% of people directly affected by disaster may develop full-blown posttraumatic stress disorder or other debilitating psychological conditions," while the National Institute of Mental Health's flyer advised persons with PTSD that they were "not alone" in that the disorder affected 5.2 million Americans annually. It added, "It's not your fault, and you don't have to suffer."

What impact did these flyers have on diagnosis after 9/11? Perhaps by raising the profile of PTSD in the minds of the general public, they directly influenced potential therapy patients. As a rule, prevailing social discourses shape the ways in which individuals make sense of their lives (Rosenwald & Ochberg 1992). In this case, widely publicized descriptions of normal reactions and abnormal symptoms closely focused individuals' attention on distressing psychic and bodily states while simultaneously authorizing particular ways of labeling them. They thus may have encouraged New Yorkers – whether they were physically present during the attack, witnessed it from a distance, or watched it unfold on television – to adopt the medicalized language of psychiatric symptoms to classify vague complaints, to diagnose themselves as suffering from mental disorders, and to seek professional help.[3] Individuals who entered mental health treatment had already been sensitized to the possibilities of specific kinds of wounds, and were primed to see certain reactions as symptoms of PTSD. One therapist noted exactly such an impact. Some of his patients presented with a resurgence of prior symptoms, while others began to wonder "if they had developed a new diagnosis, or a new disorder." As this suggests, although the flyers discussed above originally were intended to normalize responses to the attack, they may have instructed individuals to see themselves as mentally disordered.

These flyers also may have affected the ways in which mental health professionals – some of whom were struggling to find ways to classify the attack – identified their patients' reactions and states. In highlighting PTSD symptoms, they added to an already voluble chorus trumpeting this disorder. PTSD was the subject not only of numerous scientific studies and government-sponsored publicity campaigns but also of frequent newspaper and television stories that reported its signature symptoms. One therapist described conversations with colleagues who "were on the horn, saying 'PTSD, PTSD, PTSD.'" The buzz around this disorder may have inclined therapists to discover it in their patients, and to interpret the various symptoms it shared with other mental disorders as clear evidence of PTSD. Such pressures may have been especially intense for therapists who were unfamiliar with PTSD's clinical presentation. Given that "there was a lot of uncertainty about what PTSD was," therapists in doubt may have selected the diagnostic category that best conformed to external expectations. Some of those who were involved in raising the profile of PTSD were far from disinterested parties. Mental health professionals who worked for international crisis management firms – sometimes pejoratively referred to as the "trauma industry" (Sommers & Satel 2005:178) or the "grief industry" (Groopman 2004:30) – had clear stakes in convincing other therapists, as well as the government and the general public, that hundreds of thousands of individuals would be traumatized by the attack.

However, not all therapists were swayed by collegial pressures, or by other external factors; some stubbornly refused to jump on the PTSD bandwagon.[4] They resisted diagnosing patients with PTSD out of concern that publicity campaigns had trivialized it, reducing it to "a hiccup" that could quickly be repaired through brief psychological treatments. Others resisted not because they found the ubiquitous PTSD publicity misleading, but because they found it "very disturbing." Although such mental health information commonly is distributed after disasters to "reduce public fear" (Hamilton 2005:626), one therapist remarked that a number of people he treated experienced this material as a "threat"; it was "scaring people" into thinking that if they didn't admit to having psychiatric symptoms and immediately enter mental health treatment, they were doomed to "pay a price later." Instead of providing helpful information and advice, it "raise[d] the level of anxiety even higher." Another therapist wondered how individuals who were mistakenly diagnosed with PTSD in the attack's immediate aftermath would be affected by misdiagnosis. He concluded that although the label might "get stuck," as mental health professionals gained new understandings of trauma, "people would be unlabeled as time goes by."

Therapists' varying views of trauma, and of specific diagnostic criteria, not only caused them to diagnose patients differently but also led them to divergent conclusions about the studies conducted shortly after the attack that found elevated rates of PTSD (e.g., Galea et al. 2002). Those who specialized in trauma doubted that surveys administered over the telephone accurately assessed respondents for PTSD, especially when they were disoriented, in shock, or unable to describe their reactions. One therapist claimed that because people's particular responses to traumatic events did not necessarily correspond to standardized checklists of PTSD symptoms, were sometimes experienced as physical problems, or otherwise were masked, telephone researchers were likely to miss them. Equally important, many therapists doubted that severely traumatized individuals would have disclosed highly charged, confidential information to anonymous telephone researchers in the absence of trusting therapeutic relationships and outside of safe clinical settings. They also rejected the notion that researchers could accurately gauge respondents' psychological reactions to the attack without knowing about their past, because to evaluate current symptoms, "you have to know who the person is in their own history." Accordingly, these therapists concluded that post-9/11 research had underreported actual rates of PTSD.

But other mental health professionals who were equally skeptical of this research arrived at the opposite conclusion, stating that it overestimated the prevalence of PTSD.[5] First, they claimed that such surveys "put the cart before the horse," by drawing conclusions about diagnoses on the basis of isolated symptoms. By taking single symptoms – such as anxiety – that were characteristic of PTSD as definitive evidence of the disorder, they produced inflated rates of PSTD. One therapist emphasized the dangers of diagnosing patients on this basis, and of ignoring crucial differences between patients who exhibited single symptoms characteristic of PTSD and patients who fully met its diagnostic criteria, saying,

"A lot of these studies and articles talk about PTSD symptoms. How do you know it's a PTSD symptom?...Somebody who has anxiety doesn't have a PTSD symptom, they have anxiety."

Even when respondents reported symptoms that fulfilled diagnostic criteria, therapists voiced concern that, as in other epidemiological surveys, estimates of the number of people with PTSD included individuals who were symptomatic, but whose conditions were not severe enough to compromise daily functioning or to warrant professional treatment (Wakefield & Spitzer 2002). A Latina therapist also expressed reservations about this research, but for different reasons; she found fault with studies that discovered higher rates of PTSD among Latino residents of New York City (e.g., Galea et al. 2002). This therapist claimed that such studies failed to take into account that, before 9/11, many metropolitan area Latinos had elevated baseline levels of stress due to a hurricane in the Dominican Republic in 1998, and to ongoing discrimination, unemployment, and poverty. In her view, these elevated baseline levels resulted in excessive diagnoses of PTSD. The therapist further maintained that many Latinos were misdiagnosed with PTSD after 9/11 because they experienced distress in ways that non-Latino therapists frequently mistook for PTSD symptoms.[6] Latinos, she explained, "feel a lot of issues in our body." In the wake of an act of mass violence, "the body is going to try to take it in, to try to process the event." Mental health professionals who were unfamiliar with this physical presentation of suffering may have misinterpreted somatic complaints as meeting diagnostic criteria on "an American checklist for PTSD."

This therapist's report raises additional questions about studies involving intercultural telephone interviews. Diagnostic assessments have proven notoriously problematic in intercultural clinical encounters, even when they occur face-to-face. When working with patients whose cultural backgrounds differ from theirs, therapists have had significant difficulties grasping their presenting complaints, symptomatology, idioms of distress, and subjective experiences of suffering. As a result, they have failed to accurately evaluate both the nature and the gravity of their afflictions (Malgady, Rogler, & Costantino 1987; Rogler 1999; Seeley 2000; Thakker & Ward 1998). Although the authors of the DSM-IV originally intended to address the cultural dimensions of psychiatric diagnosis in greater depth than in the manual's previous editions, and established a committee expressly for this purpose, they rejected most of the committee's suggestions (Good 1996; Lewis-Fernandez 1996). The finished product evidences psychiatry's primary commitment to establishing that most mental disorders are universal diseases with culturally invariant symptoms (American Psychiatric Association 1994).

The view of PTSD as a biologically based disorder with a fixed set of symptoms (van der Kolk 2002; Yehuda 2002; Young 2001) infused telephone studies of the attack's psychological sequelae. Researchers administered a single survey instrument based on standard diagnostic criteria regardless of respondents' ethnicity. Yet the likelihood of misdiagnosis multiplies in telephone surveys in which researchers employ standardized instruments based on preset lists of PTSD symptoms. While some researchers conducted interviews in Spanish as well as in English (Galea et al. 2002), there are no indications that they used any other of the more than 130 languages spoken by New York City residents (Hamilton 2005), adapted structured questionnaires to reflect culturally specific experiences and idioms of suffering (De Jong 2002; Marsella, Friedman, & Spain 1996), or considered the impacts of concurrent environmental stressors, such as unsafe neighborhoods, social marginalization, and lack of resources and protections (Perilla et al. 2002).[7] Nor did they anticipate that members of some ethnic communities would be reluctant to discuss psychological disturbances with nameless, English-speaking researchers. Such methodological limitations compromised the accuracy of their studies. As an example, one telephone survey found that Asian residents of New York City experienced comparatively little anxiety after the attack despite the fact that many lived or worked in the vicinity of the World Trade Center. However, Peter Yee, president of the New York Coalition for Asian American Mental Health, questioned the veracity of these findings. He believed that members of Asian communities simply had been unwilling to disclose reactions over the telephone to strangers who did not speak their language (Nader & Danieli 2005). Yee's interpretation of this data casts doubt on the accuracy of similar studies that evaluated the psychological consequences of the attack for other metropolitan area minority communities.

Mutual Emotional Contagion

As the preceding sections illustrate, after 9/11, a variety of contingencies affected mental health professionals' diagnoses of their patients. Working in the thick of a national crisis, in a gravely wounded city on the watch for an epidemic of PTSD, they responded to various pressures to rapidly identify and mend the injured. Preexisting notions of trauma, subjective interpretations of diagnostic criteria, prior experiences treating traumatized patients, dominant discourses of suffering, the influence of colleagues, and cultural conceptions of emotion all were brought to bear on diagnostic decisions as therapists selected among competing categories of mental disorder. But an additional component must be added to this already extensive list of the elements in play during the process of patient assessment. Because, as noted above, "everything that the analyst knows about the patient is mediated through the analyst's own experience" (Mitchell 1993:60), therapists' subjectivities exert considerable force on psychological diagnosis and treatment. This was especially relevant after the terrorist attack on the World Trade Center. Numerous New York City therapists, whether bereaved by the deaths of relatives and friends, aggrieved by the destruction of their city, or fearful for their families' safety, were in emotional turmoil after 9/11. When psychoanalysts got together for the purpose of addressing the difficulties they experienced in treating traumatized patients, they invariably ended up discussing the attack's traumatic impact on them (Twemlow 2004). Therapists' intense despair and anxiety, combined with the phenomenon of simultaneous trauma, may have intruded on patient evaluations, causing them to misrecognize the nature and extent of patients' distress.

How are clinical encounters affected when mental health professionals are wounded? Studies conducted before 9/11 indicate that a surprisingly large number of therapists – more than 60% – had practiced while depressed. Some therapists maintained that personal experiences of mental suffering had enhanced their clinical skills, engendering greater sensitivity, tolerance, and compassion for their patients. But others admitted that practicing while depressed, or while otherwise ill or in need, had impaired their professional conduct. When therapists were in pain, or were preoccupied by sorrow and dread, they were not as able to see and hear their patients clearly (Clark 1995; Goin 2002). Their perceptions sometimes were so distorted that they could not entirely distinguish their own suffering from that of their patients, or else projected personal injuries onto them (Wong 1984). Unmotivated and lethargic, they found it more difficult than usual to pay attention to patients, and especially to those who were in heightened emotional states (Gilroy, Carroll, & Murra 2002; Sherman 1996). Some therapists in distress – like the Israeli analyst who was so anxious about ongoing terrorist strikes that he did not permit his patients to express comparable fears (Kogan 2004) – prevented patients from deeply exploring crucial material. Similarly, therapists with histories of trauma, including those who had undergone mental health treatment, discouraged patients from discussing accounts of assault or abuse, or other violent material, because they feared it would reactivate disturbing personal memories.

After 9/11, many mental health professionals who occupied roles as expert helpers were in need of psychological assistance. Under the best of clinical circumstances, and even for comparatively stable therapists, treating severely traumatized individuals can be unsettling, as it requires "taking the patient's experience into ourselves and allowing our minds and our selves to be temporarily undone" (Boulanger 2005:29). But after 9/11, a number of mental health professionals already were undone. Some who were injured by the attack resumed their clinical work prematurely, before they fully grasped its multiple repercussions for them. In consequence, therapists' uncommonly raw and powerful emotions suffused their consulting rooms. As one acknowledged,

"In such situations, one's own inner life comes to bear a little more emotionally on the analytic session. Our own anxieties come in a bit more and we listen maybe in a slightly different way."

For some therapists, listening in "a slightly different way" meant not listening as well, especially when patients brought up material pertaining to the attack. Instead of systematically pursuing such material, thereby permitting patients to examine the aspects of 9/11 they found most troubling, wounded therapists sometimes steered clear of them. Others attempted to minimize patients' emotional reactions to the attack. One mental health professional observed that when therapists were "overwhelmed," they might "shut out some of the intensity of the affective experiences of other people." These tendencies were most apparent among New York City therapists whose histories of trauma unexpectedly were triggered by the attack. The therapist who was seriously burned as a child wondered whether his early trauma had left him with clinical "blind spots." Although he realized "that one needed to be attuned, and to really stick with this material no matter how painful it was," these "blind spots" may have caused him to overlook, or not to pursue, significant aspects of patients' 9/11 experiences. In another instance, the therapist whose Japanese city had burned to the ground during World War II found that memories of these fires returned with unexpected force after the attack. As she sat in her private office with patients, she struggled to "suspend [her] own personal memories and reflections" so that she could "be there fully, for their sake." Unfortunately, as a result, "there may have been a little bit of detachment" in her work. Other therapists who were similarly concerned about being engulfed, and perhaps retraumatized, either by patients' powerful affects or by personal feelings and memories, also sought refuge in such detachment.

Alternatively, following the events of 9/11, some therapists managed their own distress by projecting it onto their patients. Inasmuch as "everyone handles threatening, disturbing fragments of mental complexity by locating and experiencing them in other people" (Mitchell 1997:1), therapists who were traumatized, retraumatized, or otherwise destabilized by the attack may have situated their most extreme and threatening reactions inside the persons they had been hired to treat. Once these reactions were safely contained in their patients, therapists could examine them, diagnose them, and employ their expertise to repair them (Frawley-Odea 2004).

Recent accounts of the clinical encounters that took place after 9/11 suggest that therapists who returned to their practices before coming to terms with the attack may have mishandled clinical interactions in other ways as well. To protect themselves from personal anxieties and feelings of vulnerability, and to reestablish a sense of security, some presented their patients with false expressions of normalcy and well-being. Similarly, to avoid having to acknowledge newly petrifying political realities, including the possibility of additional terrorist strikes, they directed clinical conversations to safer and less threatening topics, and sought sanctuary in the familiar confines of patients' inner worlds (Boulanger 2003; Seeley 2005b). Several therapists found it difficult to tolerate patients whose responses to the attack differed from theirs, and subtly pressured them to take on their own feelings and political views. Envious of patients who were coping better than they were, or frustrated with patients who were faring less well, they sometimes turned such sentiments against them. One therapist became so enraged at a patient who was resentful of the successful corporate employees who were killed in the attack that she wanted to "use my power" as his therapist "to berate and humiliate him and psychically destroy him" (Frawley-O'Dea 2004:84).

The many ways in which therapists' subjectivities influenced clinical encounters after the attack contribute to new understandings of mutual emotional contagion. Before 9/11, the clinical literature depicted the flow of virulent emotions as unidirectional, portraying therapists solely as the recipients of patients' toxic affects. Studies of secondary and vicarious trauma conformed to this pattern, describing cases where traumatized patients transmitted psychological symptoms to their comparatively stable therapists. As discussed in the previous chapter, this pattern emerged after the attack, in that patients' intense emotions affected, and infected, their therapists. However, if the boundaries between individuals are sufficiently permeable to permit affective contagion, and if therapeutic encounters are relationships of "ongoing mutual influence in which patient and analyst systematically affect, and are affected by, each other" (Aron 1996:77), then emotional contagion is bidirectional. Just as therapists are susceptible to patients' traumatic symptoms and affective states, patients are susceptible to those of their therapists, especially when they repeatedly are exposed to therapists who are highly anxious or depressed.

Numerous therapists and patients may have found themselves in precisely this situation after the attack. Whether therapists were distraught due to personal losses, unfamiliar terrors, traumatic memories, or to the battering of their city, many of them realized that they lacked their customary emotional stability and control. As one therapist said, in providing psychological treatment, "You have to be kind of centered." Yet she found it impossible to maintain her usual balance after the attack; the events of 9/11 deprived her of "the kind of even keel that I usually try to have." This applied in equal measure to seasoned disaster responders who rushed from one catastrophe to the next. Some were still reeling from eighteen months of difficult work with persons who were devastated by Hurricane Floyd, which hit the East Coast in 1999, when they were "called back into action" to help victims of the Trade Center attack (Crimando & Padro 2005:113). When therapists were overwhelmed or off-balance, they may have unintentionally transmitted their horror and misery to their patients. The transmission of emotions may have occurred when mental health professionals elected to share their experiences of the attack, or their emotional responses to it, with patients. But even therapists who did not disclose such information may have been incapable of sealing off their terror and grief, or their personal memories of the attack, so that they seeped into their practice.

Some contemporary mental health professionals argue that seepage of this nature is to be expected in therapeutic encounters. Because therapeutic interactions and interpretations are "always personally expressive of the analyst's own subjectivity" (Mitchell 1997:16), therapists' sentiments and opinions inevitably infuse their clinical conduct. One therapist noted that such seepage also occurs through multiple channels of communication, encompassing not only "the exact content of what you say" but also "how you say it and what your manner is." Further, just as therapists are attuned to their patients, and routinely notice the slightest shifts in their demeanor and mood, some patients are keenly aware of, and receptive to, their therapists' affective states.

The mutuality of emotional contagion raises the possibility that, after 9/11, therapists and patients passed traumatic affects back and forth between them, as if in a feedback loop. Several mental health professionals were concerned that they had both transmitted and received such affects. When, like their patients, they developed nightmares and flashbacks, and grew increasingly vigilant or numb, they worried that patients' violent narratives and emotions had infected them. They also feared that they served as carriers of patients' toxic material. It is common for therapists to meet with patients in back-to-back clinical sessions, with only 10- or 15-minute breaks in between. Those who kept to such schedules after 9/11, treating one highly distressed or traumatized patient after another, had very little time to process their terrible stories, or to understand how these stories affected them, before the next patient arrived. Some therapists who experienced themselves as absorbing patients' affects, who felt incapable of containing them, and who worried about transmitting them to the following patient, worked hard to prevent them from leaking from one session into the next. But given that many therapists were beset by forceful psychological reactions in the wake of the attack, their efforts may have been insufficient to disrupt ongoing processes of mutual emotional contagion.

After the attack, the mutual emotional contagion of patients and therapists exacerbated the usual complexities of psychiatric diagnosis. When therapists were injured in this situation of simultaneous trauma, their diagnostic decisions inevitably were affected.[8] Like other emotionally wounded therapists whose suffering distorted their clinical perceptions and intuition, they may not have been able to pick up on their patients' symptoms and conditions. Moreover, because therapists who are injured cannot always distinguish their wounds from those of their patients, they may have located personal injuries and disordered states inside of them. In particular, therapists who were traumatized or retraumatized by the attack, but who nevertheless continued to practice, may have projected personal traumatic reactions onto their patients, and then diagnosed them with PTSD.

Clearly, after the World Trade Center attack, when therapists evaluated patients, they brought to bear a far wider range of sensibilities and experiences than those that are included in written diagnostic criteria. This finding raises questions as to whether therapists who were severely destabilized by 9/11 should have worked as volunteers and private practitioners in its aftermath, or whether their affects were dangerously contagious and their professional judgment was excessively impaired.[9] Immediately after the attack, when thousands of therapists volunteered their assistance, there were no screening mechanisms in place to prevent those who had histories of trauma, or who were significantly disturbed by these events, from being assigned to various service centers, or from being referred numerous bereaved and traumatized patients; the only volunteers who were turned away were those who lacked up-to-date New York State licenses. Yet as this chapter suggests, in situations of simultaneous trauma where mental health professionals are profoundly shocked and aggrieved, they may not be effective healers. Rather than soothing patients and alleviating their distress, they may fan their emotional fires; rather than containing virulent emotions and preventing their transmission, they may unwittingly spread them. Accordingly, the case of 9/11 demonstrates the need for in-depth discussions of mutual emotional contagion, the reciprocal transmission of trauma, and their effects on mental health diagnosis and treatment.

CHAPTER 7

Trauma as Metaphor

ॐ

WHILE THE PREVIOUS chapter looked at the various factors in play for mental health professionals who diagnosed patients after 9/11, additional aspects of diagnosis, and of assigning diagnoses of PTSD, deserve consideration following the World Trade Center attack. This is largely due to the fact that in contrast with almost all other mental illnesses, PTSD is conceptualized as a consequence of exposure to actual catastrophic occurrences, whether they are natural, accidental, or deliberately humanly caused. Every diagnosis of PTSD thus endorses the view that violent social and political events have the power to damage the mind. At the same time, this diagnostic category brings the world at large into clinical consulting rooms. Accordingly, Chapter 7 places conceptions of trauma into wider frames, exploring multiple interactions among the psychiatric, the personal, and the political. By examining trauma's social and cultural dimensions and meanings, the place of politics in therapeutic encounters, governments' management of mood, the formation of psychological citizens, and the national trauma of 9/11, it considers the broader implications of psychological suffering after the attack, as well as the ways that notions of traumatization, and diagnoses of PTSD, were employed to achieve a number of specific political objectives.

THE MEDICALIZATION OF SEPTEMBER 11

As discussed in previous chapters, shortly after September 11, public health officials predicted that the attack would have severe and widespread psychological repercussions. Based on a rapid assessment of mental health needs conducted by Columbia University's School of Public Health, the New York State Office of Mental Health warned that residents of New York City and its environs would suffer an epidemic of psychiatric problems, including depression, anxiety, substance abuse, and especially, posttraumatic stress disorder (Herman et al. 2002b). These predictions raised such serious alarm that studies investigating the incidence of mental disorders in the attack's immediate aftermath received expedited reviews, and quickly were published in prominent medical journals (Breslau 2004). When these studies found increased rates of PTSD and substance abuse (Galea et al. 2002; Vlahov et al. 2002), they justified unprecedented government spending for mental health treatments. They also stimulated the creation of Project Liberty, which widely publicized the symptoms of PTSD and other psychiatric illnesses. Not only mental health professionals were told to be vigilant for signs of posttraumatic stress. Medical doctors were urged to look for trauma-related disorders in their patients, and to interpret "unexplained physical symptoms" as the results of exposure to traumatic events (Yehuda 2002:108).[1] Private citizens were advised to frame their shock and sorrow in the medicalized language of psychiatry, and to seek psychological help. Despite the absence of statistics indicating the total number of persons who turned to mental health professionals to relieve the emotional consequences of 9/11, it is clear that psychological services were used extensively.

Those who have positive views of mental health treatment may applaud the fact that, after September 11, the federal government chose to support it. Yet there are reasons to question the medicalization of 9/11, as well as the implications of providing free mental health treatments on such a large scale at that particular historical moment. What happens when persons harmed by acts of mass violence are turned into patients with psychiatric disorders? And what does it mean to prescribe psychological treatments to remedy individuals' emotional responses to a politically motivated attack?

TRAUMA'S SOCIAL DIMENSIONS

A central element of medicalization is the conception of major mental disorders as diseases that are biologically based, and that require professional diagnosis and treatment. Recent editions of the *Diagnostic and Statistical Manual* promote this perspective, underscoring the similarities between mental suffering and physical illnesses, and ascribing many psychiatric disorders, including PTSD, to bases in neurobiology (Thakker & Ward 1998). As previously noted, some theorists attribute individuals' susceptibilities to PTSD to innate abnormalities in the brain (cf. McNally 2003; Yehuda 1999, 2000; Young 2001). Conversely, many trauma specialists maintain that catastrophic stressors have the power to damage the brain. In support of this view, they cite preliminary studies indicating that extreme stressors disrupt the workings of neurotransmitters that regulate attention and arousal, or alternatively, that they harm those areas of the brain that are responsible for memory, cognition, and language (cf. van der Kolk 2002). They also point to research suggesting that the cortisol that is released in situations of fight or flight injures the hippocampus when its presence is prolonged or repeated (Yehuda 2002), or that early experiences of violence permanently compromise systems of stress response, increasing the probability of trauma-related disorders in adulthood (Heim, Meinlschmidt, & Nemeroff 2003). Despite the lack of agreement on the particular ways in which situations of extreme threat harm the brain, these theorists agree that traumatic injuries destroy its normal functioning, and manifest universally as symptoms of PTSD.

At first glance, medicalizing PTSD by establishing its underlying biological origins and invariant effects seems to confer a range of advantages. By converting the shock, fury, fear, and grief that disasters and atrocities engender into predictable sets of symptoms, medicalization organizes and rationalizes emotions that are otherwise chaotic and debilitating. Locating the origins of severe psychological disabilities in physiological wounds may also lessen their stigma. During World War I, when doctors diagnosed soldiers with shell shock, and attributed their psychic deterioration to brain lesions caused by exploding shells, soldiers were saved from charges of dishonorable conduct and cowardice (Davoine & Gaudilliere 2004). Transforming overpowering emotional reactions into illnesses that are based in biology has the additional advantage of defining their causes as discoverable, and of framing their symptoms as manageable – and potentially curable – by means of scientifically tested treatments (Hacking 1995). This perspective was dominant after the 1995 Oklahoma City bombing. When relatives and friends of persons who were killed in the terrorist attack were diagnosed with PTSD, they seemed to be guaranteed that unlike mourning, which might last a lifetime, their anguish would be diminished, and eventually brought to a close, with the proper professional help (Linenthal 2001).

However appealing such notions, neither PTSD nor other psychiatric categories can be reduced solely to biological entities; instead, they also are historical, social, and cultural phenomena. According to Otto Fenichel, the psychoanalyst who was a contemporary of Freud, "neuroses are social diseases ... corresponding to a given and historically developed social milieu" (1945:586). In part, emergent mental pathologies are responses to shifting social conditions that bring new pressures to bear on psychological functioning. Accordingly, the categories of illness that mental health professionals employ have proven highly susceptible to change. Forms of emotional instability – like haircuts, hats, and handbags – go in and out of fashion (Benedict 1934). Every mental disorder has a specific history, and conceptions of mental illness undergo continual revision. A quick look at successive versions of the *Diagnostic and Statistical Manual* confirms the extensive modification in notions of psychiatric disorder from one edition to the next (Gaines 1992). Substantive changes pertain to the ways diagnoses are made, the kinds of behaviors and states of mind that are regarded as disorders, the distinctive features of each diagnostic category, the types of persons who are considered most vulnerable to particular disorders, and the ostensible reasons why they occur. For instance, homosexuality used to be considered a mental disorder but is no longer, while premenstrual syndrome formerly was not included in the catalog of mental illnesses, but now is. Bipolar disorder, which used to be called manic depression, previously was thought to emerge in early adulthood, but now is diagnosed in children. Multiple personality disorder, which was diagnosed in epidemic numbers only 20 years ago, not only is out of fashion, but is nearly out of sight. After an intense controversy featuring allegations that therapists had planted memories of abuse in patients, and had coached them to display multiple personalities, this disorder was remade: its key characteristic of separate, whole personalities was eliminated, and it was renamed "Dissociative Identity Disorder" in the latest edition of the DSM (APA 2000).

Such revisions, along with the continual emergence of new diagnostic categories, also illustrate that cultural conceptions of insanity, normality, morality, and reality are constantly in flux (Gaines 1992). Indeed, Sontag's (1977) claim that physical illnesses are metaphors, in that they stand for, call up, and play out dominant social themes, anxieties, and inequalities applies to mental disorders as well. Like labels for physical diseases, labels for mental disorders designate the ills and ill fortunes of others. They distinguish the normal from the deviant, the distressed from the diseased, and the powerful from the marginal; they tell us what to think of them and how to behave toward them, and they help us anticipate what will become of them. Because mental disorders generally are more amorphous and intangible than physical disorders, they may be even more freighted with symbolic meanings.

These broader aspects of diagnostic categories are especially relevant to disorders related to trauma, and above all, to PTSD. For example, although the DSM editions portray PTSD as a culture-free, universal disorder, some theorists describe it as distinctively American, in that its core symptoms entail marked deviations from psychological norms in the United States. The chronic distress that is typical of PTSD conflicts with mainstream American views that painful emotional suffering, whether due to bereavement, violence, or disaster, is a pathological state that "can not and should not be endured" (Kleinman & Desjarlais 1995:180), and that calls for rapid repair. Common PTSD symptoms such as intrusive memories and flashbacks, in which prior traumatic events are relived, are particularly disruptive in societies where linear notions of time, and a relentless future orientation, make it aberrant to inhabit the past. Such symptoms also are most troubling for individuals who are expected to maintain a high degree of self-control, but who enact involuntary behaviors, experience unwanted states, and are otherwise powerless to prevent "the literal return of the event" (Caruth 1995b:5).

A further dimension of this disorder that speaks to its embeddedness in American society concerns its emphasis on individualism (Bracken, Giller & Summerfield 1995). Although PTSD is seen as an outcome of disasters that affect entire communities, definitions of this disorder continue to place priority on individuals' biological responses to overwhelming stress, on pathologies that are located inside individuals' bodies, and on personalized strategies of repair. Yet trauma has a "social dimension" (Erikson 1995:185). Catastrophic events, whether naturally or humanly caused, injure more than the minds of separate individuals. They also harm communities as a whole, damaging the physical environments that structure their experiences, the social ties that bind them together, their customary practices, and their collective identities (James 2004; Summerfield 1999). At the same time, community members who are exposed to the same disastrous occurrences often experience shared moods and frames of mind, common memories of the past, and diminished expectations for the future.[2]

Before the attack, New York City therapists were accustomed to framing traumatic reactions as individual problems; afterward, medicalized notions of mental disorder failed to provide them with the necessary tools for addressing its community-wide effects.[3] Nonetheless, even in their subsequent clinical work with individual patients, they were struck by its collective impacts. One therapist described the powerful communal response that ensued:

"The experience, the visceral, psychic mind-heart continuum experience, was a collective experience. We all reacted out of a collective archetypal knowledge of survival and dread. That level of communal experience out-weighed the personal story."

The collective aspects of 9/11 were illustrated not only by the subjugation of personal stories to stories of communal experience but also by the physical transformations undergone by individual bodies. In the wake of the attack, this therapist observed that patients' individual identities and idiosyncratic body languages seemed to have been erased.

"The first week or so, people just sat. They just sat. I had somebody who always sits like this, with her feet in the chair, and she was just sitting [slumps]. For the first week or two, somatically, people were just here."

Another therapist noticed sensations of pain that were so widespread that they seemed to transcend the boundaries of individuals' bodies. It was as if a collective nervous system, or a communal social body, had been damaged in the attack.

"Everybody's trauma was so raw. It didn't matter who you were talking to – relief worker, direct victim, other therapists – you were all the same body in some ways."

Just as these therapists challenged the individualism that, while inherent in PTSD, is culturally specific, a number of theorists emphasize this disorder's historical specificity. Rejecting its representation as a timeless, biologically based, individual illness, they portray it as an invention (Young 1995) – as a "pseudo-condition" that turns suffering into a "technical problem" requiring "technical solutions" (Summerfield 1999:1452). Some consider PTSD to be an artifact of postmodernism, because the fragmentation of self and meaning that is integral to this disorder is also a typical feature of fractured, postmodern selves (Bracken 2001). Moreover, they trace central aspects of PTSD to particular technological advances. In the first half of the 20th century, persons suffering from overwhelming stress rarely spoke of flashbacks. In fact, it is claimed that flashbacks were identified as key symptoms of traumatic reactions only after they gained broad popularity as cinematic devices (Jones et al. 2003).

In addition to reflecting specific cultural norms and historical periods, conceptions of mental disorders are shaped by distinctive political circumstances. Psychiatry, like psychology, psychoanalysis, and social work, always "has a political as well as a professional and scientific context" (Lee & Kleinman 2002:120). Diagnostic categories are created, revised, and invoked in response to prevailing political currents. They are applied selectively and instrumentally to justify both the power and privilege of certain segments of the population and the disadvantage and containment of others. Because trauma-related disorders are closely linked to outsize events in the outside world, and refer to the ways calamities and acts of violence damage the mind, their political implications are particularly significant.

As discussed in Chapter 1, novel conceptions of trauma, and new trauma-related diagnostic categories, frequently have emerged in the context of political movements (Herman 1997). PTSD is the most obvious example. In the late 1970s and early 1980s, the widespread diagnosis of PTSD within particular groups in the United States drew attention to their suffering, galvanized public support, and advanced their interests and aims. Originally "tailored to the needs" of Vietnam War veterans, PTSD was propelled into the DSM by a collection of groups, including psychiatrists, that were involved in the antiwar movement (Shephard 2001:355; Young 1995). To be sure, some psychiatrists lobbied for the inclusion of this category primarily to improve the mental health treatment of seriously troubled veterans of war. But asserting that Vietnam veterans had been traumatized by combat experiences, and diagnosing them with PTSD, also made several political points. A diagnosis of PTSD justified the suffering of individual veterans who had been reviled for fighting an unpopular war. At the same time, it exonerated them, shifting public anger to the government that had sent them to battle. For a growing antiwar movement, citing the high rates of PTSD among soldiers returning from battle exposed the atrocities of the Vietnam War, and by extension, of all wars; it made a statement that was antimilitary, antiestablishment, and anti-imperialist all at once. Shortly thereafter, many women who had been physically, emotionally, or sexually battered by their spouses were diagnosed with PTSD. In connection with that era's growing feminist movement, these diagnoses provided medical evidence that society's institutionalized sexism undermined women's well-being (Herman 1997). To diagnose women with PTSD was to protest the everyday violence of their lives, and to support their social and political equality.

Members of these two groups derived substantial advantages from being diagnosed with mental disorders. Before receiving diagnoses of PTSD, many of them had been marginalized. When they had dared to tell their personal stories of atrocity and abuse, they were rarely considered credible; even when their misery had been acknowledged, they were held responsible for it. Framing their troubles in the language of mental illness, and receiving a psychiatric diagnosis – especially one that attributed their predicament to external incidents of violence rather than to internal deficiencies – legitimized their suffering. PTSD also improved their social positions, as it entitled them to supportive services, legal protections, psychological care, and, in some cases, financial assistance.

Mental health professionals played central roles in both of these political movements. For many psychotherapists, the personal was political. Allying themselves with patients who had been devastated in war or abused and degraded at home, therapists encouraged them to break their silence, expose their personal suffering, attribute this suffering to societal rather than individual pathologies, and use it to inspire political action. Leaving the confines of their clinical consulting rooms, many therapists also became activists, working alongside their patients for social rather than individual change.

TRAUMA AS METAPHOR

The attack on the World Trade Center occurred at a very different historical moment. At the dawn of the twenty-first century, liberation movements seemed to have run their course. The climate of social ferment that characterized earlier decades had all but disappeared. It was replaced by what appeared to be unparalleled domestic prosperity, an unshakable national stability, and unquestioned international dominance. Nor did many individuals who were exposed to the attack, and who were diagnosed with PTSD, resemble the major groups who had previously received this diagnosis. Unlike war veterans and battered women, who had been socially and economically marginalized, large numbers of new survivors were powerful and financially successful. Also, veterans and battered women had been chastised for exaggerating their wounds, and for publicly discussing personal episodes of intense violence. In contrast, 9/11 survivors were roundly celebrated, and their stories of horror and violence were told and retold as modern heroic tales.

What common threads connected members of these groups, many of whom received the same psychiatric diagnosis? Despite their evident differences, Vietnam veterans, battered women, and survivors of the World Trade Center attack all were victims of incomprehensible, unspeakable, and undeserved acts of violence. Extending Sontag's (1977) claim that cancer is a metaphor for the repression of violent feelings, and that AIDS is a metaphor for deviance and indulgence, posttraumatic stress disorder is a metaphor for victimhood, referencing blamelessness and unprovoked assault. Indeed, more than with any other psychiatric category, conceptions of legitimate and deserving victimhood are inextricably intertwined with PTSD. When mental health professionals assign this diagnosis to individuals who have suffered catastrophes and abuse, they support their claims of victimization and assert their fundamental innocence, while simultaneously endowing these claims with the "full legitimacy of scientific knowledge" (Breslau 2004:114). When applied in the United States, this diagnosis commonly inspires "a peculiarly American notion of moral responsibility to provide compensation to victims" (French 2004:211), which helps make PTSD an especially desirable diagnosis (Summerfield 1999).[4]

Stating that trauma and PTSD are metaphors does not deny the profound suffering caused by the World Trade Center attack any more than Sontag disputed that cancer brings terrible pain. It is clear that since September 11, 2001, hundreds of thousands of Americans have experienced the nightmares, intrusive memories, and emotional numbing that are characteristic of PTSD; that millions more have been deeply anguished, desperately anxious, and deathly afraid; and that mental health treatments have been helpful to many. Yet because illness labels signify the crises that threaten societies as well as the diseases that weaken individuals, conceptualizing trauma and PTSD as metaphors permits examination of the social and political implications of reading behavioral responses to the attack in ways that endorse widespread experiences of victimization.

For one, after 9/11, conceptions of victimhood had unusually positive connotations. Instead of being seen as passive or weak, victims of the attack were
considered heroes who had made sacrifices for their country. Victim identities were privileged identities, which conferred special statuses and monetary
benefits. At the same time, victim labels were liberally distributed. They were
applied to all those who were killed, to everyone who was physically injured, displaced, bereaved, economically harmed, or emotionally wounded by the attack
(Rosenthal 2002), as well as to their friends, relatives, and acquaintances, who
were termed "tertiary and quaternary" victims (Crimando & Padro 2005:107).
The public designation of good victims, and the multiple compensations available to them, created a powerful pull. Several therapists spoke of patients who
were so envious of 9/11 victims that they had considered pretending to have
lost relatives in the attack, not only to receive the financial awards that were
offered to the kin of the deceased but also to obtain some small portion of the
public's attention and care. Whether individuals acquired victim identities, or
whether in the course of their work they assigned them by diagnosing patients
with PTSD, being involved with such identities provided opportunities for
participating in this local and national tragedy. According to one mental health
professional, diagnosing patients with PTSD was "a way to go along with the
'woe is me, we've been victimized' sensibility going on out there."

As the circumstances surrounding the designation of 9/11 victims make
clear, the assignment of victim status, including the diagnosis of psychological
patients, is an active and selective process that is shaped by social and political
as well as medical concerns (Kleinman & Desjarlais 1995). Differential assignment of victim status and selective government expenditures for humanitarian
relief denote the relative moral worth of various individuals and communities.
Previously, diagnostic labels have been key factors in determining which specific calamities – and which specific victims – merit such expenditures (Watters
2001). Because elevated rates of PTSD attest to the "public significance of the
trauma" (French 2004:213), they frequently mobilize government funding for
special programs and services for victims.[5] Despite the fact that the most common traumatic incidents involve violent assaults against women and children
by members of their families, community disasters consistently receive more
government services and greater public support (van der Kolk 2002). But even
when it comes to large-scale catastrophes, some unleash more extensive compensations than others. As an example, two months after the World Trade
Center attack, an airplane bound for the Dominican Republic crashed into a
residential neighborhood in the Belle Harbor section of Queens. The crash
resulted in the deaths of all 260 persons on board, as well as 5 people on the
ground, and ravaged scores of homes. For many members of the Dominican community, this disaster was far more devastating than the World Trade

Center attack (Batista 2005), while for neighborhood residents – who already were hard hit by 9/11 – it produced a "double trauma" (Hildebrandt 2005:106). Yet comparatively few federal resources were made available to the victims of this tragedy, who found themselves "taking a backseat" to victims of 9/11 (Hildebrandt 2005:121).

Some therapists were uncomfortable with the selective designation, and generous compensation, of deserving 9/11 victims.[6] One who specialized in treating persons harmed by catastrophes and abuse found fault with their privileged status, insisting that "other people should be compensated too," and that "we shouldn't make hierarchies based on who survived what." Another therapist was concerned about the role psychiatric categories played in identifying persons who were entitled to government aid and social support. He asked,

"How do you choose which public events are the ones that you consider worthy of putting into your diagnostic formulation? Your house burning down may be more traumatic than 9/11."

The fact that some categories of victims, and some kinds of injuries, were considered more deserving of assistance than others went beyond the government's limited response to the airplane crash in Queens. While funds for 9/11-related mental health treatments grew at a remarkable pace, during the same period, community mental health budgets were slashed. Moreover, the $95 billion that the attack initially was estimated to cost New York City meant substantial, long-term funding cuts for other human services (National Association of Social Workers 2002), causing one therapist to remark, "Children are the lowest priority and the poor are the lowest priority." A second therapist noted that while the federal government was pouring millions of dollars into Project Liberty, "community mental health funds were disappearing everywhere" and the Massachusetts psychiatric system was "going under." He asked,

"What are the priorities? If there's no money for anything, how could there be this vast amount of money for the mental health consequences of 9/11?"

MAKING PSYCHOLOGICAL CITIZENS

This therapist's question, like more general concerns regarding the designation of large numbers of deserving 9/11 victims, raises issues that are central to the politics of emotion. Numerous governing bodies seek to manipulate the emotional lives of their subjects. To augment state control, silence dissent, and gain support for military actions against supposed threats, they organize civilians' affective experience along particular lines, fostering emotions and states that are favorable to their interests (Abu-Lughod & Lutz 1990). To manage the mood of the populace – to channel its affects and passions into dispositions that support their fundamental objectives – governments identify certain emotions as normal and appropriate, or as evidence of national loyalty. In addition to prescribing the "emotional tone for the nation" (Good & Good 1988:45), political regimes develop techniques for eliciting the desired behavior.

Such projects are made possible, in part, by the underlying web of relations between governing bodies and officially recognized forms of medicine (Foucault 1963/1994). In the United States, government agencies certify medical training programs, license practitioners, track and combat diseases, approve treatments and medications, fund scientific research, provide direct patient care, organize emergency responses, and disseminate information on the latest medical discoveries. These procedures, as well as more covert collaborations,[7] provide them with multiple ways of regulating medical practice, including the practices of psychiatrists and of other mental health professionals. Because advancing medicalization, and the resultant proliferation of psychiatric illness categories, enlarges the domain in which mental health professionals have influence, and are authorized to make determinations of wellness and abnormality, it expands the chances for government control over individuals' psychological states. The "opportunistic nature" (Breslau 2004:120) of the alliance between politics and medicine is illustrated by cases where mental health professionals have collaborated with governments, for example, by diagnosing their opponents with serious psychiatric illnesses and committing them to institutions (Breslau 2000; Lee & Kleinman 2002; Littlewood & Lipsedge 1989).

According to several therapists, the American government engaged in comparable activities after 9/11. In their view, the administration sought to solidify its power, to increase its hold over the populace, and to gain popular approval for its domestic and international agendas by shaping citizens' responses to the attack in particular ways. The flyers described in Chapter 6, some of which were disseminated by FEMA, NIMH, and other federal organizations, directed individuals to take notice of mentally disordered states. One therapist maintained that, instead of encouraging people to rationally analyze the events of 9/11, the government consistently advised them to pay attention to their feelings. Because those who focused on affective reactions were more likely to become overwhelmed, "they were less able to use their minds to think about the attack." Conversely, "the people who were able to think about this weren't as confused by emotional symptoms."

Other therapists observed that, in addition to urging the public to concentrate on emotional reactions, the administration actively promoted the desired affective responses by regularly heightening the anxiety induced by the attack. The relentless "hyping of post-9/11 threats" (Rich 2005:A12), and the induction of a war on terrorism that was "undefined, unlocatable, unknowable, in a word timeless" (Aretxaga 2001:140), intensified the atmosphere of paranoia and fear. These activities had discernible impacts on individuals' emotions and states. One therapist detected a clear rise in his patients' paranoid anxiety. Another noticed a correspondence between the government's announcements of plans for military invasions and his patients' psychological conditions, saying that, "as the rhetoric escalates, patients' symptoms escalate." A third concluded that the new color-coded warning system for terrorist attacks was meant "to do nothing but create symptoms."[8] To the extent that the American government wished to keep people on edge, those who felt terrified and anxious displayed the proper – and even patriotic – affect and demeanor.

The medicalization of 9/11 provided the government with additional avenues for organizing persons' subjective experiences. After repeatedly urging Americans to closely attend to their emotions, and after stoking their terrors and insecurities, it supported the conversion of these affects into symptoms of PTSD and other officially recognized mental disorders. Overt collaborations between mental health professionals and the state, as in Project Liberty, further broadened the possibilities of government influence. Project Liberty's massive advertising campaigns both publicized mental disorders and designated state-sponsored mental health treatments as the most effective means of relieving them. Persons who were emotionally injured were offered help, free of charge. To receive it, all they had to do was to label their reactions as psychiatric symptoms, visit a licensed mental health professional, and become patients in psychological treatments.

What some therapists found especially disconcerting about the manipulation of public sentiment after the attack was that many mental health professionals were among those who were manipulated. One stated,

> "What is so striking about the psychologizing of 9/11 is the way that the mental health community has gone on board with that.... There seemed to be no questioning of it."

Rather than critically analyzing the government's motives or its version of these events, mental health professionals reacted by saying, "We're helpers, we're going to help." This therapist characterized their response as follows:

> "We are scared, we believe that the government is going to protect us, and in response to this fear, we are going to be supportive of the government and act in a solid way, joining forces and doing what we can, doing our part in this situation."

Furthermore, he found that the newly strengthened alliance between politics and mental health professionals was cause for considerable alarm. In his view, this alliance was opportunistic not only for the government, but for therapists as well. After being treated as valued experts, they were reluctant to jeopardize their positions by voicing reservations as to whether existing psychiatric categories accurately described individuals' responses to 9/11, and whether available mental health models effectively treated their wounds. This therapist observed, "There is a vast amount of research money available there – *if* you do the kind of studies that are consistent with how the government wants to see things." In consequence, some of his colleagues "put their scientific point of view away . . . and lapse[d] into the party line."

As this therapist suggests, mental health professionals may have supported the medicalization of 9/11 because they obtained significant benefits from it. When this unparalleled national emergency widened the category of therapy patient to include persons harmed by an act of international political violence, it increased mental health professionals' influence, their prestige, and the realm of their expertise. They were granted singular authority to distinguish the normal from the mentally injured, identify legitimate victims, justify expenditures of government funds, apply recognized psychiatric labels, and deliver the specialized treatments deemed essential to recovery. Such unaccustomed powers proved seductive to many. The same therapist further remarked that several of his colleagues who previously had worked with the homeless, the chronically mentally ill, and other underserved populations went to work for Project Liberty, because they found it more "chic and sexy and exciting." Yet "the problems we've been meant to address are still out there. . . . There's plenty of work to do in mainstream psychiatry."

Mental health professionals' newfound authority sometimes assumed strange forms. Some refashioned their usual helping activities as quasi-military operations. Eschewing the vocabularies of emotion and suffering that are central to the clinical project, they incorporated the jargon of the armed forces into their work. Seasoned disaster volunteers who migrated from one disaster to another were referred to as "reservists" (Crimando & Padro 2005:113), as if constituting a national guard of therapists to be called up for active duty in the event of major emergencies. Other mental health professionals described themselves as being on the "frontlines" after the attack, overstating their resemblances to soldiers on the battlefield. One therapist who worked for Project Liberty was struck by its "paramilitary" operations and language, which she described as "disasterese" (Silverman 2004:1). Mental health professionals who were "deployed" to various sites abandoned standard psychological interventions in favor of the highly regimented debriefings that were originally used in the military. Adorned with "patriotic jewelry," they behaved like "loyal troops out to comply with their commander," suggesting that their primary function was not to supply psychological help, but rather to "defend the American way" (Silverman 2004:6–7).

Although mental health professionals who enjoyed their newly elevated status may have been reluctant to critically analyze the medicalization of 9/11, a couple of therapists were concerned that the government had a stake in turning persons who were affected by the attack into psychological patients. One said that the administration's emphasis on emotional injuries, mental illnesses, and increasing rates of PTSD could be useful in advancing its agendas; that "the more people who can be brought under the umbrella of having been affected by this, the more it could get used for political ends." Another noted that the particular kinds of anxieties the government sought to elicit supplied the necessary affective link between the events of 9/11 and the alleged threats to American safety posed by Saddam Hussein. In his view, the constant "replaying of 9/11" on the first anniversary of the attack was designed to stimulate insecurities in order to drum up support for the invasion of Iraq.

In a study of the social and political fallout of a major technological disaster – the 1986 Chernobyl nuclear reactor explosion – Petryna (2002:115) described the making of "biological citizens" in the post-Soviet Ukraine. According to her account, numerous residents of the Chernobyl area sought to procure scarce government resources by claming to have suffered disabling physical injuries after exposure to radioactive particles. Those who presented doctors with physical evidence that their bodies had absorbed the requisite levels of radiation qualified for disability status. They then were taken under the government's wing and awarded its "mechanisms of benevolence," even in cases where they had deliberately increased their exposure to radiation so that their families would receive such benefits (Petryna 2002:204).

The injuries produced by the events of 9/11 were not measurable in quite the same way. However, psychiatric examinations and instruments that screened individuals for PTSD and other mental disorders, and that assessed the severity of emotional injuries, served similar functions. Where the Chernobyl nuclear explosion created biological citizens who depended on state-affiliated medical personnel to certify their illnesses so that they might secure government compensations, the World Trade Center attack created psychological citizens who permitted the state's medical representatives to define their suffering in exchange for privileged statuses and benefits. While this arrangement may have provided 9/11 sufferers with essential resources and support, the government also derived substantial advantages. Indeed, it may have served state interests to have a citizenry that saw itself as traumatized, or as otherwise psychologically disabled; a citizenry that was composed not of informed and rational political subjects, but of psychiatric patients too emotionally disturbed to think, too preoccupied with symptoms to act, and too reliant on government benefits to systematically question its actions.

THE POLITICAL IS PERSONAL

Despite the clear penetration of specific governmental interests into individuals' emotional lives after the attack, in subsequent clinical encounters, many therapists were inclined to overlook such incursions. Instead of promoting the analysis of such political machinations they stuck to their usual methods, exploring the idiosyncratic features and intrapsychic meanings of individuals' reactions to 9/11. In fact, just as politicians, with few exceptions, have kept mental health policy issues off their agendas, contemporary therapists, for the most part, have kept political issues out of their consulting rooms. In conventional clinical encounters, they expect patients to discuss the material that is most directly related to their internal and interpersonal worlds. Therapists who maintain the traditional analytic stance of neutrality (Mitchell 1997) fear that conversations about politics will expose, and perhaps impose, their own opinions and views, inhibiting patients' freedom of expression and impinging on their transferences. More to the point, many therapists believe that patients who discuss political events in clinical sessions are defending themselves against the turbulence of their inner worlds by focusing on material that is comparatively impersonal, external, and remote. Like everything else patients say in psychotherapy, their political comments are likely to be analyzed for what they reveal about the hidden world of their psyches, rather than accepted at face value.

The practice of reducing political events to the life experiences of individuals, and of subjugating political history to personal history, is typical of talk therapies. Although some describe psychoanalysis as a historical practice – as a "theory of history" that "makes sense of the present by seeing it as containing the significance of the past" (Roth 1987:9) – in every talk therapy, the history in question is that of particular individuals. Informed by psychological theories that privilege intrapsychic life and early childhood experiences, mental health professionals solicit information about the past that is narrowly biographical (Nemiah 1989). In contrast, the material they deem less relevant to the therapeutic project – including that which pertains to political events – is permitted to slide out of the clinical picture (Hacking 1995; Watters 2001). The phenomenon of medicalization greatly contributes to such exclusions, as it provides the necessary frameworks for turning persons' reactions to political events into individual psychological symptoms.

However, in the period immediately following 9/11, some therapists found it increasingly difficult to keep politics at bay. During the weeks and months of crisis that followed, ominous reminders of recent political incidents continually invaded their consulting rooms. To get to their therapists' offices, patients took subways they feared would be bombed, breathed air they thought was toxic, passed sidewalk tributes to the dead, and read missing persons flyers tacked onto trees. Even the therapeutic space, which they formerly viewed as inviolable, had been palpably breached, and felt neither protective nor safe. One therapist felt a new need to keep "an eye toward the outside all the time." While meeting with patients in her office, if she heard the sounds of airplanes, or the sirens of police cars, ambulances, and fire trucks, she no longer took them as routine. Instead, she interrupted clinical sessions to turn on the radio or look out the window, to make sure that the world was intact.

Ruptures in the usual boundaries between individuals' interior and exterior worlds forced some therapists and patients to move "out of the safety of the symbolic world, into the real." This new attention to "the real" made it more possible to consider material that usually fell outside the clinical frame, including material pertaining to politics. Political conversations frequently were initiated by patients, who wondered, "How can we sit here and talk about things when the world is falling apart?" Psychoanalysts who had practiced for decades observed that this was the first time that their patients spoke primarily of the news for weeks and weeks on end (Cabaniss, Forand, & Roose 2004). Even outside the United States, patients discussed the attack in treatment. A therapist in Germany reported that his patients spoke of 9/11 much more frequently than of disasters that hit closer to home because it had "undermined their sense of security to a greater extent than any other catastrophe of the last decades" (Wirth 2003:382). In a sharp departure from their usual practice, therapists seemed to tolerate, and sometimes even to welcome, political discussions. Working in the shadow of unfathomable violence, and with global politics suddenly close to home, therapists, like other New Yorkers, were desperate to make sense of the attack and to process breaking news. Moreover, for many mental health professionals who were personally responding to the horrors of September 11, the idea that patients' discussions of the attack, or related political comments, represented defenses against exploring their tumultuous inner worlds suddenly seemed absurd.

Yet not all mental health professionals embraced discussions of politics and of actual September 11 events. A study of psychoanalytic faculty and candidates conducted six weeks after 9/11 found that almost a third of them had failed to ask patients how the attack had affected their families. This finding is especially striking in light of the fact that 39% of these patients had lost a family member, friend, or colleague in the attack. Once they learned of patients' losses, most analysts offered condolences – but nearly half of them also analyzed patients' emotional reactions in terms of their individual psychological histories and intrapsychic lives (Cabaniss et al. 2004).[9]

Nor was therapists' new openness without negative repercussions, as political discussions sometimes triggered new kinds of clinical conflicts. Some therapists were appalled by patients' political views after 9/11, and struggled with the tensions such exchanges brought to their work. As one therapist explained, "Your client might say, 'They did this! We should go kill them all!' – and you are on the opposite side of the political spectrum." Even though "the instinct for a moment is to challenge them, that's not your job. You have to do something else." For many mental health professionals, doing "something else" entailed returning conversations to the underlying psychological dynamics that were responsible for patients' heightened aggression or other marked reactions to the attack.

However, as the period of crisis receded, and as therapists regained their bearings, they once again began to relegate political conversations to the sidelines. Therapists assisted patients in assimilating 9/11 to prior experiences of suffering and violence, encouraging them to revisit earlier emotional injuries in light of this fresh assault, and to weave this societal catastrophe into their individual life stories. One therapist explained that helping patients who were injured in the attack was no different from helping them with other personal difficulties, in that the primary aim was to understand,

"Why are they hurt? What really is it pulling up? What is it really about and what are they really saying?"

In privatizing patients' experiences of the attack, mental health professionals chose a clinical course of action that was diametrically opposed to the one many of their colleagues had employed in the 1970s and 1980s when they worked with Vietnam veterans and abused women. For their earlier counterparts, the personal was political. They believed that individuals' psychological difficulties were produced by insidious structures of violence, discrimination, and disparity that placed specific communities at risk. In their view, psychological analysis was inadequate unless it was accompanied by political analysis and activism. In direct contrast, for many contemporary therapists, the political is personal. These therapists commonly hold that damaging societal and political conditions are best understood and addressed through the categories of psychology and psychiatry, and through the psyches of individuals. Despite their brief engagement in political discussions immediately after 9/11, they

quickly resumed their emphasis on intrapsychic conflicts, interpersonal relationships, and individual psychiatric symptoms. Rather than inviting patients
to make sense of the attack within the frameworks of national policies, they
unhooked this act of mass violence from its political and historical moorings
and tethered it to personal histories of violence and loss. As a result, the work of
psychotherapy involved the transformation of a monumental, global event that
occurred in a city of millions, and that echoed around the world, into thousands
and thousands of self-contained individual histories, traumatic narratives, and
psychiatric diagnoses.

THE TRAUMA OF THE NATION

What are the implications of reducing the political to the personal following
acts of mass violence, and of creating psychological citizens who are prescribed
courses of mental health treatment? First, these perspectives imply that, even in
cases of community and national catastrophe in which injuries are widespread,
recovery is best accomplished through a practice that is medicalized, and that
repairs one person at a time. Given that the designation of deserving victims
involves processes of selection and exclusion, it is to be expected that certain
categories of individuals invariably will be privileged, and will be awarded all
kinds of aid, while others will be deprived of assistance. Second, because these
perspectives focus on alleviating the psychological miseries that political violence engenders, they call for improving mental health treatments, enhancing
service delivery, and conducting more sophisticated studies on PTSD, rather
than for altering the political policies that contribute to such violence. They
also displace the burdens of managing the consequences of political violence
from politicians to mental health professionals, while simultaneously relieving
civilians of the responsibilities of political engagement.

Third, the medicalized frameworks in which such perspectives operate
employ principles of confidentiality that hold that the material patients disclose
is fundamentally private. With very few exceptions, therapists are prohibited
from discussing patients' accounts of injury outside clinical settings. When such
material is published or presented at scientific conferences, key details must be
disguised and composite portraits created to preserve patients' anonymity, and
the audiences reached are narrow. Confidentiality restrictions may complicate
efforts to compile a corpus of information that documents the myriad repercussions of political violence, and that informs public health strategies, provides
forums for public witnessing, and shapes adequate responses to future disasters.
After 9/11, these restrictions had the more pernicious effect of reinforcing the
suppression of public dissent, which occurred when the Bush administration

suggested that those who contested American foreign policies were traitorous. On the first anniversary of the attack, this "audible silence" continued, as speakers at a ceremony at Ground Zero refrained from making statements that were inconsiderate, contentious, or "stained with vile political content" (Lapham 2002:8).

Yet even as the government silenced public discussions, it encouraged New Yorkers to talk about their responses to the attack with mental health professionals. Through federally funded Project Liberty programs alone, almost 1.5 million New York state residents accepted its invitation (New York State Office of Mental Health 2006). Some of them, like uncounted numbers of additional persons who met with therapists outside Project Liberty's auspices, spoke of the attack hour after hour, month after month, with great emotion and in great detail – but they did so behind closed doors, in the privacy of therapists' offices. Indeed, by making the political personal, and by offering individual mental health treatments that were private and confidential, therapists unwittingly may have contributed to the formation of a depoliticized and silent citizenry.

A final implication of reducing the political to the personal, and of diagnosing political subjects with mental disorders, concerns the fact that diagnostic labels represent more than the diseases that afflict individuals, but equally are metaphors for the crises that threaten societies. As noted above, pervasive notions of trauma, and large numbers of PTSD diagnoses in the wake of 9/11, provided a means of designating legitimate victims and certifying that they were blameless. But traumatic notions and diagnoses acquired additional significance following the World Trade Center attack. Not only were they invoked to attest to the innocence of hundreds of thousands of individual victims of the attack, who neither provoked nor deserved their fate, but they also came to symbolize the victimization of an ostensibly innocent, peace-loving nation, which was struck by a horrific act of violence for no apparent reason.

Notions of national victimization are evident in the dominant narrative of September 11, 2001. Like other narratives of trauma, it features a violent, catastrophic assault that seems to come out of nowhere, as if nothing provoked or preceded it. Individuals' traumatic narratives commonly portray such assaults as turning points that irrevocably alter their lives. In the same way, the national traumatic narrative portrays the terrorist attack as a turning point for the United States, which suddenly finds itself in a world that – through no fault of its own – has fundamentally and irreversibly changed. Although the dominant narrative of 9/11 unhooks the assault from the nation's political past, like all traumatic events, it haunts and inhabits the present, and definitively carves the shape of its future.

Further, just as Vietnam veterans and battered women profited from being diagnosed with PTSD, and from being identified as genuine victims who merited special benefits and support, the United States sought to capitalize on its new identity as an innocent and traumatized victim of a malignant, unwarranted attack. The systematic elevation of deserving September 11 victims at home found its global counterpart in the privileging of American victims of terror – and of America itself as a victim – in the international sphere. Just as the Holocaust commonly is portrayed as an incomparable atrocity that requires a separate category to set it apart from "ordinary evil" (Alexander 2002:27), the United States distinguished 9/11 from acts of mass violence in other parts of the world. While claiming that this terrorist attack was exceptional, and required an exceptional response, it simultaneously universalized its impact by representing it as an assault on all humanity (Das 2001). By doing so, the United States invited other nations to share its sense of innocence, identify with its undeserved injuries, and support its military ventures in the name of self-defense.

If the events of 9/11 demonstrate the general complexity of the ties that bind individuals, psychiatry, and the state, then they also provide specific examples of the ways that mental health professionals knowingly or unknowingly advance government interests – especially when they are in a position to gain. In this case, therapists legitimated psychological experiences that accorded with government aims. Moreover, these events, and their medicalization, illustrate that therapeutic settings may be designated the necessary and sufficient spaces in which to recoup from acts of mass violence. As such, they suggest that political events – including acts of spectacular violence – can be managed and contained within conventional therapist-patient relationships. There have been various attempts to further strengthen these relationships. In November of 2001, Senator Edward Kennedy introduced the Post Terrorism Mental Health Improvement Act to the Senate. This act would ensure the supply of trained practitioners, and guarantee funding for mental health services, following terrorist attacks (Martin 2002). In addition, since the attack, PTSD has been redefined as "a post-disaster mental health problem" (New York City Dept of Mental Health and Hygiene 2003:1), making the links between acts of mass violence and accepted psychiatric illnesses even more naturalized and routine.

Despite the tendency of mental health professionals to transform the political into the personal, and to concern themselves primarily with the histories of individuals, such narrow and medicalized understandings of the connections between personal biography and political history are open to revision. Thus far, the diagnostic category of PTSD, which allows social and political events to be written into individuals' life stories (Breslau 2004), has provided the key nexus for translating the political into the personal. Similarly, trauma has been described as "a symptom of history," in that persons who are traumatized "carry an impossible history within them" (Caruth 1995b:5). But rather than emphasizing the individual and psychological components of such formulations, it is equally possible to foreground their historical and societal elements. In this perspective, those who were injured by 9/11 have more than psychiatric symptoms, and carry more than reified, depoliticized, and medicalized personal histories; they also carry the political history of the nation. Psychiatric symptoms, and other emotional reactions to acts of mass violence, may be reinterpreted as the means by which persons manifest impossible political histories. To the extent that such psychological wounds are the inevitable results of American foreign policy, then the individuals who bear them are not sufferers of mental illnesses, but rather are political subjects who pay the price of American domination.

Revisions of this nature directly affect mental health professionals. Once they view their patients as political subjects, the terms of clinical engagement are significantly altered. Mental health professionals who treat individuals harmed by acts of mass violence are not only witnesses to individual history, but simultaneously are witnesses to national and international history. Such notions are further elaborated in the following and final chapter.

CHAPTER 8

Mental Health in Traumatic Times

ॐ

PREVIOUS CHAPTERS described the particular difficulties New York City mental health professionals encountered, and the overall inadequacies of their field, in responding to the World Trade Center attack. Yet before mental health professionals were able to complete the necessary project of addressing such deficiencies, they found themselves under pressure to prepare for future attacks on American ground. This concluding chapter examines their varied attempts to meet the urgent and unfamiliar demands posed by the arrival of international political terror in their midst. After discussing emerging plans for mental health preparedness, it examines significant and lingering uncertainties within the mental health field concerning the psychological impacts of the attack, the treatment of trauma-related disorders, and the definition of post-traumatic stress disorder. It then explores mental health professionals' efforts to make their work more relevant to these traumatic times by revising clinical assumptions, altering therapeutic practices, and reformulating notions of social and political responsibility.

ARE WE PREPARED?

As the fifth anniversary of the attack on the World Trade Center approached, the events of September 11, 2001, remained very much in the news. Newspaper stories reported that many of the 1,600 persons who had called emergency operators on the morning of September 11 seeking information on safe pathways out of the towers had been instructed to stay inside (Dwyer 2006a); that 760 fragments of bone had been discovered in the Deutsche Bank building across from the Trade Center site, 74 of which were mixed in with the gravel on the roof (Dunlap 2006a; Dwyer 2006b); that 13,790 human remains that were too small or too degraded to be identified were being stored in vacuum-sealed plastic bags labeled with bar codes in climate-controlled containers inside a big white tent set up near 30th Street and First Avenue (Dunlap 2006c); and that numerous first responders who had labored at Ground Zero, and who had developed chronic respiratory ailments, were having difficulties receiving workers' compensation (Chan 2006).[1a]

In addition to these daily stories, continuing media coverage of escalating violence in Iraq, the ongoing Israeli-Palestinian conflict, the month-long war between Israel and Lebanon, and terrorist plots in London supplied constant, unsettling reminders that additional acts of mass violence perpetrated against the United States, and targeting American civilians, were to be expected.

In the absence of cogent strategies for preventing such attacks, the nation's next best recourse was to ready itself to receive them. "Preparedness" became the new buzzword, and this somewhat hazy concept was rapidly translated into numerous concrete programs and plans. The federal government spent close to $70 million on grants to academic institutions, and almost 100 colleges across the country created new courses on terrorism, counterterrorism, homeland security, and emergency management (Dreifus 2004; Hoffman 2004).[2] Intelligence officials asked Hollywood screenwriters to contribute to national readiness by imagining the kinds of destructive productions terrorists might stage (Nacos 2002). Some attempts to increase disaster preparedness were aimed directly at the public. The Centers for Disease Control posted information on their Web site listing "Common sense principles that might be useful in a bombing event"; these included leaving the area immediately after the explosion, avoiding damaged buildings, and calling 911 (Centers for Disease Control and Prevention n.d.). The Department of Homeland Security declared September "National Preparedness Month," and published a brochure with detailed instructions for coping with biological, chemical, nuclear, and radiological threats (U.S. Department of Homeland Security, "Ready America," n.d.). In a similar spirit, the Federal Emergency Management Agency invited children to become "Disaster Action Kids" or "Ready Kids." The treasure hunts, comic strips, crossword puzzles, and coloring books on its Web site were loaded with information on how to pack emergency supplies, make family disaster plans, and respond to different types of calamities, including national security emergencies. Children who mastered this material, and who passed the online quizzes, qualified for downloadable certificates of graduation from "Readiness U" (U.S. Department of Homeland Security, "Ready Kids," n.d.).

But if New Yorkers were any example, public attitudes toward disaster preparedness would prove difficult to change. According to one survey, significant numbers of city inhabitants had failed to ready themselves for the next catastrophe. They had neglected to stockpile food, water, and cash, and to assemble disaster supply kits containing gas masks, personal documents, battery-operated radios, and bandages. They had neither made plans to communicate with family members from whom they might become separated nor specified locations for their reunion. As for evacuation plans, 15% of those surveyed said that they simply would ignore orders to leave the city. Numerous others intended to depart by taxi, despite the impossibility of finding a cab in New York City when it is merely raining. Residents of Manhattan, the borough directly hit on 9/11, were the least prepared of all New Yorkers (New York University 2006). Such findings caused Dr. Irwin Redlener, the director of Columbia University's Center for Disaster Preparedness, to observe that though 9/11, together with Hurricane Katrina in 2005, should have been wake-up calls, instead they were more like "'snooze alarms,'" and New Yorkers had gone back to sleep (Ramirez 2006a:B2).[3] Dismissing the need for tangible plans, one therapist remarked that 9/11 itself had provided the best preparation for future acts of mass violence, as it had caused New Yorkers to form a protective shell that "inoculated" them against further traumatic injuries.

MENTAL HEALTH PREPAREDNESS

Persistent calls to enhance disaster preparedness also were aimed at the mental health field. In light of their uneven post-9/11 performance, New York City mental health professionals acknowledged the importance of developing more comprehensive, coordinated, and effective mechanisms of response. To be sure, many were pleased with their field's efforts. Some claimed that Project Liberty had generated new understandings of the kinds of mental health programs that were required after disasters (Pfefferbaum 2006). Others thought that their work after 9/11 had engendered personal and professional growth. One said that she was "a much bigger person and a sturdier analyst after 9/11," and another agreed that she had become a better therapist "for having sat in that grief and that fear and not run away." Yet even those who took pride in their clinical work, in government-funded initiatives, or in colleagues' spontaneous volunteerism under extremely pressured conditions, and in sites of unfathomable destruction, were dismayed by the insufficiency of their training, the woeful inadequacy of clinical models, and the confusion and disorganization that compromised service delivery. In their view, attempts to provide psychological services after 9/11 had plainly and publicly revealed their field's theoretical, methodological, and organizational shortcomings.

Although confronting these shortcomings and achieving mental health preparedness constituted enormous and ill-defined tasks – and although clinical work generally is based on precedent, rather than on anticipating events that might happen – mental health professionals began to take steps in this direction. To mention a few examples, they published books examining the psychological effects of terrorism, and the specific lessons they learned after 9/11 (e.g. Danieli & Dingman 2005b; Danieli, Brom, & Sills 2005; Knafo 2004), and they held conferences on traumatic loss and on the latest interventions for trauma survivors. The New York State Psychiatric Institute at Columbia University founded the Center for the Study of Trauma and Resilience to investigate post-9/11 psychological injuries, and to train practitioners in delivering trauma treatments (Columbia University Medical Center n.d.). The Disaster Trauma Working Group met monthly, providing mental health professionals with basic disaster mental health training, practice exercises in which they acted out catastrophic scenarios, and detailed information on various kinds of attacks. In addition to initiatives undertaken by the mental health community, the federal government funded three scientific meetings where disaster mental health researchers, policymakers, and trauma specialists discussed the psychological consequences of 9/11. The National Institute of Mental Health unveiled a new grant program supporting "research in response to terrorist acts against America," which called for studies of 9/11's psychological effects and of the mental health response (National Institute of Mental Health 2001).

However important such efforts, some mental health professionals claimed that preparedness could not be achieved without the establishment of a permanent mental health infrastructure that could be mobilized immediately following catastrophic events. Such an infrastructure would not be hampered by funding rules like those that were in place at the time of the Trade Center attack, which stipulated that federal moneys for emergency psychological services could only be obtained by applying for grants after the catastrophe occurred and was officially declared a disaster (Felton 2004). Rather, a permanently funded mental health infrastructure would have the capacity to rapidly organize and streamline the delivery of mental health services, dispatch mental health professionals to sites in need of relief, implement services for crisis intervention and for continuing psychological care, create centralized databases of survivors and of the deceased, and disseminate up-to-date information on all relevant aspects of the catastrophe. Rather than relying on unskilled and unpaid volunteers, it would employ a cadre of mental health professionals trained expressly for this purpose. To ensure a steady supply of practitioners, it would integrate findings on optimal treatments into clinical training programs, and arrange to bring in national mental health professionals in cases where those near the areas of impact were disabled by the disaster. Standard clinical perspectives would be complemented by public health approaches to terrorism (Institute of Medicine 2003). They also would be informed by historians, sociologists, and anthropologists, whose understandings of political violence, collective trauma, and indigenous modes of suffering and healing would foster the design of services that reached out more effectively to minority groups and immigrants, and that were community based and culturally informed (Flynn 2004; Seeley 2005b).[4]

But how likely was the creation of an extensive and efficient disaster mental health system in a nation whose basic mental health services were given such low priority that they were grossly underfunded and in a state of disrepair? In April of 2002, President Bush formed the New Freedom Commission on Mental Health to evaluate public and private psychological systems nationwide. Its final report, which was completed a year later, unambiguously condemned existing services as inadequate, fragmented, disorganized, expensive, and generally unavailable in rural areas and minority communities (President's New Freedom Commission on Mental Health 2003).[5] Far from facilitating access to high-quality treatment, these services presented "barriers" that "add to the burden of mental illnesses."[6] They also failed to connect individuals with the medical care, housing, and employment that were essential to full recovery. Rather than recommending minor changes to the services on hand, the New Freedom Commission concluded that the nation's mental health system was a "patchwork relic" that required nothing less than a "fundamental transformation."[7]

CONTINUING CONTROVERSIES IN MENTAL HEALTH

Even under ideal conditions, in which a brand-new mental health infrastructure would be established and existing mental health services would be totally transformed, mental health preparedness would not necessarily ensue. Instead, mental health preparedness is equally contingent on having a comprehensive and reliable body of knowledge concerning both the psychological repercussions of acts of mass violence and the most successful methods for relieving them. Such knowledge was unavailable before 9/11, and neither the wide array of mental health services that were delivered after the attack nor the hundreds of postattack studies on its psychological effects managed to produce it.[8] As discussed in Chapter 6, many therapists regarded the epidemiological studies that were conducted in the wake of 9/11 as too flawed to provide solid evidence on rates of psychiatric disorder. None of these studies was based on the face-to-face clinical evaluations that are essential to diagnosis, and none was culturally adapted for New York City's diverse inhabitants (Marshall & Suh 2003).[9] Moreover, because they measured divergent psychological phenomena among different populations using an assortment of instruments that were administered in varying ways, it was impossible to compare their results or to reconcile contrasting findings (North & Pfefferbaum 2002; Rosack 2002; Schlenger et al. 2002b).[10] Key questions regarding the psychological damage inflicted by 9/11 thus remained unresolved, including whether the attack had engendered the expected mental health epidemic, or whether the majority of New York metropolitan area residents had proven resilient, making 9/11 "the mental health crisis that wasn't" (Sommers & Satel 2005:177).[11]

One way to get a basic sense as to whether or not 9/11 produced an extensive mental health crisis is to examine the rates of utilization of psychological services after the attack. Yet adequate data in this area are lacking. To cite a major gap, there are no baseline statistics on the number of New Yorkers who were in mental health treatments with private practitioners before 9/11, and there are no means of collecting information on their use of these treatments afterward. To further complicate matters, persons who were injured in the attack still were entering treatment more than five years later. The American Red Cross's 9/11 Mental Health and Substance Abuse Program, which referred survivors and family members for long-term psychological help, did not go into effect until January 1, 2005, and was not scheduled to terminate its services until December 31, 2007 (American Red Cross 2004; 9-11 Mental Health 2005).[12]

In the absence of information on the number of people who entered private mental health treatments, Project Liberty's utilization rates would appear to provide some indication as to the extent of New Yorkers' distress. However, these figures are unclear, and they have been variously interpreted.[13] For example, preliminary statistics showed that, as of March 31, 2003, mental health professionals working under Project Liberty's auspices had counseled 643,710 individuals, which fell far short of estimates that more than 2.5 million people would use such services (cf. New York State Office of Mental Health, "2005–2009 Statewide Comprehensive Plan," n.d.). There was little agreement as to what this shortfall signified. Did it mean that actual rates of mental disorder were substantially lower than predicted, or that Project Liberty had failed to reach nearly two million individuals who were in dire need of help (Gittrich 2003)?[14] Similarly, when New York City mental health clinics did not have an influx of new patients after the attack, did this prove that New Yorkers' needs for professional help had been grossly overstated (Satel 2002)? Or, as some therapists claimed, did it mean that persons who were directly affected remained too fragile or fearful to speak of what they had endured? And did elevated rates of alcohol and drug use (Stein et al. 2004) confirm that numerous individuals were indeed suffering, but had chosen less professionalized methods of coping with anxiety and grief?

Additional controversies arose following reports that, counter to expectations, as the chronological distance from September 11, 2001, increased, Project

Liberty's numbers also continued to grow. The highest volume of sessions – 54,097 in total – was delivered in May of 2003, nearly two years after the attack. Data processed in October of 2004 showed that Project Liberty had provided a total of 40,283 group and 442,907 individual public education sessions on various mental health topics, and had delivered individual or family crisis counseling to 741,977 inhabitants of New York City and the ten surrounding counties included in the federally declared disaster area – the vast majority of them to New York City residents. These new statistics showed that close to 1.5 million New Yorkers had utilized Project Liberty's services (New York State Office of Mental Health 2006). According to another report, the response to Project Liberty remained robust until August 2003, nearly two years after the attack, and only declined then because its services began to be phased out (Donahue et al. 2006). The continuing strength of these numbers appears to challenge findings that in the majority of cases, high rates of psychiatric disturbance decreased within two months of the attack, leaving only a small percentage of individuals with longer term mental dysfunctions (Stein et al. 2004).

Just as studies of 9/11 failed to provide definitive understandings of ensuing rates of psychiatric disorder, mental health professionals' activities after the attack failed to help them reach a consensus as to whether such extraordinarily destructive incidents placed everyone in their path at equal psychological risk, or whether particular persons and populations were especially susceptible to them. In June 2005, nearly four years after the attack, the American Red Cross allocated more than $16 million to treat the medical and mental health conditions of approximately 15,000 first responders. In doing so, it recognized that long-term mental disabilities afflicted individuals who had been continuously and closely exposed to the events of 9/11. Many therapists agreed that the individuals who were affected most seriously were those who directly experienced the crash of the airplanes, the collapse of the towers, the crush of the escape, or the loss of family and friends.[15] However, several of their colleagues maintained that the persons who were most destabilized were those with preexisting psychological conditions. In addition, the attack raised new questions regarding the impact of indirect exposure to disasters and acts of mass violence. Clearly, people did not have to experience the attack firsthand, have relatives who were wounded, or reside near the sites that were hit to feel psychologically harmed. In Massachusetts, 80,000 persons, most of whom were "severely impacted" by the events of 9/11, used state mental health services (Donato 2005:115); this high number is only partially explained by the fact that both airplanes that hit the World Trade Center took off from Boston's Logan Airport, and contained passengers and crew from that area.[16] More strikingly, substantial numbers of individuals across the United States, many of whom watched the attacks on the

World Trade Center and on the Pentagon on television, suffered significant psychological distress (Schuster et al. 2001; Silver et al. 2005; Stein et al. 2004).[17] These unanticipated and far-reaching effects fueled disputes as to which populations would be most at risk, and to whom mental health services should be provided, in the event of future acts of mass violence.

Nor did the events of 9/11 produce a substantive body of knowledge regarding the optimal therapeutic interventions for individuals who were subjected to catastrophic stressors and, more specifically, to massive attacks on the nation. Instead, evidence-based treatment approaches that therapists broadly endorsed were still "missing in action" (Moran 2003:42). Persisting questions, which were crucial to the establishment of an effective mental health infrastructure, included the following: "What interventions, delivered by whom, at what time . . . and tailored to what type of events, to produce the most efficacious results?" (Flynn 2005:763–764). As one therapist who specialized in trauma stated, "We really are not clear on how to move trauma out of people's heads."

A couple of studies suggested that a treatment known as cognitive behavioral therapy-prolonged exposure (CBT-PE) was effective in treating PTSD (Marks, Lovell, Noshirvani, Livanou, & Thrasher 1998; Taylor et al. 2003). Such treatments were funded by NIMH grants, and were provided on a limited basis to workers and first responders involved in rescue and recovery efforts. Their eight sessions of CBT-PE, in which they imagined being reexposed to the specific incidents that still troubled them, were meant to help them "reprocess" irrational fears and beliefs, thereby reducing stress-related symptoms (Gabriel n.d.). Yet many therapists had never heard of CBT-PE, and those who knew about it were reluctant to employ it because they had not been trained in it or found it overly structured. They also feared that reexposing patients to stressors, even if imaginary, would retraumatize them (Amsel, Neria, Marshall, & Suh 2005).

Given their objections to CBT-PE, it is curious that so many mental health professionals implemented psychological debriefings after 9/11, as these interventions also require persons to revisit recent traumatic incidents. Proponents of psychological debriefings claim that, when they are delivered soon after the occurrence of catastrophic events, they actually reduce individuals' chances of developing trauma-related disorders, including PTSD. The most common type of psychological debriefing is known as critical incident stress debriefing (CISD). To promote psychological integration, it calls for individuals to immediately tell their trauma stories in a highly structured manner, and in groups with other persons who are affected by the same stressor. Group members are asked to describe exactly what they thought and felt while these events were unfolding, and to specify the most difficult parts of their experiences (Mitchell 1983).[18]

Although debriefings were widely employed, they were highly controversial. Prior to the attack, there was little conclusive evidence that debriefings decreased psychological distress; in fact, because they stimulated disturbing emotions, alarming memories, and feelings of endangerment, they sometimes were counterproductive (Friedman, Hamblen, Foa, & Charney 2004; Lamprecht & Sack 2002:232; Litz, Gray, Bryant, & Adler 2002; Southwick & Charney 2004).[19] While some therapists considered psychological debriefings too risky to administer, others found them hard to resist. Their clear-cut protocols, single session formats, one-size-fits-all approach, and suitability for large groups appealed to therapists who faced an enormous urban crisis and "want[ed] to be able to do something," or who were expected to quickly relieve the distress of hundreds of individuals in corporate or organizational settings. In addition, persons with "vested interests" in supplying the specific kinds of debriefings they had developed heavily promoted their use (Miller 2002:87).

In consequence – and often in spite of their reservations or inadequate training – therapists conducted debriefings for first responders, employees of firms in the Trade Center area, and numerous other groups. The results were decidedly mixed. For every therapist who considered debriefings indispensable in structuring their work, and in providing people with "the only place they could talk about what was going on," another therapist concluded that they had done more harm than good. One noted the absurdity of requiring group members to identify the hardest thing they had to deal with when "they had just run out of a building that collapsed and killed thousands of people." A second therapist recalled that some group members had grown angry when they were asked to recount their experiences. When persons told one highly disturbing 9/11 story after another, there was "too much affect" in the room, increasing the possibility of emotional contagion; those who were less exposed to the attack were infected by the horror of others' graphic accounts. A third concluded that asking individuals who were directly exposed to the attack to describe what they had witnessed, thought, and felt "was the last thing you would do" because "people would melt down." In his view, the only way for some people to maintain their psychological balance entailed keeping silent about their experiences.[20]

Finally, the attack and its aftermath failed to clarify fundamental aspects of PTSD. Perhaps the most significant area of ongoing controversy concerns indirect exposure to catastrophic stressors. The three most recent editions of the *Diagnostic and Statistical Manual* state that persons may develop traumatic reactions after witnessing disasters and acts of violence, or after learning about the experiences of family members or friends who were directly exposed to them (American Psychiatric Association 1987, 1994, 2000). While these manuals do not explicitly discuss indirect exposures consisting of media representations of disasters, clinical conventions discourage practitioners from taking them into account in diagnosing PTSD (North & Pfefferbaum 2002).[21] The subcommittee that formulated the DSM-IV definition of PTSD did not consider events like 9/11, where millions of people across the United States developed psychological symptoms after watching the attacks on television (Schlenger, Cadell, Ebert, Jordan, & Batts 2002a; Schuster et al. 2001; Stein et al. 2004).[22] It cannot be said for certain whether these elevated rates of distress reflected individuals' fears for their personal well-being, for the safety of their families and friends, or for the security of the nation, and this topic merits further investigation. But it is clear that such intense and pervasive reactions, which extended thousands of miles beyond the actual sites of destruction, caught mental health professionals off guard.

Current diagnostic guidelines for PTSD clearly distinguish between direct and indirect exposure to traumatic stressors, and between direct and indirect victims. However, terrorism and other acts of political violence are waged with the intent to damage not only the particular individuals who are captured, held hostage, or physically wounded, but as many people as possible. Their victims include everyone who is affected by the suffering of those they harm directly, as well as everyone who witnesses them from a distance through any available medium. These acts thus raise questions about the DSM's distinctions between direct and indirect victims and exposure, and challenge its conceptions of PTSD. In doing so, they suggest that the current diagnostic criteria for this disorder do not provide a solid basis for developing mental health responses to future acts of mass violence.

IS THERAPY RELEVANT?

Perhaps because mental health professionals did not gain clear understandings of the psychological injuries caused by the attack, or of the most effective methods of treating them, some began to worry about the relevance of the therapeutic enterprise. Not only were therapists concerned that they lacked the necessary expertise to intervene after acts of mass violence (Twemlow 2004) but they also feared that, by exposing the deficiencies of their customary practices, the attack had revealed the limits of therapeutic discourses. If suffering could not be alleviated through analysis, catharsis, interpretation, narration, empathy, or support; if disseminating information about psychological disorders caused some individuals to see themselves as diseased; and if, in a city with millions of inhabitants, it was impossible to diagnose and treat every single person in need, then standard clinical approaches plainly were inadequate.[23] Further, the attack raised difficult questions as to whether these approaches were relevant following a devastating act of violence that destroyed individuals' sense of security, dashed their hopes for the future, and produced an extensive crisis of meaning. As one mental health professional stated, perhaps therapy simply "was not the right project" for events like 9/11.[24]

Additional indications that therapy might not be the right project for large-scale, humanly caused catastrophes centered around the fact that, after the attack, the delivery of psychological services proved hazardous to mental health professionals, so that their immersion in the suffering of others caused them emotional harm. If they were injured by their work in the wake of September 11, was it because they had been out of their depth, or had faced material that was of a different scale, or of a different kind, than what their professional tools could handle? Or had the situation of simultaneous trauma made therapeutic endeavors especially problematic, as it destabilized both members of the clinical dyad? Certainly, mental health professionals who did not take time to work through their own reactions before providing treatment to others were unusually receptive to patients' intense affects. In addition, because the emotional consequences of 9/11 were contagious, professional strategies that were designed to reduce psychological harm sometimes transmitted it instead. Therapists and patients who were in heightened states of anxiety and anguish may have injured and reinjured each other, just as therapists who sought support from their colleagues may have spread distress throughout their professional community. Indeed, these events raised the possibility that, in extraordinarily devastating circumstances, no type of clinical training can equip therapists to heal the wounded, no quantity of support can shield them from the emotional risks of their work, and no mental health infrastructure can fully address the psychological fallout.

PARADIGM SHIFTS

In response to such troubling notions, many therapists attempted to modify their practices. Some focused attention on particular areas where the field's theoretical foundations had proven disconcertingly thin. As an example, September 11 had made it clear that the field lacked comprehensive models for the treatment not only of simple trauma and of bereavement but also of trauma and bereavement that co-occurred, or were deepened by multiple losses, worsened by physical injuries, heightened by exposure to environmental toxins, delayed by the lack of a body to bury, complicated by losses of housing and employment, caused by incomprehensible terrorist acts, or experienced in a climate of unrelenting threat. Nor did the field offer appropriate models for the treatment of trauma and bereavement that occurred on a massive scale, were contagious rather than contained, afflicted communities as well as individuals, and required alleviation on both social and individual levels. When existing concepts provided insufficient guidance for assisting persons who were bereaved on 9/11, therapists committed themselves to developing new understandings of how to mourn in cases of extremity, or after a collective tragedy.[25] One therapist became a "mourning activist." Another helped families with neither bodies nor remains to bury invent new memorial ceremonies and rituals.

In addition, therapists abandoned norms of practice that they had consistently adhered to in less traumatic times. Even many orthodox psychoanalysts temporarily loosened conventional restraints, whether by acknowledging the reality of the catastrophe, offering patients reassurance and advice, answering questions about their families' well-being, or revealing personal reactions to the attack (Cabaniss et al. 2004). Less classically trained therapists also altered their customary modes of practice. For several of them, such modifications commenced on the morning of September 11, when they overstepped their usual clinical boundaries by telephoning patients to let them know that they were unharmed. Others permitted themselves greater degrees of emotional openness or more physical contact with patients. Several therapists hugged patients for the first time, because this was "the human thing to do" in an exceptional situation that "transcended" regular clinical rules.[26]

In another shift, therapists who previously focused on exploring patients' histories, or on "imagining new possibilities," which is central to posttraumatic therapies (van der Kolk 2002), changed their clinical emphases. With the past overshadowed by the present, and with the future suddenly in question, a sense of immediacy infused their work. One therapist became more directive with her patients, and advised them to make crucial changes in their lives. Although before 9/11, she waited for patients to initiate conversations on key psychological issues, given the volatile postattack atmosphere, she began to "speed it up a little," and to "help people figure out what's important to them."

Others found that the events of 9/11 unsettled their basic clinical premises and, in some cases, called for substantial revision. Unlike prior mental health treatments where patients' personal problems had unfolded against the backdrop of a stable social world, after 9/11 individuals had to adapt to an unpredictable environment, and to dramatically different notions of what was normal, expectable, and possible. The threatening external climate meant that therapists could no longer assure patients that they were out of danger or that their clinical spaces were safe, both of which are essential to the treatment of trauma (Herman 1997). As one therapist remarked, recent circumstances had shown that "things can happen that we didn't imagine, and it's an unstable world, and it's an unstable life." He noted,

"As a field we've emphasized creating a stable environment.... What if that's impossible? What if to do that is sort of delusional at this point?"

Rather than providing patients with a false sense of security, he determined that it would be more useful to help them "tolerate the instability."

Moreover, because standard clinical narratives emphasize patients' psychological progress following a course of mental health treatment, they minimize the possibilities of unresolved losses, unrelenting grief, and chronic emotional pain. But after the attack, therapists who recognized that many of their patients would never fully heal developed more open-ended conceptions of human suffering. After treating many individuals who lost family members in the attack, the therapist above observed, "One of the biggest mistakes we make as therapists is that we believe in the whole concept of happiness and feeling better." In this case, however, he said, "If you try to help them, you've lost." Instead of trying to ease their misery, he decided to "take a stand to be with them in this bad place," and to teach them to "suffer better." A second therapist agreed that, to work with patients who were bereaved by 9/11, she had to "truly believe that suffering is a part of life, and we can deal with it, and loss is a normal part of life, and we will get past this." She tried to provide "a container for this pain until they can process it, little by little by little." As she explained,

"The therapist is like a transitional object, and you're what they hold onto until they can put both their feet on the ground again. And I think you literally loan your hope and your strength and your sense of survival and hold up a mirror to them, that you believe that they can survive this, and feed it back to them."

Along similar lines, as the year after September 11 wore on, therapists began to reconsider the fundamental nature and purpose of their work. Some concluded that the best way to make sense of the anguish caused by the attack was to see it not as evidence of mental disorders, but as part of the human condition, and as similar to "things that humans have been dealing with since the beginning of time." Accordingly, they questioned both the utility of psychological analysis and the prospects for emotional repair. As one stated,

"I'm much more inclined now to see the kinds of human suffering that life contains as part of what life contains. Life is filled with suffering. Ultimately, life cannot be fixed."

Such shifts in perspective led them to question additional therapeutic conventions that they had formerly taken for granted. They no longer viewed psychological healing as contingent on therapists working out of particular kinds of offices, spending a specified amount of time alone with persons they identified as patients, enacting certain kinds of professional relationships, and applying specialized theories and techniques. Instead, they believed that healing took place in the context of humane interactions, and by virtue of a "therapeutics based on love." Equipped with these more comprehensive notions of suffering and cure, numerous mental health professionals vowed to do "anything and everything, in any way you can," in the name of mental health.

Spirituality

Doing everything that was possible in the name of mental health led several therapists to incorporate spirituality into their clinical work. Despite initial concerns that spiritual beliefs had no place in a humanistic practice that was grounded in rationality and that promoted self-knowledge and personal growth, some therapists turned to spirituality when their customary clinical approaches failed to diminish patients' profound despair. A couple of therapists who lost faith in their usual methods of healing, and who believed that they had reached the limits of what their field had to offer, discovered that spirituality was "far more important than mental health," because it helped people find "some meaning in their suffering," or "when death comes in." For relatives of the deceased, spiritual practices helped defuse the violent anger they felt toward the federal government for its failure to prevent the attack. Some therapists thought that individuals' spiritual capacities were directly related to their ability to cope. One therapist remarked that people with strong spiritual beliefs were best able to handle tragic events like 9/11, and made it a point to identify each patient's spiritual "source of strength." She found it extremely difficult to work with those who lacked spiritual beliefs, because "it's like there's a void there, and there's nothing to reach, there's absolutely no hope whatsoever." On a more practical note, therapists may have been aware of the national preference for spiritual rather than mental health counselors. According to a poll that was conducted shortly after 9/11, Americans were more likely to seek help from spiritual advisors than from mental health professionals (Davidowitz-Farkas & Hutchinson-Hall 2005), perhaps because spiritual counselors were less likely to delve into personal psychological matters.[27]

Therapists who incorporated spirituality into their practices found that it required them to modify their usual clinical roles. Instead of providing psychological insights or emotional support, they had to connect their patients with what was positive in life. In one therapist's view, when patients were in the depths of despair, it was her job to help them "hold on until the light comes," and to assure them that "you will eventually find reasons for continuing, and for living, and some meaning and a way to survive this." Rather than enacting an anonymous and distanced therapeutic stance, they initiated closer and more genuine personal connections with their patients. Recalling her work with rescue workers at the World Trade Center site after 9/11, a therapist compared herself to other healers who ministered to the suffering:

> *"I wanted to use whatever spiritual capacities I have to connect in a real, authentic, humane way, in a present way, with other human beings, for even that five minutes, for even that one minute, for even that glance. . . . Because it seemed to me that humanity is what mattered more than anything."*

However beneficial for their patients, serving in such capacities sometimes placed mental health professionals under considerable strain. To assist others, they had to keep themselves "not only in a good psychological place, but in a good spiritual place and a good human place." Feeling unusually burdened, a number of therapists turned to spirituality to attain some measure of personal relief. One volunteer who worked at Ground Zero stressed the importance of regular contact with her spiritual advisor, as it allowed her to take the horrific stories she heard every day and "offer them up to God in prayer instead of having them fester inside my soul" (Garrison 2005:268).

INTERNATIONALIZING THERAPY

While some mental health professionals turned to spirituality to help the individuals they treated find meaning after the attack, others attempted to make therapy more relevant by looking at the ways their colleagues in other countries responded to massive catastrophes (e.g. Awwad 2005; Berger 2005; Campbell, Cairns, & Mallett 2005; Kinzie 2005; Kutz & Bleich 2005; Somasundaram 2005). New York City mental health professionals consulted with specialists from nations that were more familiar with terrorism and political violence. Trauma experts from Israel made the rounds, presenting talks and workshops in training institutes, psychological clinics, and other professional settings to teach American therapists the models they employed in the aftermath of attacks. In addition, mental health professionals attended international conferences on terrorism and trauma. According to a therapist who specialized in trauma, Americans had much to learn in these forums. Compared to their international counterparts, their experiences of terror were quite limited; for many, they were comprised of the single case of 9/11. Although some were inclined to assume "that this is terrorism, [and] that this is the response to terrorism," and to cast themselves as experts on its universal psychological effects, this therapist discouraged them from doing so. Instead, she urged American mental health professionals to broaden their understandings of the varying ways in which acts of mass violence were experienced and classified in other parts of the world. As an example, the Irish therapist stated that mental health professionals in Northern Ireland did not refer to civilians' injuries as "post-traumatic," because this term did not accurately describe circumstances in which acts of political violence had persisted for decades. Another therapist pointed to research suggesting that people who were committed to political causes were more resilient in the face of violence because their convictions protected them against severe psychological injuries.

Some international mental health professionals were troubled by American therapists' exclusive interest in the events of 9/11, and by their failure to understand that other people all over the world had endured devastating acts of mass violence. The Irish therapist was impatient with American colleagues who considered the World Trade Center attack more deserving of international attention than other instances of terror. She urged them to "get a bit wise about what's going on in the rest of the world," and to get beyond the "very narrow and dangerous perspective" that the United States and Israel "are the only important entities where trauma is concerned – that the rest of us can put up with it." Furthermore, having seen her relatives, who took part in "Ireland's fight for freedom and justice," labeled as terrorists, this therapist took issue with the mechanisms by which particular political actors were identified. She asked her colleagues to consider, "What moves a freedom fighter from acceptable fighting behavior, or war behavior, to becoming what people now consider a terrorist?"

COMING OUT FROM BEHIND THE COUCH

As an alternative to trying to learn from other nations' experiences of, and responses to, acts of mass violence, many mental health professionals sought to make therapy more relevant by using their knowledge of the mind to enhance the public good. The attack had caused them to realize that their usual clinical practices made them insular and isolated, and left them without the means to serve their communities. They were determined to become more socially and politically engaged, whether by teaching people how to cope with the attack and its aftershocks, or by speaking out against injustices and working for political change. Despite the fact that classical notions of the therapist's neutrality (Mitchell 1997) still exerted strong pulls, predisposing practitioners to keep their political views and commitments to themselves, several longed for the days when mental health professionals had publicly advocated for social causes. One said that his admiration for "the old-time European analysts," who had been political activists, was central to his decision to become a psychoanalyst. Another therapist argued not only that neutrality was impossible but also that mental health professionals had a responsibility to speak out, "and if we are perceived to be biased by a certain element of the population, then so be it."

Just as mental health professionals searched for ways to have larger social and political roles, general psychologists rapidly became involved in political affairs. Members of the American Psychological Association formed a new subcommittee called "Psychology's Response to Terrorism," in order to use the discipline's expertise to "contribute to the national cause" (Martin 2002). Before long, psychologists not only were expanding academic curricula on trauma and developing public stress management programs but also were consulting with the Federal Aviation Authority, the Federal Bureau of Investigation, and the newly formed Department of Homeland Security.[28] Mental health professionals were less certain than general psychologists that their distinctive knowledge and skills would be beneficial to society (Altman & Davies 2002). Would their understandings of the mind be useful in advising government agencies, educating the public, or resolving social and political problems? And if so, were they willing to forsake their traditional clinical roles – and to risk the disapproval of conservative colleagues – by "com[ing] out from behind the couch" (Twemlow 2004:711)?

Those who opted to come out took part in a wide range of activities, all of which were designed to bring clinical insights to bear on the events of 9/11 and the ensuing political climate. Some of their approaches resembled the work of the Culture and Personality School, which flourished in the middle decades of the twentieth century (Bock 1999). During that period, prominent social scientists, including Ruth Benedict and Margaret Mead, analyzed societies from a distance, investigating predominant personality structures and locating their antecedents in cultural practices. They were especially interested in discovering how the childrearing patterns of a specific cultural group contributed to the formation of typical adult personalities and psychic abnormalities among members of that society.[29]

After the World Trade Center attack, contemporary therapists engaged in similar pursuits. In a number of articles, they analyzed the motives, traits, and behaviors of persons whom they identified as religious fanatics and terrorists in terms of their childhood experiences. These articles were informed by the supposition that widespread early traumas involving parental cruelty and mistreatment were the source of these individuals' enormously destructive actions. As an example, one of the first such articles claimed that terrorists had been brutalized as children. This traumatic abuse had impeded their cognitive growth, fixating them at a prerational stage of development and producing "paranoid styles" of thinking (Godwin 2002:375). According to a second article, terrorists – and suicide bombers in particular – suffered from early experiences of emotional neglect and abandonment, which caused them to develop borderline personality disorders. Osama bin Laden – himself "a pathological borderline" (Lachkar 2002:357) – typified this pattern, as he had lost his father in an airplane crash when he was in his youth. Terrorists' histories of abandonment prevented them from developing good judgment, impulse control, and affect regulation, and made them irrational and vengeful. While a third article agreed that religious fanatics had personality disorders, it diagnosed them as narcissistic personalities who were socially disconnected, incapable of understanding how their actions affected others, and possessed of a "basic fear of their own emotional inner world" (Wirth 2003:366). Like the other articles, it traced religious fanatics' exceptional aggression to the "extreme forms of violence, powerlessness, helplessness, and hopelessness" that they had previously endured (Wirth 2003:374). A final article concurred that terrorists came from "extremely abusive families" (DeMause 2002:340). However, it located the roots of their violent behaviors in the misogyny of their societies, which produced angry, punitive mothers who physically abused their children. Those who grew enraged with their mothers as the result of such treatment displaced their venom onto others, whom they then sought to eliminate. Moreover, terrorists managed forbidden aspects of themselves, such as secularity, sexuality, egotism, and materialism, by projecting them onto Westerners and seeking to destroy them.[30]

To be sure, not all mental health professionals accepted this kind of analysis. Opposed to the reduction of the political to the personal, and uncomfortable with the idea that terrorists were pathological deviants whose destructive acts were rooted in emotional disturbances rather than in political grievances, they situated their behavior in broader historical and social contexts. They proposed that individuals who engaged in political violence believed in a set of socially shared ideals, had specific messages to communicate, and wanted to be understood. They also wondered whether therapists could help terrorists be listened to and forgiven (Hough 2004; Twemlow 2004).[31]

PSYCHOTHERAPISTS FOR SOCIAL RESPONSIBILITY

Uncertain of the value of psychoanalyzing whole societies at a distance, or frustrated with mere theorizing, many therapists looked for more practical ways to come out from behind the couch. Their desires to become accountable to society, and to find a political voice, assumed more concrete form when they established an organization called "Psychotherapists for Social Responsibility" (PSR). Although many of the organization's founding members were psychoanalysts, and were trained in a specific kind of theory and technique known as relational psychoanalysis,[32] they invited the New York City mental health community at large, including mental health professionals who were neither analysts nor clinicians, to join PSR.

PSR had several objectives. In light of the simultaneous trauma engendered by 9/11, it sought to provide mental health professionals, many of whom were isolated in private practices, with a supportive community of colleagues. Its meetings gave therapists a place to sort through their personal reactions to the attack, and to better understand the multiple ways these reactions were spilling into clinical sessions and other professional encounters. In addition, PSR was intended as an educational body that would inform mental health professionals about pressing issues in domestic and international politics. To this end, it sponsored numerous meetings in which specialists gave presentations about such topics as Islam, the Middle East, and the conflict between Israel and Palestine. Of equal importance, PSR offered a platform from which mental health professionals could articulate political responses to the attack and communicate their messages to the public. According to Steven Kuchuck, the organization's former co-leader, PSR's founders initially saw mental health professionals as a potential political bloc, and believed that they were capable of influencing government policies. Their intent was to "show people in the government what we thought were dangerous policies being formed in terms of war efforts...and the erosion of civil rights." They also hoped to have more concrete political impacts:

"That if we couldn't be part of stopping the war, then we could be part of shortening the war. That if we couldn't be part of shortening the war, then at least we could be part of helping to elect a different president after Bush's first term."

Finally, key founders of the organization wanted to apply psychoanalytic categories to examine the Bush administration's hidden motives, as well as the underlying reasons for its emotional grip on the nation, and then to convey their analytic insights to the public. At an organizational meeting held in a Greenwich Village elementary school in December 2002, one of its founding members asserted that the events of 9/11 were more than a national political crisis.[33] In her words, "The threat of violence, and the failure of our government to protect us, constitute a mental health crisis that we are uniquely able to analyze" (Psychotherapists for Social Responsibility n.d.). The leaders of PSR also invoked their professional duty to caution civilians about the hazards of the current political situation. Mental health professionals are ethically and legally bound to warn individuals when they learn that they are in danger of being harmed. After the attack, they considered it their obligation to inform American civilians that the federal government's domestic and international agendas posed significant threats to their well-being.

The organization accomplished several of its goals. PSR initially attracted considerable interest among mental health professionals who were still reeling from the attack, and who were searching for new sources of connection and support. At its peak, which coincided with the run-up to the war in Iraq, it counted several hundred members, and its mailing list numbered almost a thousand. PSR also had some success in mobilizing therapists politically. Hundreds of mental health professionals turned out for a speak-out in May 2002 following the invasion of Baghdad, and many of its members attended other rallies where they disseminated literature explaining the group's positions. However, when it came to communicating their observations to the public, and educating society at large regarding the Bush administration's true motives, PSR's leaders fell short. Despite their efforts to translate the organization's positions into a language that resonated with the lay public, and that stimulated widespread political action, they were unable to convey psychoanalytic insights in terms that were widely comprehensible or credible.

For example, a position paper posted on PSR's Web site, which employed psychoanalytic frameworks to understand "the workings of dysfunctional political processes," interpreted the strong public support for President Bush after 9/11 in terms of the psychological dynamics of parent-child relationships. After comparing Bush to a "terrifyingly irresponsible or dangerous parent," it noted that paradoxically, the child "look[s] for help from the very parent who has just rejected or abused him." At a time when the nation desperately needed a "good parent" who "does not take sides when children are fighting but tries to show them how to behave," the president missed every opportunity to "display the well-known signs of parental confidence and respect for all the children." This paper further claimed that because Bush's leadership style "unconsciously appeal[ed] to the kind of protection offered by the bully/gang leader," it represented "an identification with the adolescent" rather than with a "competent nurturing parental protector who recognizes reality." Remaining loyal to this kind of leader was "equivalent to getting into a car with a driver who has been drinking," whereas the smarter choice entailed "refusing to get into the car and finding another way home" (Benjamin n.d.).

PSR's inability to articulate powerful and convincing views that resonated with the public may have been indicative of its broader difficulties in developing a clear sense of mission and direction. Was PSR primarily a support group for mental health professionals? Or was it an antiwar group – and if so, was it against the war in Iraq exclusively, or was it also opposed to the Bush administration's wars on civil rights, the poor, and social service organizations? Was its principal function to bring psychoanalytic insights to bear on political issues, to inform the public of the government's genuine motivations, to help citizens comprehend their unconscious reasons for supporting the president, or to stimulate political action and change? This confusion of identity and purpose was compounded by the fact that some therapists who were involved in PSR were inexperienced in community organizing, uncomfortable with their newly politicized roles, unfamiliar with large parts of the world, and unaware of international politics. Members who were involved in building the organization's Web site had so much trouble coming up with content that they wondered whether they were ambivalent about the overall project. On another occasion, two PSR members who attended a meeting on the public health consequences of the war in Iraq were taken aback to find that it focused on Iraqis rather than on Americans. They were also unable to answer questions concerning how they would translate mental health professionals' vague warnings about pervasive traumatic reactions among civilians due to the war in Iraq into concrete public health programs.

The combination of these factors doubtless contributed to the organization's demise. In January 2006, three years after its first meeting, PSR came to an end. At that time, interest in the organization had declined so precipitously that only a handful of therapists regularly attended its meetings. A few mental health professionals broke with PSR after taking issue with its psychoanalytic orientation. Others reduced their involvement so they could channel their energies into defeating President Bush in the 2004 election. PSR's original founders – among them highly respected psychoanalysts who were crucial to the organization's legitimacy, identity, and political philosophy – went on to other projects, creating a vacuum at the top. But according to Kuchuck, the most devastating blow to the organization was the growing consolidation of Republican power. With each successive Republican triumph, the members of PSR became increasingly exhausted and demoralized. After the reelection of President Bush in November 2004, PSR ran out of steam. Over the course of the following year, when its leaders announced their plans to step down, no one offered to take their place.

In some respects, the timing of PSR's dissolution was curious. When the organization folded in the winter of 2006, the war in Iraq, which had provided an early rallying point, still had not come to an end. Threats of terrorism persisted, and American military aggression in the Middle East seemed to be on the verge of escalation. Despite such alarming developments, Kuchuck believed that therapists' "sense of urgency" had diminished. This apparent contradiction between the worsening state of international affairs and mental health professionals' waning interest in PSR suggests that the organization's primary function was to fill a void for therapists who felt alone in their horror and grief, and who were unsure how to proceed professionally, in the wake of the attack. No matter how dire the political situation, once they had adapted to the new domestic and international realities, and had integrated such understandings into their clinical practices, they no longer required the supportive community offered by PSR.

Missed Opportunities

Like their colleagues who were involved in Psychotherapists for Social Responsibility, the larger mental health community also proved ineffective in engaging in political advocacy and getting its messages out to the public. According to Ester Fuchs, a Columbia University professor and a Special Advisor to New York City Mayor Michael Bloomberg after the attack, exceptional crises provide rare opportunities to modify public attitudes, and to alter the direction of government policies. However, in the wake of 9/11, mental health professionals neglected to capitalize on the opportunities that were presented to them. Even when the medicalization of 9/11, together with therapists' generous volunteerism, enhanced their public profile and generated increased support for their services, they did not utilize their new leverage to change perceptions of mental illness, to fight for improvements in the nation's mental health system, or to press for parity between psychological treatments and medical treatments. Following the anthrax attacks in the fall of 2001, specialists in public health vigorously lobbied for federal moneys to establish permanent programs addressing biological and chemical weapons. In contrast, the mental health community focused on securing temporary funding for time-limited services related to the immediate crisis.[34] As Fuchs correctly observed, "The odds of somebody suffering from mental illness are much greater than us getting another chemical attack." Yet because mental health professionals neglected to lobby for services that would continue after the initial period of emergency had passed, they were unable to gain a foothold in the nation's public health system.

Fuchs offered various explanations for such oversights and failures. First, many therapists who volunteered after the attack were private practitioners who withdrew to their consulting rooms as soon as the crisis abated. Rather than using the attack as a catalyst for transforming national mental health policies, or for developing new notions of public mental health, they preferred to take care of their patients, and to "sit down and do psychotherapy." Their interest in returning to their practices may have been intensified by economic considerations. Fuchs compared private practice to "piece work." Therapists are paid by the hour, and their incomes are dependent on conducting as many sessions as possible. When therapists volunteered, or when they donated their time to public education or political action, they sacrificed billable hours. Fuchs further remarked that many mental health professionals did not have the political skills that were necessary to navigate complex government systems. Their professional associations lacked political organs that might have turned short-term crisis funding into long-term mental health programs, or that might have more generally advanced their professions' goals. Nor had they cultivated partnerships with political allies, advocacy groups, and policymakers who might have lobbied on their behalf. As a result, psychological services repeatedly were "zeroed out" of public health proposals.

At the same time, mental health professionals were not responsive to the needs of funding agencies, which typically require scientific evidence showing that particular programs are effective before awarding them financial support. Therapists seemed reluctant to make such data available. Either they had not been formally trained to assess the practical value of their work, did not consider it quantifiable, were hesitant to subject it to outside evaluation, or believed that its benefits were so apparent as to make formal studies superfluous.[35] Fuchs also believed that therapists' extensive volunteerism after the attack had amounted to "shooting yourself in the foot," because "the more you engage on a volunteer basis, the less the public sector thinks they have to support it."[36] She argued that mental health professionals had created the expectation they would once again volunteer – and that, in fact, they had a civic obligation to do so – if additional catastrophes occurred. They thus inadvertently perpetuated the view that financial compensation for their services and full-time, well-trained, government-sponsored mental health workers were unnecessary.

Finally, Fuchs maintained that mental health professionals had failed to effectively communicate the psychiatric consequences of the attack to the public, as well as to initiate broader societal conversations about mental illness. As a consequence, they were unable to reframe mental disorders as social rather than individual problems, and to convince the public that permanent mental health programs were needed.

Therapists' failures to directly address society about mental health issues in this specific instance were in line with their customary aversion to placing themselves in the public eye. But while mental health professionals have remained largely silent and unseen in an effort to protect their anonymity and neutrality, other parties have eagerly stepped into the breach. Before 9/11, pharmaceutical corporations – to a much greater degree than mental health professionals – conducted extensive media campaigns that provided information about mental disorders, minimized the stigma that is attached to them, and publicized treatments that relieved them. Of course, their primary aim was neither to educate the public nor to develop comprehensive mental health programs, but rather to sell psychiatric medications. This objective informed their approach to PTSD prior to the attack. The more that pharmaceutical corporations shaped public perceptions of this disorder in ways that expanded its definition, reduced its negative connotations, and encouraged primary care physicians to diagnose and treat it, the more they increased their earnings (Young 2001). These corporations have consistently proven that they are willing and able to create comprehensible messages about common psychological problems, utilize the mass media to present them directly to society, and market concrete and simple solutions. Consequently, even after 9/11, they – rather than state-licensed, professionally trained, and highly experienced mental health professionals – continued to control the public discourse on mental disorders.

Bearing Witness to Atrocities

Although not explicitly mentioned by New York City mental health professionals, a final way for them to make therapy more relevant following acts of mass violence entails using clinical sessions to allow individuals to bear witness to the horrific events they have experienced. It is not unusual for therapists to see themselves as witnesses, or to conceptualize the act of witnessing as central to their occupation; for example, in treating traumatized persons who have been victimized, therapists are "called upon to bear witness to a crime" (Herman 1997:135). While bearing witness is considered important for patients who have been exposed to interpersonal violence, some claim that it is especially critical for those who have endured large-scale atrocities, such as the events of 9/11. Psychiatrist Robert Lifton, who has written several books on genocide and war, observes that survivors of mass violence must bear witness in order to carry out their responsibilities to the dead, and to defuse their guilt at being alive (Caruth 1995a). For Dori Laub (1995:63), a survivor of the Holocaust as well as a psychoanalyst who has worked with numerous survivors, and who co-founded Yale University's archives for their testimonies, telling personal stories of atrocity is necessary for psychological survival, even when it seems impossible to fully or accurately recount them.[37] According to Laub, Holocaust survivors "did not only need to survive so that they could tell their stories; they also needed to tell their stories in order to survive."

Many mental health professionals agree that patients have strong needs to tell their traumatic narratives, yet they are markedly less certain what this means for the therapists who hear them. To be sure, therapists must be able to listen to patients' accounts of their experiences without being destroyed by them; they must be "a witness who is stable enough to bear witness" (Boulanger 2003:134). Lifton claims that listening to survivors' stories is transformative for therapists, because as they listen to, symbolize, internalize, and relive patients' vivid accounts, they become "survivor[s] by proxy" (Caruth 1995a:143, 145). But some therapists who repeatedly bear witness to patients' stories of abuse and atrocity find themselves grappling with complex ethical questions. Having received patients' disturbing material, what are they to do with it? Do principles of confidentiality, and of protecting patients' privacy, forbid them from writing about or discussing it? Alternatively, are they morally obligated to override these principles and to share this information – and if so, with whom and for what purposes? As one therapist asks, "What is it we tell, and what right do we have to tell it" (Thomas 2002:7)? Thomas poses this question after having observed her colleagues relate their patients' disturbing stories of violence at professional meetings and conferences. She worries that by presenting this material, they place their audience at risk for secondary trauma. But she is equally concerned that therapists who tell such stories in professional forums do so for their own benefit; to gather emotional support, to fend off personal fears of being victimized, to purge themselves of intolerably brutal material, or to show off their clinical prowess. However, according to Thomas, the only valid reason for therapists to retell the traumatic narratives they hear in clinical sessions is to enrich colleagues' understandings of how to work with patients who have endured similar horrific experiences.

Mental health professionals' roles as witnesses raise additional questions regarding their obligations to society. As Lifton remarks, the significance of bearing witness goes beyond the fact that it is "therapeutic for the individual survivor," in that it is also "valuable to society" (Caruth 1995a:138).[38] Taking this notion one step further, Sandra Bloom (1999) argues that because therapists are privy to information that reveals the causal links between interpersonal violence and trauma-related disorders that are pervasive, contagious, inheritable, and sometimes fatal, they have a "moral burden" to share their knowledge with the public. In her view, acts of assault and abuse constitute "the most critical public health problem facing this nation" (Bloom 1999:268), and it is therapists' "professional, personal, political, and moral responsibility to say so." Mental health professionals who fail to publicly attest to the severe and widespread consequences of violence, and who do not work to eradicate all forms of brutality, are complicit in its escalation.

What are the implications of Bloom's argument for therapists who bear witness to survivors of large-scale political violence? Do they have an ethical obligation to publicly disseminate what they know about the psychological consequences of acts of mass violence, and to take political action against the events that produced them? Is it possible that such activities might reduce current levels of violence? Herman (1997) sidesteps this question by contending that all clinical discussions of traumatic experiences have an intrinsic political value. Yet their political impact undoubtedly is minimized when they are kept within the confines of the therapist-patient couple. Previously, therapists treating patients who were victims of political violence created innovative clinical models to amplify the impact. In Chile, two therapists who worked with targets of state-sponsored terror and torture during the Pinochet government developed a form of testimony therapy, in which they encouraged patients to testify to the abuses they had endured (Cienfuegos & Monelli 1983). The therapists then recorded and transcribed their accounts, making permanent documents of government brutality that later could be used to indict members of the regime. In taking, recording, and distributing such testimonies, these therapists not only offered opportunities for psychological release but also actively engaged in political resistance. More recently, American therapists who worked with refugees from Bosnia collected testimonies in which they elaborated on what they had witnessed, and what their communities had experienced, during the genocide in the Balkans. Like the Chilean therapists, they turned these testimonies into written documents that could be disseminated throughout the refugee community, and that might eventually serve as evidence for tribunals investigating war crimes (Weine, Kulenovic, Pavkovic, & Gibbons 1998). In both of these cases, therapists encouraged individuals to bear witness to personal experiences of calamity, to collective trauma, and to the larger social contexts and political situations within which they occurred. They thus exemplify one of the means by which mental health professionals who are the recipients of personal narratives of societal violence and catastrophe may discharge the moral burden that Bloom describes.

While testimony therapy clearly offers an important means of making psychological treatments more relevant following incidents of mass violence, it does not seem to have been implemented after the events of 9/11. These events might have been used to further expand notions of therapeutic witnessing, but New York City mental health professionals appeared to be less interested in creating historical records or political documents than in alleviating patients' suffering.[39] One therapist saw delivering mental health treatments as the best way for her to be of service in a time of national crisis:

> *"All I can do is keep doing what I'm doing. I can't go dig, I have a bad back. I don't know how to fly a plane, I don't know how to carry a gun. [But] I can talk to people. I can try to help them. I can cheer them up. I can help them cry. I can hold their hands."*

Another therapist renewed her commitment to helping persons who were harmed by acts of violence. As she stated, "There is great suffering. And the only meaning one can make out of suffering is in some way to be in opposition to it."

New Directions in Mental Health

Like the World Trade Center attack itself, the mental health community's response to September 11 will continue to be revisited and reassessed. While many central questions remain unanswered as to how this community will address future large-scale violent catastrophes, several trends are clear. For one, because the events of 9/11 "provide an opportunity to refine future DSM definitions" (Marshall, Galea, & Kirkpatrick 2002:2683), they are certain to engender substantive modifications in conceptions of PTSD. As discussed above, the next version of the *Diagnostic and Statistical Manual* is likely to explicitly acknowledge the risks of traumatic injury for persons who are indirectly exposed to catastrophic stressors, including those who are exposed through the media. In addition, in contrast with the DSM-IV-TR (American Psychiatric Association 2000), which does not emphasize the connections among political violence, national catastrophes, and widespread PTSD, the fifth edition of the *Diagnostic and Statistical Manual* can be expected to single out terrorism as a precipitant of PTSD and to identify PTSD as a common reaction to terrorism. This constitutes a clear departure, given that at the time of the attack, the association between PTSD and military service was so entrenched that the National Center for PTSD was located within the Veterans Administration. Although the DSM-V has yet to be completed, revised characterizations of PTSD already have emerged. When, as noted in the previous chapter, the New York City Department of Mental Health and Hygiene (2003:1) characterized PTSD as a "post-disaster mental health problem," this disorder was stripped of its customary associations with combat, and with interpersonal abuse.[40]

Such modifications demonstrate the extent to which trauma-related psychiatric categories are made and remade in response to particular social and political occurrences. In consequence, they raise significant questions for mental health professionals. Do shifting definitions of mental disorder imply that unprecedented and unthinkable incidents, or drastic ruptures in external environments, result in novel kinds of psychic disturbances? To pose this question somewhat differently, do enormous atrocities and acts of violence negatively influence individuals' behavior and emotions in ways that invariably fall outside the boundaries of existing diagnostic categories? If so, will mental health professionals continually have the task of altering definitions of existing disorders to contain them, of generating entirely new classifications of mental disorders to describe them, and of developing new treatments to heal them? To what extent do other diagnostic categories – including those that are unrelated to trauma – also describe individuals' reactions to historically specific predicaments, pressures, and catastrophes? As a result of the September 11 attacks, it is likely that questions such as these, which require mental health professionals to investigate the multiple relationships between individual psychologies and historical conditions, will become more central to the therapeutic project and to critical studies of psychiatry.

Moreover, the fact that diagnostic categories are contingent on specific external occurrences calls attention to the limitations of medicalization in addressing human suffering. After 9/11, many therapists recognized that medicalized notions of mental diseases were not useful for understanding the ways in which the attack and its myriad consequences suffused the everyday lives of individuals, disrupting social relationships, damaging collective identities, threatening economic security, and undoing community ties. Nor did medicalized perspectives foster crucial examinations of the politics of mental health treatments, the wider meanings of psychiatric diagnoses, the federal government's management of public sentiment, or the nature of the partnership between political institutions and the mental health community. In interrogating such perspectives, mental health professionals will create spaces in which they may examine more effectively specific instrumental uses of mental health discourses in times of crisis. At the same time, they may diminish their complicity in depoliticizing individual experience and in creating psychological citizens.

Finally, the events of 9/11 may encourage mental health professionals to enlarge their professional roles and sense of social responsibility. These events have already inclined them not only to more broadly minister to individuals who are wounded by social and political violence but also to apply what they have learned through numerous therapeutic encounters in ways that enhance the public good. Abandoning their traditional stance of clinical anonymity and neutrality, they may choose to publicly testify that sociopolitical violence engenders widespread psychological casualties. In addition, mental health professionals may work to prevent traumatic reactions by developing public policies that decrease the prevalence of catastrophic stressors, or by conducting research on the root causes of interpersonal, societal, and political violence (International Society for Traumatic Stress Studies n.d.; Lamprecht & Sack 2002).

As mental health professionals participate in these endeavors, and as they develop new approaches, they will further challenge the conventional therapeutic project, which privileges the interior worlds of those they treat, and which conceptualizes individuals as separated from, and as virtually untouched by, social and historical circumstances. The events of 9/11 clearly demonstrate the deficiencies of this project. Without question, therapists who listened to patients' accounts of the attack, and of its multifaceted consequences, were privy to information concerning the psychological problems and personal histories of individuals. But they also heard significant material regarding the collective emotional casualties caused by a specific act of mass political violence. When therapists are the recipients of material of this nature, they inevitably are the "receiver[s] of testimony" (Weine 1999:172) pertaining to large-scale societal conditions and historical occurrences. Accordingly, it is essential to revise foundational understandings of mental health professionals' roles and of the larger therapeutic project. In the course of their clinical work, therapists bear witness not only to individuals' intrapsychic struggles and interpersonal conflicts; they simultaneously bear witness to national and international history.

Notes

Introduction

1. New York City hospitals used at least 15 different codes related to external causes of mortality and morbidity for victims of the attack until emergency procedures introducing terrorism-related categories were implemented (National Center for Health Statistics n.d.).
2. Concepts of vicarious and secondary trauma are further discussed in Chapter 1.
3. For more information on post-9/11 mental health programs, their funding, and their recipients, see Lowry and McCleery (2005). Rosner and Markowitz (2006:45) discuss the network of services set up by the New York City Department of Mental Health – which at one point was running 988 emergency mental health programs – and by city hospitals. See New York State Office of Mental Health ("New York State Office of Mental Health's Response to the World Trade Center Disaster," n.d.) for services set up after 9/11 by this office.

Chapter 1. Trauma Histories

1a. Of the tens of thousands of persons who were in or near the World Trade Center when the attack occurred, less than a thousand wound up in the emergency room at St. Vincent's Hospital (Haberman 2006). In one account, only 400 people arrived within the first two hours of the attack; most had minor injuries, none required surgery, and there was no "second wave" (Eth & Sabor 2005:43). According to another account, 600 persons went to St. Vincent's, 150 of whom were admitted and 4 of whom died (Jones 2004). St. Vincent's and other local hospitals, which had emptied rooms and beds in preparation for large numbers of seriously wounded individuals, bore the financial burden for this emergency mobilization (Rosner & Markowitz 2006).
2a. Shortly after the World Trade Center attack, President George W. Bush declared New York City and its ten surrounding counties a federal disaster area. As a result, they were eligible for government funding for various kinds of relief, including crisis

counseling services (Donahue et al. 2006). The 1974 Robert T. Stafford Disaster Relief and Emergency Assistance Act authorizes the federal government to provide short-term mental health services; however, these services can be provided only after state mental health personnel have submitted grant applications containing a needs assessment and program descriptions to FEMA, the Federal Emergency Management Agency (Myers & Wee 2005). Some find that the Stafford Act's provisions for disaster mental health services are sorely out of date (e.g. Oldham 2004).

3. There is no single, authoritative definition of disasters. Myers and Wee (2005) counted 48 separate definitions of this term in a course that was offered by FEMA.

4. Terrorist acts also are psychologically debilitating because they disrupt everyday life, undermine individuals' sense of reality and control, destroy symbolic and sentimental targets, and expose the shortcomings of local and federal governments (Myers & Wee 2005).

5. No one knows exactly how many people were in the World Trade Center vicinity at the time of the attack. City and state agencies estimate that 370,000 persons worked in lower Manhattan, 50,000 of them in the twin towers (Rife 2002). The 9/11 Commission Report (2004), using data from the National Institute of Standards and Technology, states that between 16,400 and 18,800 people were in the World Trade Center complex when the first airplane hit.

6. For a review of early studies on the mental health impacts of 9/11, see Schlenger (2005). It is important to note that some studies of postattack mental disorders address the effects of the World Trade Center attack on New Yorkers, while others examine the combined psychological impacts of the World Trade Center attack, the attack on the Pentagon, and the crash of Flight 93 in Pennsylvania across the nation.

7. Despite public health officials' concerns about outbreaks of major mental disorders, individuals experienced a broad range of psychological reactions to the attack, ranging from brief periods of mild emotional distress to severe and enduring mental disturbances (North & Pfefferbaum 2002).

8. There is no precise count of the number of therapists who volunteered, and estimates vary. One report states that 31,000 mental health professionals, 26,000 who were from New York City, volunteered between September 11, 2001 and January, 2002. But it adds, "How this number was arrived at and what it really means is unclear," as is "What these volunteers actually did, with whom, and for how long" (Strozier & Gentile 2004:419).

9. By December 2003, Project Liberty had contracted with 160 social service agencies, employing more than 2,600 workers and training 5,000 crisis counselors to reach out to individuals and communities (Danieli & Dingman 2005a).

10. The media campaign that publicized Project Liberty cost nearly $9.4 million. Heavy expenditures, especially for television advertising, seemed to increase telephone calls to the LifeNet hotline, which in turn referred callers to Project Liberty's services (Donahue et al. 2006).

11. It is important to distinguish the short-term crisis counseling that was most commonly provided by Project Liberty from long-term talk therapies. Crisis counseling addresses the immediate emotional reactions and practical problems that are caused by the emergency and aims to restore coping capacities within a few sessions, rather than investigating individuals' psychological histories and functioning in depth and on an open-ended basis (Myers & Wee 2005).

12. In many cases, this was due to more than generosity. The federal government mandated the extension of employer-based health insurance plans for 18 months after the attack. After that, the American Red Cross temporarily covered health insurance premiums for the injured and for families of the deceased (www.redcross.org/press/disaster/030201). However, because some insurance plans did not cover long-term mental health treatment, additional government funding was necessary (Rosner & Markowitz 2006).

13. In August 2002, the Red Cross set up the "September 11 Recovery Program," which supplied $204 million for individuals' long-term needs, including those pertaining to mental health (American Red Cross 2005).

14. Therapists are not the only ones who experience secondary or vicarious trauma. Journalists whose daily work includes rushing to the scenes of earthquakes, floods, car accidents, murders, house fires, and kidnappings often suffer "crankiness, sleeplessness, bad dreams, foggy thinking, depression, impotence, unfocused anger, [and] sadness that wraps around us like a shroud"; yet editors, news directors and producers have not been sympathetic to this "worker overload" (Casey 2001). Secondary traumatization also occurs among humanitarian aid workers who assist refugees and victims of war (Cardozo & Salama 2002; Jessen-Petersen 2002). In addition, many members of the clergy who volunteered after 9/11 were at risk for compassion fatigue, which is comparable to secondary trauma (Roberts, Flannelly, Weaver, & Figley 2003).

15. Notions of indirect trauma were relevant to 9/11. Polls showed that between 99% and 100% of Americans followed news reports of the attack; indeed the attack may have been "the most watched made-for-television production ever" (Nacos 2002:38). September 11 also was one of the first occasions when the Internet, cell phones, and other new digital technologies made it possible for persons all over the world to witness an intensely violent catastrophe (Kaplan 2005).

16. To cite a few distinctive features of each discipline, psychiatrists are the only mental health professionals who attend medical school. They commonly endorse neurobiological notions of mental disorder, and in most states, they are the only mental health professionals who can prescribe medication. Clinical psychologists are trained in university psychology departments, and they often are involved in research as well as in practice. They have special expertise in administering cognitive, personality, and other psychological tests. Social workers, who historically have worked with disenfranchised populations, have more holistic perspectives. They attend to psychological, biological, and social factors in addressing individuals' experiences and provide both concrete and psychological support. Psychoanalysts typically undertake more intensive examinations of the mind, looking at the deeper and unconscious roots of psychological motivations and patterns. Psychiatrists, psychologists, and social workers may become psychoanalysts by undergoing additional training in independent psychoanalytic institutes.

17. As an example, the New York State Psychiatric Institute was overwhelmed with requests from clinicians seeking education and training in trauma. In response, the newly created New York City Consortium for Effective Trauma Treatment offered comprehensive trainings by world-renowned trauma experts (Marshall & Suh 2003).

18. The proliferation of scientific meetings on mental health treatment after 9/11 conforms to prior patterns in which the more therapists are exposed to traumatized patients, the more they participate in professional conferences. Therapists make use of such meetings to sort through their personal emotional reactions, locate sources of support, and learn new clinical skills (M. Miller 2003).

Chapter 2. Volunteers for America

1. Previous generations of mental health professionals were also attracted to working with victims of atrocities; some felt "privileged" and excited at the prospect of treating Holocaust survivors (Danieli 1984:36).

2. Although therapists "who are attracted to disaster relief work love it passionately," there are concerns that it is "too much about working out their own problems" (Stoller 2005:461–2). John Draper (2005:65), the director of public education for the LifeNet Hotline Network for the Mental Health Association of New York City at the time of the attack, agrees that therapists address personal psychological problems through their professional work. He states that, "For many of us helpers, that's the way we get better."

3. While well intentioned, spontaneous and extensive volunteerism can cause problems for communities in crisis, which must devote scarce resources and time to the management, training, and coordination of volunteers (Dreifus 2004). After the attack, the flood of mental health professionals into lower Manhattan was a source of "consternation" to city officials, who instructed them to "go elsewhere" (Rosner & Markowitz 2006:45). When the New York City Fire Department's Counseling Service Unit was deluged with calls from mental health professionals who wanted to help, attention and energy were distracted from more urgent matters. Therapists who arrived, uninvited, at firehouses, and who offered professional services without prior FDNY authorization, were considered especially burdensome (Greene, Kane, Christ, Lynch, & Corrigan et al. 2006).

4. The optimum response to disasters requires responding organizations to have existing disaster mental health teams, as well as the capacity to send mental health professionals to sites where their particular expertise is needed (Myers & Wee 2005). On 9/11, however, the New York City chapter of the Red Cross lacked such teams, and did not have procedures for determining which volunteers to use, or for matching their skills to the settings that needed them (Hamilton 2005).

5. The usual Red Cross practice of excluding unlicensed mental health professionals was especially problematic in New York City, which has a large number of psychoanalysts who are extremely experienced, but who in 2001 were ineligible for licensing by New York State (Strozier & Gentile 2004).

6. New York City's extensive network of public health and social services allowed city officials to quickly assemble a broad disaster response. To supplement local resources, 5,000 National Guard troops, 500 state troopers, 100 Bureau of Criminal Investigation staff members, and 2,500 crisis counselors were sent to the city (Rosner & Markowitz 2006).

7. The organizations represented at Pier 94, which were "in confessional-like booths" (Bloom 2005:346), included the New York State Crime Victims Board/Safe Horizons, the Department of Labor, the New York State Workers' Compensation Board, the New York State Courts Family Support, the United States Attorney's Office, Immigration and Naturalization Services, Veterans Affairs, FEMA, FBI Crime Victims Assistance, Legal Services, Disabled American Veterans, the Social Security Administration, and private insurance companies.

8. The fact that every conceivable kind of service was contained under one roof, and provided with relatively few questions asked, moved one reporter to describe it as a "paradise" for the welfare state (Rosner & Markowitz 2006:52).

9. Although the therapy pets that were stationed at various service centers and on boat trips to Ground Zero consoled many people who were harmed by the attack, some animals

were negatively affected; they lost hair, had difficulty eating and sleeping, and showed other signs of stress (Bloom 2005). Their handlers took special care of them, "telling them what a great job they did, [and] taking them to a hunting reserve where they can chase deer, rabbits, and squirrels" in order to ease their stress (Canzoneri & Canzoneri 2005:439).

10. After several months of recovery work at Ground Zero, of the 2,749 people killed in the attack, the bodies of only 293 persons were found intact. Identifying the other 2,456 entailed matching the DNA samples their relatives supplied to small pieces of muscle, tissue, or bone found in the debris (Lipton 2005).

11. Although the Family Assistance Center's services were supposed to be provided with a minimum of red tape, some of those who applied for aid found the procedures onerous. The lengthy forms and other bureaucratic obstacles that typically complicate applications for disaster assistance have been called "the second disaster" (Myers & Wee 2005:28).

12. For more on the multiple and shifting meanings of Ground Zero dust, see Sturken (2004:312–314).

13. The cleanup was expected to take two and a half years, but was finished in nine months. Mayor Giuliani ordered the accelerated pace of work "to prove that his city was not crippled by the attack" (DePalma 2007b:A1). Construction crews and other workers on the pile risked being penalized or fired if they did not work quickly enough. The Mayor's rush to clean the site has been blamed not only for restricting the search for remains but also for causing serious respiratory ailments in tens of thousands of rescue and recovery workers. The U.S. Environmental Protection Agency describes how difficult it was to persuade Ground Zero workers to wear respirators and other protective equipment (EPA 2002). However, Giuliani, who was well aware of the abundance of toxins at the site, neither forced workers to wear protective masks nor shut down the site until they complied with federal safety regulations. By ignoring these regulations and speeding up the cleanup, he sacrificed workers' health. More than eight thousand workers with serious medical problems have sued New York City for negligence (DePalma 2007b). The observation that "Americans have never made ruins their home or allowed ruins to define – and thereby shape – their future" (Young 2003:17) also pertains to the fast pace of the cleanup.

14. One Ground Zero volunteer likened her role to "that of a bartender," and used her background in improvisational comedy "to reduce the tension with a well-needed joke" (Garrison 2005:269). She also noticed instances of inappropriate behavior among mental health professionals, who confided their problems to the police and firefighters they were supposed to be serving, or who developed romantic feelings toward them (Garrison 2005).

15. This therapist is referring to the wash stations that were set up for Ground Zero workers to clean their boots, gloves, and masks, and to vacuum their clothing, before they left the site. Given the extent of the contamination, there were concerns that workers who wore their work clothes home would spread poisonous materials off-site. Workers did not consistently use these wash stations, and the Environmental Protection Agency (2002) claims that there was no way to enforce their compliance. When a central wash station was installed in a gigantic, heated white tent known as the Taj Mahal, the most effective means of inducing workers to use it involved setting up food services inside the same tent.

Chapter 3. "Get Me Counselors!"

1. Immediately following the attack, the mental health response was ad hoc and uncoordinated. The situation improved when the Red Cross began to organize social service sites (Strozier & Gentile 2004). Still, the rapid proliferation of emergency post-9/11 programs, and the fact that they were sponsored by numerous nonprofit organizations, as well as by city, state, and federal government agencies, led to a lack of organization, leadership, and a clear chain of command, and to rampant competition for power and turf (Rosner & Markowitz 2006).

2. For instance, the Fire Department of New York's (FDNY) in-house Counseling Service Unit (CSU), which is located in lower Manhattan, experienced greatly increased demands for psychological help. Prior to 9/11, the CSU treated approximately 600 FDNY personnel annually, many for alcoholism and other addictions, and rarely saw firefighters' families. In contrast, in the first few years after the attack, an average of nearly 200 persons per month sought help from the CSU. To meet accelerating demands for treatment, the CSU, with funds from FEMA and Project Liberty, expanded its staff of mental health professionals from 12 to 59; hundreds of additional consultants also provided care. Furthermore, the CSU opened five new offices located across the New York metropolitan area, and developed a number of innovative services for active FDNY personnel, their families, the families of the deceased, and retirees (cf. Greene et al. 2006).

3. To cite an example of large-scale counseling to organizations, the Environmental Protection Agency (EPA), whose regional office was close to the World Trade Center, held a voluntary trauma counseling session for employees, many of whom either witnessed or responded to the attack. More than 600 employees attended the session, which was held at the Grand Hyatt Hotel in midtown. Because the financial district was cleaned up very quickly, the EPA reopened its offices less than two weeks later, on September 24. Counselors were made available to employees who had difficulty with this rapid return (EPA 2002).

4. Models of psychological debriefing, which were widely implemented after the attack with varying results, are discussed in Chapter 8.

5. See Perilla, Norris, & Lavizzo (2002), who report that in the aftermath of Hurricane Andrew in southern Florida, ethnic minority communities that had less access to services and benefits and fewer resources experienced worse mental health outcomes.

6. Organizations other than Project Liberty also attempted to make services more culturally accessible and inclusive. A program sponsored by HOPE NY reached out to Muslim communities by training imams at local mosques to recognize psychiatric symptoms in those who came to pray (Gheith, Abu Ras, & Cournos, in press).

7. Despite the cultural diversity of New York City, like the rest of the country, it has a severe shortage of bilingual and bicultural mental health professionals. To make matters worse, the city's hospitals and clinics lack trained mental health interpreters (Gurvitch 2005). This situation is indicative of therapists' broader failures to take culture into account, and it is reflected in the literature on 9/11 and mental health. Most of this literature fails to examine the culturally specific responses of particular persons and communities, and the kinds of services they would have found most helpful. Marshall and Suh (2003) note that patients' presentations of distress and expectations of treatment were influenced by their culture and ethnicity, but do not provide specific examples.

Nader and Danieli (2005:404) refer to culture-specific remedies, stating that a "New York Asian community used cleansing (e.g., to clear away the evil), and other protection practices to reduce anxiety," but do not identify the particular community or describe the cleansing practices.

8. Criticism was directed at both federally and privately funded mental health programs that were made available to Latino communities. Because these programs made the mistake of offering individual rather than family services, ignoring culturally specific manifestations of distress, and failing to partner with community-based providers, they were unable to engage community members, with "disastrous" effects (Batista 2005:129).

9. This obituary was part of the series called "Portraits of Grief," which is discussed further in Chapter 4.

10. A group of African American women in Los Angeles found the attack considerably less terrifying than many other violent events they encountered in their daily lives (Mattingly, Lawlor, & Jacobs-Huey 2002).

11. Death tolls commonly are inflated in the immediate aftermath of disasters because the same individuals are reported missing by multiple persons. This applied to the World Trade Center attack, where initial estimates put the death toll at more than 6,000. The Office of the Chief Medical Examiner was charged with producing an accurate count of victims by the first anniversary of the attack (Jones 2005).

12. According to Ribowsky (2005:78), who was the director of identifications for the World Trade Center Incident Command Center at the Medical Examiner's Office, many victims were "fragmented." The fragments then were exposed to water, high heat, fires, physical force, changes in temperature, and other environmental conditions that degraded their DNA. This made identification impossible, despite the use of innovative technologies.

13. Although, as noted above, the fact that so many victims' remains were never identified was attributed initially to their degraded condition, more recently there have been charges that the pressured pace of the cleanup at the World Trade Center site precluded searching for remains in numerous nearby areas (Dunlap 2007). The discovery of human bones in manholes near the site in the fall of 2006 led Mayor Michael Bloomberg to reopen the search for remains, promising that it would be "as extensive as humanly possible" (Dunlap 2006d:B2). There was hope that this would lead to the discovery of more remains and to the identification of more victims (Dunlap 2006b).

14. Greene et al. (2006) point out that, within the field of mental health, theories of trauma and theories of grief evolved along separate lines. Theories of trauma were based on the psychological difficulties suffered by combat veterans and victims of abuse, whereas theories of bereavement grew out of studies of grieving adults and children. As a result, conceptions of traumatic mourning were slow to emerge. Therapists' experiences with traumatic loss and traumatic mourning are discussed further in Chapter 4.

15. See Yaeger (2003) for more details on the means by which crushed debris from the World Trade Center site was turned into the sacred ash of the dead. Yaeger describes the transportation of this debris – which had been put into 55-pound drums – from Ground Zero to One Police Plaza, as well as the rituals surrounding its handling. She also says that prior to the ceremonial treatment and distribution of this dust, persons had sold stolen fragments of the towers to the relatives of the deceased.

16. Not all family members were able to see World Trade Center dust, or the contents of the urn, as distinct from the rest of Ground Zero rubble, or as "something hallowed and

new" (Yaeger 2003:188). In the view of one father whose son was killed in the attack, it was "just a bunch of dirt" (Morikawa n.d.).

Chapter 4. The Psychological Treatment of Trauma

1. Like other psychological defenses, dissociation is thought to protect the mind against fully experiencing overwhelming events. According to one therapist, the dissociative process operates "immediately and instinctively in situations where our essential being is threatened with extinction." When persons dissociate, they commonly feel that they are disconnected from themselves, that the events they are experiencing are not really happening to them, or that they are watching events unfold from a place outside their bodies. People who dissociate during a traumatic event may also do so later when traumatic memories are triggered (Herman 1997). The therapist quoted above observed "the glazed look" characteristic of dissociation in many first responders. As he stated, "The cops I spoke to, who were cut, bruised, and covered in white dust – they weren't there."

2. Bergmann (2004) suggests that the attack may have been helpful to some psychotherapy patients because it helped them recall and reflect on prior traumatic incidents that they had not been able to access before 9/11.

3. In fact, the federal government set up the Fund in part to protect the airline industry and companies connected with the World Trade Center against the thousands of lawsuits they feared would be brought against them by victims' families. Those who accepted payment from the Fund waived the right to litigate.

4. Their status as heroes became official when on September 9, 2005, President George Bush awarded a Public Safety Officer Medal of Valor – which is among the nation's highest honors – to every firefighter who died on 9/11. The gold-colored medals feature an "H" for heroes, as well as engraved images of the twin towers, the Pentagon, and the State of Pennsylvania. Police officers who perished were similarly honored (Janofsky 2005).

5. Although the extensive media coverage and public memorial ceremonies may have comforted individuals who were indirectly affected by the attack, they upset some who were personally bereaved. The families of deceased firefighters eventually sought to mourn more privately; by the fourth anniversary of 9/11, many avoided public memorial ceremonies (Greene et al. 2006).

6. For more on Ground Zero's development as a site for international tourism, see Lisle (2004).

7. Some claim that the media's focus on the specific individuals who die in a given atrocity or disaster not only turns a political story into a personal story (Alexander 2002) but also obscures the differential impacts along the lines of class, gender, race, and ethnicity (Button 2002). In contrast, N. Miller (2003:41) commends the democratic impulse behind the "Portraits of Grief," in which "everyone was given equal space and equal treatment" regardless of vastly different social locations. Miller notes the "archetypal plots" (42) of these Portraits, compares their standardized photographs to those in high-school yearbooks, and likens their prose to that of wedding announcements. She characterizes the whole series as a "collective history of life before the disaster" (44).

8. Mayor Bloomberg's recent commitment to reopening the search for remains makes it likely that more victims will be identified, and that there will be additional funerals.

Chapter 5. The Trauma of Psychological Treatment

1. Other terms have been proposed for these and similar phenomena. Some reduce simultaneous trauma to transference-countertransference dynamics (e.g. Altman & Davies 2002). Others (Danieli & Dingman 2005a:10, emphasis in the original) discuss "event countertransference," which describes "therapists' reactions to patients' *stories* of their traumatic *events* rather than to patients' *behavior*." The term "shared trauma," which emerged after the Oklahoma City bombing, applies to situations in which both members of the clinical dyad experience the same traumatic event (Saakvitne 2002:443; Tosone & Bialkin 2004). Yet all of these terms have limitations. For one, it is impossible to speak of the "transference-countertransference implications" (Altman & Davies 2002:359) of New York City therapists' post-9/11 clinical work without considering that therapists and patients were not simply responding to each other's distinctive emotions but were also reacting to personal experiences of the attack and to prior traumatic events. As for the concept of event countertransference, after 9/11, as in other cases of simultaneous trauma, therapists reacted to more than their patients' stories, as they concurrently were grappling with the intense affects produced by their own exposure to these events. Finally, I prefer to speak of simultaneous trauma rather than shared trauma as this term more clearly denotes therapists' and patients' separate, and perhaps disparate, exposures and responses to a common traumatic stressor.
2. The collected reactions of Israeli therapists were unlike those of disaster mental health workers who responded to the Oklahoma City bombing. These workers suffered unusually high rates of stress; 65% of Project Heartland's crisis counselors tested positive for PTSD, and 77% were at risk for burnout. Their difficulties have been linked to the horrific nature of the attack, its extensive repercussions, and their long-term involvement in delivering services (Myers & Wee 2005). The fact that their reactions might have been unusually severe because they belonged to the local community and suffered simultaneous trauma has not been sufficiently considered.
3. Foucault (1963/1994:9) notes that the doctor-patient relationship depends on "maintaining the maximum difference between them" as it turns "the ideal configuration of the disease" into "a concrete, free form" whose essential nature is readily recognized.
4. Although the evidence is mixed, according to one study, it is extremely common for therapists who specialize in trauma to have personal histories of trauma; of 56 trauma specialists, 54 acknowledged such histories (Truman 1997). For those with histories of trauma, even "radically different traumas can be experienced as similar" (Kacandes 2003:168).
5. Therapists' discussions of the resurgence of traumatic memories, and of their simultaneous trauma, support the claim that many mental health professionals experienced "multiple levels of traumatization" after the attack (Saakvitne 2002:444).
6. It is possible that therapists' self-disclosures tend to increase in situations of shared or simultaneous trauma, where clinicians' intense personal reactions compromise their ability to maintain a neutral professional stance (Tosone & Bialkin 2004).
7. Saakvitne (2002:48) states that in addition to safeguarding their physical and emotional well-being, therapists "need opportunities that allow us to turn away, to escape from harsh reality into fantasy, imagination, art, music, creativity, and sheer foolishness."

Chapter 6. Diagnosing Posttraumatic Stress Disorder

1a. Many therapists mentioned that the smells produced by the attack constituted an additional, and continuing, exposure. Rosner and Markowitz (2006) trace the smells to the incineration or vaporization of the towers' 210 stories of furniture, windows, girders, fluorescent bulbs, carpets, and wallboard. Strozier and Gentile (2004:417, 418) note that the smells were produced not only by "all the incinerated computers and rugs and drapes and doors and mountains of cement and some asbestos and a lot of chemicals" but also by "the bodies of thousands of people." Indeed, for many New Yorkers, the smells evoked "echoes of Auschwitz." These echoes also were present in the dust that covered New York City after the attack. One woman who lived uptown refused to clean her windows after 9/11 because she was sure that the dust on them was composed of victims' remains (Tylim 2004).

2. The failure to distinguish clearly between psychiatric symptoms and normal expressions of distress also was characteristic of post-9/11 epidemiological studies (North & Pfefferbaum 2002).

3. A similar phenomenon occurred after the atomic bombing of Hiroshima. The local media felt morally obligated to publicize the typical symptoms of radiation-related illnesses, and other effects of the bomb, which came to be known as A-bomb disease. However, there were worries that such reports would intensify survivors' fears of contamination, or would cause them to discover these symptoms in themselves and behave as if they were doomed (Lifton 1967). The fact that in A-bomb disease – as in PTSD – ill effects could be invisible, were often delayed, and emerged as ambiguous symptoms exacerbated individuals' anxieties about their condition.

4. Some lamented the lack of opposition to "advocates of the PTSD diagnosis" after 9/11. In their view, the "narrow symptom approach" not only engendered "competition for media attention and the funds offered to hospitals and relief programs" but also, by spreading unrealistic and oversimplified explanations of reactions to the attack, discouraged individuals from seeking more thorough psychological treatments (e.g., Roth 2004:431).

5. Public health officials responded to concerns that epidemiological surveys produced inflated estimates of the prevalence of actual PTSD by introducing the less stringent construct of "probable PTSD" (cf. Rosack 2002). However, one mental health professional was concerned that this new construct amounted to "creating diseases," and another worried that future mental health policies would be based on this poorly defined and dubious construct. Baseline rates of PTSD are estimated to be around 8% of the general population (Taylor et al. 2003).

6. As an example, mental health professionals do not seem to have recognized *ataques de nervios*, which are common ways of expressing mourning and distress among Latinos (Batista 2005).

7. It is extremely difficult to accurately translate standardized American diagnostic instruments into languages other than English. There are no instruments for assessing PTSD that are universally valid, and the concept of "cultural equivalence" has not yet been fully realized (Keane, Kaloupek, & Weathers 1996:189).

8. After 9/11, diagnoses may have been most greatly affected when therapists used their postdisaster clinical work as a means of processing personal responses to the attack (Draper 2005; Stoller 2005).

9. Myers and Wee (2005) ask whether mental health professionals who are personally affected by disasters should deliver psychological services in their aftermath. They also wonder whether therapists with personal histories of trauma are especially vulnerable to the psychological risks of such work.

Chapter 7. Trauma as Metaphor

1. Although there are new screening instruments that would allow primary care physicians to routinely check patients for psychiatric disorders, including PTSD, doctors have been reluctant to adopt them because they take too long to administer – around 6 minutes per patient (Oldham 2004).

2. The notion of the "traumatized worldview" has been proposed to describe the shared fear, mistrust, and pessimism that were predominant among residents of an El Salvadoran community after state-sponsored political terror (Dickson-Gomez 2002:416).

3. Although existing clinical frameworks foreground individual rather than collective trauma, and although individual treatments were widely provided after the attack, some mental health professionals – like the consultant to the elementary school described in Chapter 3 – offered group treatments or developed community approaches to mental health. To cite other examples, Saul (2005) describes another downtown school's efforts to promote collective resilience and recovery. Its activities contributed to the formation of the Downtown Community Resource Center for Lower Manhattan. Waizer et al. (2005) discuss several community-based interventions used after 9/11, some of which targeted particular minority populations.

4. Its desirability is enhanced by the fact that this diagnosis requires an external precipitant. This means that persons with PTSD are able to sue the individuals or groups they hold responsible for their condition.

5. Diagnoses of PTSD are gateways to benefits in other countries as well, where individuals seeking government services or refugee status have learned to report the necessary trauma histories and trauma-related symptoms (cf. James 2004; Salis Gross 2004).

6. See Rosner and Markowitz (2006) for a brief discussion of how moneys might have been differently distributed to victims of the attack. This discussion considers whether those with private means or with access to private sources of reimbursement should have received funds from the federal government and from 9/11 charities, or whether these funds should have been reserved for those without other resources.

7. See Soldz (2007) for a discussion of recent claims that an American Psychological Association task force on ethics was under the covert control of the Department of Defense.

8. Close examinations of the timing of heightened terror alerts suggest that government efforts to keep people afraid – and in a sustained state of "pre-traumatic stress" – also were used to increase support for military expenditures and domestic activities in the name of homeland security (Zimbardo 2003). However, there are signs that these campaigns eventually lost their potency. Americans became desensitized to elevated terror alerts, perhaps because prior alerts had not been followed by attacks (Carey & O'Connor 2004).

9. Similarly, therapists who treated survivors of Hiroshima and Auschwitz steered patients away from political topics and redirected them toward childhood memories (Caruth 1995a).

Chapter 8. Mental Health in Traumatic Times

1a. As previously noted, several thousand Ground Zero workers who blame worsening respiratory problems on their work at the site are now suing New York City for damages (DePalma 2006, 2007b). Although mental health professionals who worked at Ground Zero may have developed similar illnesses, I know of no studies on this topic.

2. New York City's two largest universities developed comprehensive programs in these areas. Columbia University's National Center for Disaster Preparedness, which was established a year before 9/11, redoubled its efforts to formulate public health strategies and prepare public health practitioners for bioterrorism and disasters (Columbia University Mailman School of Public Health n.d.). Soon after the attack, the Department of Homeland Security funded New York University's Center for Catastrophe Preparedness and Response. This interdisciplinary center examines the legal and security dimensions of disasters, and develops medical and mental health responses (New York University Center for Catastrophe Preparedness and Response n.d.).

3. Despite the fact that they failed to make such preparations, a poll conducted five years after the attack found that one-third of New Yorkers thought about September 11 daily, and that two-thirds were still very worried that further attacks would occur, compared to 22% nationwide (Toner & Connelly 2006). They may have felt that it was pointless for them to be prepared when the federal government lacked the ability to protect the nation against future attacks (Ramirez 2006b). The Bush administration gave the public mixed messages after the anthrax attacks in the fall of 2001; officials "urge[d] us to return to a sense of normalcy" while also "encouraging us to maintain our vigilance and heightened state of preparedness" (Rosner & Markowitz 2006:51).

4. Chemtob (2005:725) claims that "if terrorism is a psychological weapon, then we must develop psychological countermeasures as part of our defense posture," so that civilians can resist, and rebound from, the fears that terrorism triggers. However, he fails to specify what these "protective attitudes" might entail. Friedman (2005) also describes a public mental health approach for survivors of terrorist acts. It includes preparing the general public for catastrophes, promoting early intervention for the groups considered most vulnerable, and alleviating severe symptoms among individuals with chronic mental illnesses. While most of his suggestions are thoughtful, Friedman's (2005:530) claim that "psychological vaccines" can boost resilience erroneously suggests that psychoeducational programs are capable of eradicating negative emotional responses to catastrophic events.

5. The public health infrastructure was equally decrepit, with the majority of local health departments lacking high-speed Internet access, modernized laboratories, well-trained directors, and the capacity to share information and coordinate programs across state lines (Rosner & Markowitz 2006).

6. As noted in Chapter 4, mental health services across the nation are further compromised by severe shortages of bilingual and bicultural mental health professionals and interpreters (Gurvitch 2005).

7. If new, disaster-related public mental health systems are housed in the Department of Homeland Security rather than in their traditional location in the Department of Health and Human Services, as the Institute of Medicine's (2003) report implies, they may be able to bypass the wreckage of existing services. However, this will produce new problems of coordination with existing mental health practitioners and programs, as well as a two-tiered mental health system.

8. Although more than 300 studies were conducted on the mental health impacts of 9/11, they were not coordinated, resulting in both gaps in knowledge and duplication (Rosner & Markowitz 2006).

9. Some mental health professionals emphasize that when clinical assessments are based solely on survey instruments, their accuracy is compromised (Pfefferbaum et al. 2002; Schlenger 2005).

10. North and Pfefferbaum (2002) discuss the difficulties involved in conducting postdisaster research, the requirements of such research, specific studies conducted after 9/11, and their limitations. In their view, there is a "tradeoff" between collecting data immediately after a disaster and conducting sophisticated and methodologically sound research, and the latter is often sacrificed for the former.

11. The validity of early telephone surveys is also compromised by the fact that thousands of downtown residents lacked phone service during the period in which they were administered. As a result, sampling procedures that involved random digit dialing could not have been properly implemented (Henzlova 2002).

12. With more than a year left to go, this program had already provided long-term mental health assistance to more than 8,000 people in 44 states, as well as in the District of Columbia, Puerto Rico, the Virgin Islands, and 13 foreign countries (American Red Cross 2005).

13. Project Liberty's data on the number of people who used its services are less than clear because individuals who received multiple services – for example, who attended educational presentations and group therapy sessions as well as individual counseling – may have been counted more than once, and because New York City providers did not submit data on all their activities before September 1, 2002.

14. It is also impossible to know whether those who used Project Liberty's services were those who were the most seriously psychologically injured, who were closest to service sites, or who were most receptive to its ads.

15. Trauma expert Bessel van der Kolk (2002:381) states that traumatization may be more likely to occur among those who are most closely exposed to "sensory realities," such as being "physically immobile and helpless while trying to escape," having "first-hand experiences of the sounds, smells, and images of a calamity," or directly witnessing "the death and dismemberment of human beings."

16. In September, 2006, workers at Logan International Airport expressed guilt at having provided "a launching pad" for the attack, and stated that airline workers' emotional responses to the attack had received insufficient attention. Since 2001, approximately 170,000 aviation employees have left the industry (Daniel 2006).

17. According to one report, a huge number of Americans – more than 10 million persons, 75% of whom resided outside the Washington, D.C., and New York metropolitan areas – claimed to have relatives, friends, or colleagues who were killed or injured in the attack (Schlenger et al. 2002b). Lists of victims' home states and countries attest to the broad geographic impact of 9/11 (cf. Feinberg 2005).

18. My usage of these terms reflects the ways they were employed by the mental health professionals I interviewed and the literature I cite. For a detailed discussion of the finer distinctions among psychological debriefing, critical incident stress debriefing, critical incident stress management, crisis management briefing, defusing, and demobilization, see Myers and Wee (2005:156–176, 188).

19. Although critical incident stress debriefing has been studied extensively, so many methodological flaws plague this research that there still is no solid evidence as to its effectiveness or lack thereof. This is due both to the difficulties of conducting random-ized controlled studies following traumatic incidents and disasters, and to the imprecise use of relevant terms (Myers & Wee 2005).

20. Debriefings should never be mandatory, should not be provided to groups of persons with varying levels of exposure to given catastrophes, should not be provided by clinicians who are less than fully skilled in their delivery, and should not be the only interventions

people receive (Myers & Wee 2005). All of these guidelines were disregarded after 9/11.

21. This is curious, since terrorist attacks are carefully orchestrated to be visually spectacular and emotionally gripping. The more theatrical they are, the more media play they will receive and the more people they will harm (Nacos 2002). The Internet may be the perfect vehicle for the communication of terrorists' messages as it is freely accessible, comparatively uncensored, and not subject to broadcasting restrictions (Weimann 2005).

22. In one interpretation, this association did not mean that television watching induced psychological symptoms, but that watching television was a way for persons to cope with preexisting emotional distress (Schlenger et al. 2002b).

23. Some of those who were severely destabilized by 9/11 entered unconventional treatments as a last resort. A number of firemen took part in detoxification programs designed by the founder of Scientology and partially paid for by the actor Tom Cruise. These treatments, which included saunas, workouts, and medication, were designed to extract the poisons they absorbed during their work after the attack. Some fireman reported eliminating black and blue beads of sweat the size of quarters (O'Donnell 2003). Others took advantage of software using videogame technology that exposed them to three-dimensional images of the attack, and that allowed them to gradually overcome their reactions to it (Lake 2005).

24. It has been suggested that if national leaders had encouraged coping behaviors, provided support, promoted social cohesion, and disseminated accurate information, they might have been as effective as mental health services – and much less costly – in lessening the attack's negative psychological consequences (Flynn 2004; Reissman 2004). However, many of the messages government officials disseminated, especially those concerning the quality of the air in downtown Manhattan and the links between the attack and Iraq, contained conflicting, ambiguous, and patently false information (Rosner & Markowitz 2006).

25. As an example, Malkinson, Rubin, and Witzum (2005) discuss what is psychologically distinctive about the traumatic bereavement that results from terrorist acts.

26. From an intersubjective perspective, the simultaneous trauma of 9/11 might be clinically useful in that it might foster "joint observation and introspection" (Kretsch, Benyakar, Baruch, & Roth 1997:32). However, it is unclear whether psychoanalysts and other mental health professionals consciously chose to deviate from customary techniques in order to more effectively address patients' fears, or whether they did so in an attempt to master personal feelings of helplessness and anxiety (Cabaniss et al. 2004).

27. It has been reported that approximately 90% of Americans coped with 9/11 by turning to religion (Schuster et al. 2001).

28. The darker side of using psychological knowledge to defend the nation emerged when in 2005, the American Psychological Association (APA) was charged with adopting a policy supporting psychologists' participation in interrogations of political prisoners. One of the psychologists who drafted this policy had directed a behavioral sciences group that was involved in interrogations at Abu Ghraib, the Iraqi prison notorious for severe abuses of prisoners. Some psychologists were appalled that their discipline's expertise had been used to systematically break down detainees, thereby violating the professional obligation to do no harm (Benjamin 2006). This controversy has not yet been resolved. At the APA's annual convention in 2006, its Council of Representatives adopted a resolution that affirmed the organization's unequivocal opposition to

torture and abuse, and condemned psychologists who participated in such activities (www.apa.org/releases/notorture.html). However, a speaker at the same meeting denied that there were conflicts between the APA's ethical stance and the work of psychologists who consulted with interrogation teams at U.S. military facilities (Farberman 2006).

29. Culture and Personality theorists also were hired to create psychological portraits of enemy populations and their leaders during World War II. The federal government used this information to shape military strategy (Bock 1999).

30. Although the United States is known worldwide for its societal and military violence, I know of no psychological studies that examine the cultural roots of American aggression. However, there have been a couple of broad analyses of the United States and its residents. Wirth (2003:385–386) suggests that Americans suffer from mass psychological disturbances, stating that the United States, "the greatest economic and military power in the history of mankind, is subject to a collective narcissistic delusion of grandeur," and that it must abandon its "self-idolization." Volkan (2001) argues that as a rule, societies that are destabilized by traumatic events regress, returning to earlier stages of development in order to repair shattered group identities. He claims that America regressed after the attack, resulting in xenophobia, the war on terror, reductions in civil liberties, the suppression of dissent, and simplistic distinctions between good and evil.

31. For other analyses of terrorism from psychosocial rather than clinical perspectives, see Moghaddam and Marsella (2004).

32. Relational psychoanalysis holds that "all ideas, including psychoanalytic wisdom, are historical, linguistic, political, and contextual" (International Association for Relational Psychoanalysis and Psychotherapy n.d.). It also incorporates feminist perspectives on marginalization and powerlessness, and intersubjective notions of ongoing reciprocal influence. Consequently, it was considered an appropriate framework for understanding the world after 9/11, and for instigating political organization and action.

33. Along with numerous other therapists, I attended this meeting, at which the unusual mixture of high theory, moral purpose, and personal confession that characterizes gatherings of mental health professionals was on display. Where else would a key speaker interrupt a dense analysis of the federal government's political rhetoric to recount her recent dream? And where else would members of the audience stand up and reveal their private anxieties, or announce that they had overcome personal insecurities? In addition, I took part in drafting a PSR press release until it became clear that those in charge of this activity were intent on emphasizing psychoanalytic rather than public health, sociological, or political frames of analysis.

34. For a more pessimistic account of public health after 9/11, see Rosner and Markowitz (2006). They provide a detailed report of the federal government's failure to deliver billions of dollars for specific improvements in the nation's public health infrastructure as memories of 9/11 receded. They also discuss emerging conflicts as to whether post-9/11 federal moneys should fund broad public health programs, such as those regarding childhood immunization and the prevention of chronic, infectious, and sexually transmitted diseases, or whether they should be more narrowly directed toward bioterrorism. Some public health specialists feared that the emphasis on bioterrorism was designed to drum up support for the Bush administration's agendas, and thus would cement the ties among public health, law enforcement, and the military. As the federal budget deficit ballooned and billions of dollars were spent on the war in Iraq, shrinking the moneys available for public health, these conflicts gained in intensity.

35. In contrast, Project Liberty planned to systematically assess its services in "the first-ever evaluation of an emergency mental health program" funded by the federal government (Felton 2004:147). The results, which are contained in the September, 2006 volume of *Psychiatric Services*, were published too late to be fully discussed in this book. The soundness of this research, some of which is based on service recipients' self-reports through mail and telephone surveys, promises to be the subject of debate.

36. Fuchs's comments were prescient. Soon after 9/11, there was a call for a "mental health reserve corps" composed of therapists who would "contribute their time and expertise on an emergency basis" (Susser et al. 2002:59). In September 2006, Thomas Frieden, Commissioner of the New York City Department of Health and Mental Hygiene, sent New York City practitioners a letter asking them to join the Medical Reserve Corps (MRC), "a multidisciplinary group of volunteer health professionals who agree to help their friends and neighbors here in NYC during a public health emergency" (New York City Department of Mental Health and Hygiene n.d.). In October 2006, the MRC intensified its drive to register new volunteers, stating, "We challenge every volunteer to introduce at least one health professional friend/colleague to the MRC program and encourage them to join this year." Although MRC volunteers will be "pre-identified, pre-credentialed, and pre-trained," the events of 9/11 suggest that this will not necessarily protect them against intense and disabling reactions to their work after disasters and attacks.

37. Questions of timing are crucial in telling traumatic narratives. Models of psychological debriefing require persons to tell their stories immediately. In contrast, some Holocaust survivors did not speak of their experiences for decades. Laub (1995) considers the reasons for the delay, as well as its dangers. Leys (2004) discusses the alternative view that social and individual recovery are best accomplished not by recalling and telling the truth about traumatic events, by but repressing them.

38. There is disagreement as to whether bearing witness to massive acts of violence helps prevent future atrocities. Some fear that it spreads hostilities, revenge, and trauma to the next generation (Weine 1999). Others maintain that repeated media exposure to catastrophes produces numbness and desensitization rather than corrective action (Kleinman & Kleinman 1997). Langer (1997:59 emphasis in original) doubts that we learn from history. He states, "Perhaps it is time to admit that atrocity in the past does not discourage but in fact *invites* atrocity in the future."

39. Alternatively, the goal of creating a historical and political document underlies the Columbia Oral History Project (Clark 2002), which has recorded the testimonies of hundreds of people directly exposed to the World Trade Center attack. People who participated in this project not only yearned to comprehend what they had experienced, but also felt obliged to tell a story that diverged from the dominant narrative of 9/11, to express political dissent, or to testify for posterity.

40. It bears repeating that, at the time of this writing, the connections between combat and PTSD also were being reassessed as thousands of destabilized American soldiers were returning home after tours of duty in Iraq.

Works Cited

9/11 Commission Report. (2004). *Final report of the National Commission on Terrorist Attacks Upon the United States*. New York: W.W. Norton.

9-11 Mental Health. (2005). *The 9-11 Mental Health and Substance Abuse Program*. Retrieved August 1, 2006, from www.9-11mentalhealth.org.

Abu-Lughod, L., & Lutz, C. (1990). Introduction: Emotion, discourse, and the politics of everyday life. In C. Lutz & L. Abu-Lughod (Eds.), *Language and the politics of emotion* (pp. 1–23). New York: Cambridge University Press.

Alexander, J. (2002). On the social construction of moral universals: The "Holocaust" from war crime to trauma drama. *European Journal of Social Theory, 5*(1), 5–85.

Altman, N. 1995. *The analyst in the inner city: Race, class and culture through a psychoanalytic lens*. Hillsdale, NJ: Analytic Press.

Altman, N., & Davies, J. 2002. Out of the blue: Reflections on a shared trauma. *Psychoanalytic Dialogues, 12*(3), 359–360.

American Psychiatric Association. (1980). *Diagnostic and statistical manual of mental disorders: Third edition*. Washington, DC: American Psychiatric Association.

American Psychiatric Association. (1987). *Diagnostic and statistical manual of mental disorders: Third edition, revised*. Washington, DC: American Psychiatric Association.

American Psychiatric Association. (1994). *Diagnostic and statistical manual of mental disorders: Fourth edition*. Washington, DC: American Psychiatric Association.

American Psychiatric Association. (2000). *Diagnostic and statistical manual of mental disorders: Fourth edition, text revision*. Washington, DC: American Psychiatric Association.

American Psychological Association. (2006, August 10). American Psychological Association reaffirms unequivocal position against torture and abuse. *APA press release*. Retrieved September 13, 2006, from www.apa.org/releases.

American Red Cross. (2004, October 25). American Red Cross to fund continuation of 9/11 Mental Health and Substance Abuse Program. *Press room*. Retrieved August 2, 2005, from www.redcross.org/pressrelease/.

American Red Cross. (2005). *American Red Cross Liberty Disaster Relief Fund: Quarterly report, March 31*. Retrieved August 1, 2006, from www.redcross.org/press/disaster/030201.

American Red Cross. n.d. *Disaster services*. Retrieved August 1, 2006, from www.redcross.
org/services/.

American Red Cross in Greater New York. (2004a). 9/11 Commission proves emotional
wounds from the attacks still not healed for New Yorkers. *American Red Cross News*.
Retrieved August 3, 2005, from www.nyredcross.org.

American Red Cross in Greater New York. (2004b). *The history of the Red Cross in New York.
9/11 Timeline: The Red Cross response*. Retrieved August 2, 2005, from www.nyredcross.
org/media/.

Amsel, L., Neria, Y., Marshall, R., & Suh, E. (2005). Training therapists to treat the psychological consequences of terrorism: Disseminating psychotherapy research and researching
psychotherapy dissemination. In Y. Danieli, D. Brom, & J. Sills (Eds.), *The trauma of
terrorism: Sharing knowledge and shared care, an international handbook* (pp. 633– 647).
Binghamton, NY: Haworth Press.

Aretxaga, B. (2001). Terror as a thrill: First thoughts about the "war on terrorism." *Anthropological Quarterly, 75*, 138–150.

Aretxaga, B. 2003. Maddening states. *Annual Review of Anthropology, 32*, 393–410.

Aron, L. (1996). *A meeting of minds: Mutuality in psychoanalysis*. Hillsdale, NJ: Analytic
Press.

Awwad, E. (2005). Defeated dreams: The tragedy of survivors. In D. Knafo (Ed.), *Living
with terror, working with trauma: A clinician's handbook* (pp. 201–228). Lanham, MD: Jason
Aronson.

Baird, B. (2004). WTC families to sue over remains at landfill. *Voices of September 11th*.
October 27. Retrieved June 25, 2005, from www.voicesofsept11.org.

Ballenger, J. C., Davidson, J. R. T., Lecrubier, Y., et al. (2000). Consensus statement of
posttraumatic stress disorder from the International Consensus Group on Depression
and Anxiety. *Journal of Clinical Psychiatry, 61*(Suppl 5), 60–66.

Barrett, M., Demaria, T., & Comforto, B. (2005). A community World Trade Center trauma
and bereavement counseling program. In Y. Danieli & R. Dingman (Eds.), *On the ground
after September 11: Mental health responses and practical knowledge gained* (pp. 353–361).
Binghamton, NY: Haworth Press.

Barrett, R. (1988). Clinical writing and the documentary construction of schizophrenia.
Culture, Medicine and Psychiatry, 12, 265–299.

Batista, G. 2005. On the ground after September 11: Lessons learned from the relief efforts
to the Latino community in New York City. In Y. Danieli & R. Dingman (Eds.), *On the
ground after September 11: Mental health responses and practical knowledge gained* (pp. 124–
129). Binghamton, NY: Haworth Press.

Beck, A. (1962). Reliability of psychiatric diagnoses: A critique of systematic studies. *American
Journal of Psychiatry, 119*, 210–216.

Beltsiou, J. n.d. *Money in the mix: Interviews with psychoanalysts about money as a topic in the
therapeutic discourse*. Unpublished doctoral dissertation.

Benedict, R. (1934). Anthropology and the abnormal. *Journal of General Psychology, 10*,
59–92.

Benjamin, J. (n.d.). *Position paper: Psychotherapists for Social Responsibility*. Retrieved July 19,
2006, from www.psr.org.

Benjamin, M. (2006). Psychological warfare. Retrieved August 7, 2006, from www.salon.
com/new/feature/.

Berger, R. (2005). Early interventions with victims of terrorism. In D. Knafo (Ed.), *Living with terror, working with trauma: A clinician's handbook* (pp. 233–271). Lanham, MD: Jason Aronson.

Bergmann, M. Terrorism on U. S. soil: Remembering past trauma and retraumatization. In D. Knafo (Ed.), *Living with terror, working with trauma: A clinician's handbook* (pp. 449–459). Lanham, MD: Jason Aronson.

Bishop, I., & Geller, A. (2005, September 9). Sept. 11 heroes' precious medal. *New York Post*, 2.

Bloom, J. 2005. The Family Assistance Center at Pier 94. In Y. Danieli & R. Dingman (Eds.), *On the ground after September 11: Mental health responses and practical knowledge gained* (pp. 345–352). Binghamton, NY: Haworth Press.

Bloom, S. (1999). The germ theory of trauma: The impossibility of ethical neutrality. In B. Stamm (Ed.), *Secondary traumatic stress: Self-care issues for clinicians, researchers, and educators* (pp. 257–276). Baltimore: Sidran Press.

Bock, P. (1999). *Rethinking psychological anthropology: Continuity and change in the study of human action*. New York: W.H. Freeman.

Bonanno, G. (2004). Loss, trauma and human resilience: Have we underestimated the human capacity to thrive after extremely aversive events? *American Psychologist, 59*(1), 20–28.

Boss, P. (2004). Ambiguous loss research, theory and practice: Reflections after 9/11. *Journal of Marriage and Family, 66*(3), 551–566.

Boss, P., Beaulieu, L., Weiling, E., Turner, W., & LaCruz, S. (2003). Healing loss, ambiguity, and trauma: A community-based intervention with families of union workers missing after the 9/11 attack in New York City. *Journal of Marital and Family Therapy, 29*(4), 455–467.

Boulanger, G. (2002a). The cost of survival: Psychoanalysis and adult onset trauma. *Contemporary Psychoanalysis, 38*(1), 17–44.

Boulanger, G. (2002b). Wounded by reality: The collapse of the self in adult onset trauma. *Contemporary Psychoanalysis, 38*(1), 45–76.

Boulanger, G. (2003). The strength found in innocence: Resistance to working psychodynamically with trauma survivors. *Psychoanalysis and Psychotherapy, 20*(2), 119–136.

Boulanger, G. (2005). From voyeur to witness: Recapturing symbolic function after massive psychic trauma. *Psychoanalytic Psychology, 22*(1), 21–31.

Bracken, P. (2001). Post-modernity and post-traumatic stress disorder. *Social Science and Medicine, 53*, 733–743.

Bracken, P., Giller, J., & Summerfield, D. (1995). Psychological responses to war and atrocity: The limitations of current concepts. *Social Science and Medicine, 40*(8), 1073–1082.

Bracken, P., Giller, J., & Summerfield, D. (1997). Rethinking mental health work with survivors of wartime violence and refugees. *Journal of Refugee Studies, 10*(4), 431–442.

Brennan, T. (2004). *The transmission of affect*. Ithaca, NY: Cornell University Press.

Breslau, J. (2000). Globalizing disaster trauma: Psychiatry, science, and culture after the Kobe earthquake. *Ethos, 28*(2), 174–197.

Breslau, J. (2004). Cultures of trauma: Anthropological views of postttraumatic stress disorder in international health. *Culture, Medicine and Psychiatry, 28*, 113–126.

Brown, L. (1995). Not outside the range: One feminist perspective on psychic trauma. In C. Caruth (Ed.), *Trauma: Explorations in memory* (pp. 100–112). Baltimore: Johns Hopkins University Press.

Button, G. (2002). Popular media reframing of man-made disasters: A cautionary tale. In S. Hoffman & A. Oliver-Smith (Eds.), *Catastrophe & culture: The anthropology of disaster* (pp. 143–158). Santa Fe, NM: School of American Research Press.

Cabaniss, D., Forand, N., & Roose, S. (2004). Conducting analysis after September 11: Implications for psychoanalytic technique. *Journal of the American Psychoanalytic Association, 52*(3), 718–734.

Campbell, A., Cairns, E., & Mallett, J. 2005. Northern Ireland: The psychological impact of "the Troubles." In Y. Danieli, D. Brom, & J. Sills (Eds.), *The trauma of terrorism: Sharing knowledge and shared care, an international handbook* (pp. 175–184). Binghamton, NY: Haworth Press.

Canzoneri, M., & Canzoneri, K. (2005). Therapy dogs and 9/11. In Y. Danieli, D. Brom, & J. Sills (Eds.), *The trauma of terrorism: Sharing knowledge and shared care, an international handbook* (pp. 437–440). Binghamton, NY: Haworth Press.

Cardozo, B., & Salama, P. (2002). Mental health of humanitarian aid workers in complex emergencies. In Y. Danieli (Ed.). *Sharing the front line and the back hills: Peacekeepers, humanitarian aid workers and the media in the midst of crisis* (pp. 242–255). Amityville, NY: Bayworth Publishing.

Carey, B., & O'Connor, A. (2004, August 3). As public adjusts to threat, alerts cause less unease. *New York Times*, A9.

Carter, R. (1995). *The influence of race and racial identity in psychotherapy: Toward a racially inclusive model*. New York: John Wiley.

Caruth, C. (1995a). An interview with Robert Lifton. In C. Caruth (Ed.), *Trauma: Explorations in memory* (pp. 128–147). Baltimore: Johns Hopkins University Press.

Caruth, C. (1995b). Introduction. In C. Caruth (Ed.), *Trauma: Explorations in memory* (pp. 3–12). Baltimore: Johns Hopkins University Press.

Casey, G. (2001, October 8). After 9/11 – Journalism – Trauma, stress and coping. *TV spy*. Retrieved May 30, 2002, from www.tvspy.com.

Centers for Disease Control and Prevention. (n.d.). *Emergency preparedness response. Preparing for a terrorist bombing: A common sense approach*. Retrieved August 12, 2006, from www.bt.cdc.gov/masscasualties/.

Chan, S. (2006, May 22). City workers' 9/11 claims meet obstacles. *New York Times*, B4.

Charity Wire. (n.d.). Retrieved June 22, 2004, from www.charitywire.com.

Chemtob, C. (2005). Finding the gift in the horror: Toward developing a national psychosocial security policy. In Y. Danieli, D. Brom, & J. Sills (Eds.), *The trauma of terrorism: Sharing knowledge and shared care, an international handbook* (pp. 721–729). Binghamton, NY: Haworth Press.

Chemtob, C., Tolin, D., van der Kolk, B., & Pitman, R. (2000). Eye movement desensitization and reprocessing. In E. Foa, T. Keane, & M. Friedman (Eds.), *Effective treatments for PTSD: Practice guidelines from the International Society for Traumatic Stress Studies* (pp. 139–155). New York: Guilford Press.

Chen, D. (2005, February 24). As 9/11 remains go unnamed, families grieve anew. *New York Times*, B3.

Cienfuegos, A., & Monelli, C. (1983). The testimony of political repression as a therapeutic instrument. *American Journal of Orthopsychiatry, 53*(1), 43–51.

Clark, M. M. (2002, September). The September 11, 2001, Oral History Narrative and Memory Project: A first report. *Journal of American History*, 569–579.

Clark, R. (1995). The Pope's confessor: A metaphor relating to illness in the analyst. *Journal of the American Psychological Association, 43*, 137–149.

Cohen, N. (2005). Reflections on the public health and mental health response to 9/11. In Y. Danieli & R. Dingman (Eds.), *On the ground after September 11: Mental health responses and practical knowledge gained* (pp. 24–28). Binghamton, NY: Haworth Press.

Collogan, L., Tuma, F., Dolan-Sewell, R., Borja, S., & Fleischman, A. (2004). Ethical issues pertaining to research in the aftermath of disaster. *Journal of Traumatic Stress, 17*(5), 363–372.

Columbia University Mailman School of Public Health. (n.d.). *National Center for Disaster Preparedness: Public health preparedness.* Retrieved July 21, 2006, from www.ncdp. mailman.columbia.edu.

Columbia University Medical Center. (n.d.). *Center for the Study of Trauma and Resilience.* Retrieved August 29, 2005, from www.columbiatrauma.org.

Corry, J. (2002). New York, New York: America's hero. In W. Plezczynski (Ed.), *Our brave new world: Essays on the impact of September 11* (pp. 119–136). Stanford, CA: Hoover Institution Press.

Crimando, S., & Padro, G. (2005). Across the river: New Jersey's response to 9/11. In Y. Danieli & R. Dingman (Eds.), *On the ground after September 11: Mental health responses and practical knowledge gained* (pp. 107–114). Binghamton, NY: Haworth Press.

Daniel, M. (2006, August 30). At Logan, the pain of 9/11 runs deep. *Boston Globe.* Retrieved September 2, 2006, from www.boston.com/news.

Danieli, Y. 1984. Psychotherapists' participation in the conspiracy of silence about the Holocaust. *Psychoanalytic Psychology, 1*, 23–42.

Danieli, Y. (Ed.). (1998). *International handbook of multigenerational legacies of trauma.* New York: Plenum Press.

Danieli, Y., Brom, D., & Sills, J. (Eds.). (2005). *The trauma of terrorism: Sharing knowledge and shared care, an international handbook.* Binghamton, NY: Haworth Press.

Danieli, Y., & Dingman, R. (Eds.). (2005a). Introduction. In Y. Danieli & R. Dingman (Eds.), *On the ground after September 11: Mental health responses and practical knowledge gained* (pp. 1–25). Binghamton, NY: Haworth Press.

Danieli, Y., & Dingman, R. (Eds.). (2005b). *On the ground after September 11: Mental health responses and practical knowledge gained.* Binghamton, NY: Haworth Press.

Das, V. (2000). The act of witnessing: Violence, poisonous knowledge, and subjectivity. In V. Das, A. Kleinman, M. Ramphele, & P. Reynolds (Eds.), *Violence and subjectivity* (pp. 205–225). Berkeley: University of California Press.

Das, V. 2001. Violence and translation. *Anthropological Quarterly, 75*, 105–112.

Davidowitz-Farkas, Z., & Hutchison-Hall, J. (2005). Religious care in coping with terrorism. In Y. Danieli, D. Brom, & J. Sills (Eds.). *The trauma of terrorism* (pp. 565–576). Binghamton, NY: Haworth Press.

Davies, M. (2004, June 18). Marriage, partner rights, 9/11 burials taken up by Executive Council. *Episcopal News Service.* Retrieved July 18, 2005, from www.faithstreams.com.

Davoine, F., & Gaudilliere, J. (2004). *History beyond trauma.* New York: Other Press.

DeJong, J. (2002). Public mental health, traumatic stress and human rights violations in low-income countries. In J. De Jong (Ed.), *Trauma, war and violence: Public mental health in socio-cultural context* (pp. 1–92). New York: Kluwer Academic/Plenum.

DeMause, L. (2002). The childhood origins of terrorism. *Journal of Psychohistory, 29*(4), 340–348.

DePalma, A. (2006, September 6). Illness persisting in 9/11 workers, big study finds. *New York Times*, B1.

DePalma, A. (2007a, May 24). For the first time, the city connects a death to 9/11 dust. *New York Times*, B1.

DePalma, A. (2007b, May 14). Ground Zero illnesses cloud Giuliani's legacy. *New York Times*, A1.

Dickson-Gomez, J. (2002). The sound of barking dogs: Violence and terror among Salvadoran families in the postwar. *Medical Anthropology Quarterly, 16*(4), 415–438.

Didion, J. (2003, January 16). Fixed ideas since September 11. *New York Review of Books*, 54–59.

Dimen, M. (2002). Day 2/month 2: Wordless/the words to say it. *Psychoanalytic Dialogues, 12*(3), 451–455.

Disaster Psychiatry Outreach. (n.d.). *History*. Retrieved June 4, 2006, from www.disasterpsych.org.

Donahue, S., Lanzara, C., Felton, C., Essock, S., & Carpinello, S. (2006). Project Liberty: New York's crisis counseling program created in the aftermath of September 11, 2001. *Psychiatric Services 57*(9), 1253–1258.

Donato, D. (2005). Massachusetts behavioral response to September 11. In Y. Danieli & R. Dingman (Eds.), *On the ground after September 11: Mental health responses and practical knowledge gained* (pp. 115–123). Binghamton, NY: Haworth Press.

Draper, J. (2005). LifeNet and 9/11: The central role. In Y. Danieli & R. Dingman (Eds.), *On the ground after September 11: Mental health responses and practical knowledge gained* (pp. 63–71). Binghamton, NY: Haworth Press.

Dreifus, C. (2004, September 7). A sociologist with an advanced degree in calamity. *New York Times*, F2.

Doughtery, J. (2003, January 4). *Homeland insecurity*. Retrieved July 23, 2005, from www.worldnetdaily.com.

Dunlap, D. (2006a, August 26). Expert supports search methods for 9/11 remains at bank building. *New York Times*, B2.

Dunlap, D. (2006b, October 25). Officials try to identify sites where body parts still lie. *New York Times*, B3.

Dunlap, D. (2006c, August 29). Renovating a "sacred space," where the remains of 9/11 wait. *New York Times*, B3.

Dunlap, D. (2006d, November 2). Where the city will search for remains from Sept. 11. *New York Times*, B2.

Dunlap, D. (2007, February 1). Search for remains will go on beneath asphalt lot. *New York Times*, B2.

Dwyer, J. (2006a, August 17). More tapes from Sept. 11: "They have exits in there?" *New York Times*, A21.

Dwyer, J. (2006b, April 6). Pieces of bone are found on building at 9/11 site. *New York Times*, B4.

Dwyer, J., & Flynn, K. (2005). *102 minutes: The untold story of the fight to survive inside the twin towers*. New York: Times Books.

Environmental Protection Agency. (2002). *EPA response to September 11*. Retrieved February 10, 2003, from www.epa.gov/wtc/stories.

Epstein, H. (1979). *Children of the Holocaust: Conversations with sons and daughters of survivors*. New York: Penguin Books.

Erikson, K. (1976). *Everything in its path: Destruction of community in the Buffalo Creek flood.* New York: Simon & Schuster.

Erikson, K. (1995). Notes on trauma and community. In C. Caruth (Ed.), *Trauma: Explorations in memory* (pp. 183–199). Baltimore: Johns Hopkins University Press.

Eth, S., & Sabor, S. (2005). Healing in the aftermath of 9/11: Recovery from suffering and grief for the community and its caregivers. In Y. Danieli & R. Dingman (Eds.), *On the ground after September 11: Mental health responses and practical knowledge gained* (pp. 42–50). Binghamton, NY: Haworth Press.

Farberman, R. (2006, October). Council action at convention. *APA Online Monitor on Psychology, 37*(9). Retrieved November 1, 2006, from www.apa.org/monitor.

Federation Reference Centre for Psychological Support. (n.d.). *Family Assistance Center – Pier 94, New York City September 20.* Retrieved September 1, 2004, from wysiwyg://20http://www1.drk.dk/sw3317.asp.

Feinberg, K. (2005). *What is life worth?: The unprecedented effort to compensate the victims of 9/11.* New York: Public Affairs.

Felton, C. (2002). Project Liberty: A public health response to New Yorkers' mental health needs arising from the World Trade Center terrorist attacks. *Journal of Urban Health, 79*(3), 429–433.

Felton, C. (2004). Commentary on "A national longitudinal study of the psychological consequences of the September 11, 2001 terrorist attacks: Reactions, impairment, and help-seeking": Lessons learned since September 11, 2001 concerning the mental health impact of terrorism, appropriate response strategies, and future preparedness. *Psychiatry, 67,* 146–152.

FEMA. (n.d.). *Region 1: Advocacy needs.* Retrieved September 1, 2004, from www.fema/gov/regions/.

FEMA.(n.d.). *Region 1: Family Assistance Center of New York.* Retrieved September 1, 2004, from www.fema/gov/regions/.

Fenichel, O. (1945). *Psychoanalytic theory of neurosis.* New York: W.W. Norton.

Figley, C. R. (Ed.). (1995). *Compassion fatigue: Coping with secondary traumatic stress disorder in those who treat the traumatized.* New York: Brunner/Mazel.

Firth, S. (2002, September/October). When the search is over. *Pennsylvania Gazette,* 40–45.

Flynn, B. (2004). Commentary on "A national longitudinal study of the psychological consequences of the September 11, 2001 terrorist attacks: Reactions, impairment, and help-seeking": Can we influence the trajectory of psychological consequences to terrorism? *Psychiatry, 67*(2), 164–166.

Flynn, B. (2005). Mental health response to terrorism in the United States: An adolescent field in an adolescent nation. In Y. Danieli, D. Brom, & J. Sills (Eds.), *The trauma of terrorism: Sharing knowledge and shared care, an international handbook* (pp. 755–768). Binghamton, NY: Haworth Press.

Foa, E., Dancu, C., Hembree, E., Jaycox, L., Meadows, E., & Street, G. (1999). A comparison of exposure therapy, stress inoculation training and their combination for reducing posttraumatic stress disorder in female assault victims. *Journal of Consulting and Clinical Psychology, 67,* 194–200.

Foa, E., Keane, T., & Friedman, M. (Eds.). (2000). *Effective treatments for PTSD: Practice guidelines from the International Society for Traumatic Stress Studies.* New York: Guilford Press.

Foner, N. (Ed.). (2005). *Wounded city: The social impact of 9/11*. New York: Russell Sage Foundation.

Foster, R. P., Moskowitz, M., & Javier, R. A. (Eds.). (1996). *Reaching across boundaries of culture and class: Widening the scope of psychotherapy*. Northvale, NJ: Jason Aronson.

Foucault, M. (1978). *The history of sexuality: An introduction, Vol. 1*. New York: Vintage Books. (Originally published in 1976)

Foucault, M. (1988). *Madness and civilization*. New York: Vintage Books. (Originally published in 1965)

Foucault, M. (1994). *The birth of the clinic: An archeology of medical perception*. New York: Vintage Books. (Originally published in 1963)

Foucault, M. (1995). *Discipline and punish: The birth of the prison*. New York: Vintage Books. (Originally published in 1975)

Frawley-O'Dea, M. (2004). When the trauma is terrorism and the therapist is traumatized too: Working as an analyst since 9/11. *Psychoanalytic Perspectives, 1*(1), 67–89.

French, L. 2004. Commentary. *Culture, Medicine, and Psychiatry, 28*, 211–220.

Freud, S. (1961). *Beyond the pleasure principle*. In J. Strachey (Ed.), *The standard edition of the complete works of Sigmund Freud*. New York: Norton. (Originally published in 1920)

Freud, S. (1961). Introductory lectures on psychoanalysis. In J. Strachey (Ed.), *The standard edition of the complete works of Sigmund Freud, v. 16* (pp. 448–463). London: Hogarth Press. (Originally published in 1917)

Freud, S. (1961). Character and anal eroticism. In J. Strachey (Ed.), *The standard edition of the complete works of Sigmund Freud, v. 9* (pp. 167–175). London: Hogarth Press. (Originally published in 1908)

Freud, S. (1998). The aetiology of hysteria. In J. Masson. *The assault on truth: Freud's suppression of the seduction hypothesis* (pp. 259–290). New York: Pocket Books. (Originally published in 1896)

Freud, S. (1912). A note on the unconscious in psychoanalysis. In J. Rickham, ed. *A general selection from the works of Sigmund Freud* (pp. 46–53). New York: Doubleday.

Friedman, M. (2005). Toward a public mental health approach for survivors of terrorism. In Y. Danieli, D. Brom, & J. Sills (Eds.), *The trauma of terrorism* (pp. 527–539). Binghamton, NY: Haworth Press.

Friedman, M., Hamblen, J., Foa, E., & Charney, D. (2004). Commentary on "A national longitudinal study of the psychological consequences of the September 11, 2001 terrorist attacks: Reactions, impairment, and help-seeking": Fighting the psychological war on terrorism. *Psychiatry, 67*(2), 123–136.

Gabriel, B. (n.d.). America's heroes one year later: Researchers learn from 9/11 survivors. *American Association of Medical Colleges*. Retrieved July 31, 2006, from www.aamc.org/newsroom/.

Gaines, A. (1992). From DSM-I to III-R; Voices of self, mastery and the other: A cultural constructivist reading of U.S. psychiatric classification. *Social Science and Medicine, 35*(1), 3–24.

Galea, S., Ahern, J., Resnick, H., Kilpatrick, D., Bucuvalas, M., Gold, J., et al. (2002). Psychological sequelae of the September 11 terrorists attacks in New York City. *New England Journal of Medicine, 346*(13), 982–987.

Garfinkel, I., Kaushal, N., Teitler, J., & Garcia, S. (2005). Vulnerability and resilience: New Yorkers respond to 9-11. In N. Foner (Ed.), *Wounded city: The social effects of the World Trade Center attack on New York City* (pp. 28–75). New York: Russell Sage Foundation.

Garrison, B. (2005). Reflections on volunteer self-care at the site. In Y. Danieli & R. Dingman (Eds.), *On the ground after September 11: Mental health responses and practical knowledge gained* (pp. 268–270). Binghamton, NY: Haworth Press.

Geertz, C. (1973). *The interpretation of cultures: Selected essays.* NY: Basic Books.

Gheith, A., Abu Ras, W., & Cournos, F. (in press). Mental health services for the New York City Muslim community. In L. Cristillo (Ed), *Muslims in New York City.* New York: New York University Press.

Gilroy, P., Carroll, L., & Murra, J. (2002). A preliminary survey of counseling psychologists' personal experiences with depression and treatment. *Professional Psychology: Research and Practice, 33*(4), 402–407.

Gittrich, G. (2003, May 27). Millions unspent as relatively few seek counseling. *New York Daily News.*

Godwin, R. (2002). The land that developmental time forgot. *Journal of Psychohistory, 29*(4), 368–382.

Goin, M. (2002). When it really hurts to listen: Psychotherapy in the aftermath of September 11. *Psychological Services, 53*(5), 561–562.

Good, B. (1992). Culture and psychopathology: Directions for psychiatric anthropology. In T. Schwartz, G. White, & C. Lutz (Eds.), *New directions in psychological anthropology* (pp. 181–205). New York: Cambridge University Press.

Good, B. (1996). Culture and DSM-IV: Diagnosis, knowledge and power. *Culture, Medicine and Psychiatry, 20*(2), 127–131.

Good, B., & Good, M. J. (1988). Ritual, the state, and the transformation of emotional discourse in Iranian society. *Culture, Medicine and Psychiatry, 12*, 43–63.

Goodnough, A. (2002, May 2). Post 9-11 pain is found to linger in young minds. *New York Times.*

Greene, P., Kane, D., Christ, G., Lynch, S., & Corrigan, M. (2006). *FDNY crisis counseling: Innovative responses to 9/11 firefighters, families, and communities.* Hoboken, NJ: Wiley & Sons.

Groopman, J. (2004, January 26). The grief industry. *New Yorker*, 30–38.

Gurvitch, A. (2005). What did we learn? A call to action to improve immigrants' access to mental health services. In Y. Danieli & R. Dingman (Eds.), *On the ground after September 11: Mental health responses and practical knowledge gained* (pp. 541–550). Binghamton, NY: Haworth Press.

Haberman, C. (2006, September 8). In a gallery of faces, the names come to life. *New York Times.*

Hacking, I. (1995). *Rewriting the soul: Multiple personality and the sciences of memory.* Princeton, NJ: Princeton University Press.

Hamilton, S. (2005). Volunteers in disaster response: The American Red Cross. In Y. Danieli, D. Brom, & J. Sills (Eds.), *The trauma of terrorism: Sharing knowledge and shared care, an international handbook* (pp. 621–632). Binghamton, NY: Haworth Press.

Harvard College. (2002, January 1). General review – Disaster and trauma. *Harvard Mental Health Letter, 18*(7).

Heim, C., Meinlschmidt, M., & Nemeroff, C. (2003). Neurobiology of early-life stress. *Psychiatric Annals, 33*(1), 18–25.

Henzlova, M. (2002). Letters to the editor. *Journal of the American Medical Association, 288*(21), 2685.

Herman, D., Felton, C., & Susser, E. (2002a). Mental health needs in New York State following the September 11th attacks. *Journal of Urban Health, 79*(3), 322–331.

Herman, D., Felton, C., & Susser, E. (2002b). *Rates and treatment costs of mental disorders stemming from the World Trade Center terrorist attacks: An initial needs assessment.* Albany, NY: New York State Office of Mental Health.

Herman, J. 1997. *Trauma and recovery.* New York: Basic Books.

Hildebrandt, M. (2005). Double trauma in Belle Harbor. In. N. Foner (Ed.), *Wounded city: The social impact of 9/11* (pp. 106–132). New York: Russell Sage Foundation.

Hill, R. (2002). *Disaster response in the mental health community.* Retrieved June 30, 2005, from www.naswnyc.org.

Hoffman, C. (2004, September 1). As anxiety grows, so does field of terror study. *New York Times,* B4.

Hoffman, E. (2004). *After such knowledge: Memory, history and the legacy of the Holocaust.* New York: Public Affairs.

Hoffman, I. (1992). Some practical implications of a social-constructivist view of the analytic situation. *Psychoanalytic Dialogs 2,* 287–304.

Hollander, N. (1997). *Love in a time of hate: Liberation psychology in Latin America.* New Brunswick, NJ: Rutgers University Press.

Holmes, J. (1998). Money and psychotherapy: Object, metaphor or dream. *International Journal of Psychotherapy, 3*(2), 123–134.

Hough, G. (2004). Does psychoanalysis have anything to offer an understanding of terrorism? *Journal of the American Psychoanalytic Association, 52*(3), 813–828.

Howell, A. (2005, September 26). Red Cross program offers emotional support to disaster survivors. *In the News.* Retrieved October 23, 2005, from www.redcross.org/article/.

Ingleby, D. (1995). The interplay between science and culture. In N. Goldberger & J. Veroff (Eds.). *The culture and psychology reader* (pp. 108–123). New York: NYU Press.

Institute of Medicine. (2003). *Preparing for the psychological consequences of terrorism: A public health strategy.* Washington, DC: National Academy of Sciences.

International Association for Relational Psychoanalysis and Psychotherapy. (n.d.). Retrieved July 19, 2005, from www.iarpp.org.

International Society for Traumatic Stress Studies. (n.d.). *What is ISTSS?* Retrieved May 31, 2006, from www.istss.org/what/history.cfm.

Itzhaky, H., & Dekel, R. (2005). Helping victims of terrorism: What makes social work effective? *Social Work, 50*(4), 335–343.

Jack, K., & Glied, S. (2002). The public costs of mental health response: Lessons from the New York City post-9-11 needs assessment. *Journal of Urban Health, 79*(3), 332–339.

James, E. C. (2004). The political economy of 'trauma' in Haiti in the democratic era of insecurity. *Culture, Medicine and Psychiatry, 28,* 127–149.

Janofsky, M. (2005, September 10). With medals, Bush honors public servants killed on 9/11. *New York Times,* B4.

Jessen-Petersen, S. (2002). Caring for staff in UNHCR. In Y. Danieli (Ed.), *Sharing the front line and the back hills: Peacekeepers, humanitarian aid workers and the media in the midst of crisis* (pp. 53–60). Amityville, NY: Bayworth Publishing.

Jones, A. (2005). The days of the remains. In Y. Danieli & R. Dingman (Eds.), *On the ground after September 11: Mental health responses and practical knowledge gained* (pp. 326–331). Binghamton, NY: Haworth Press.

Jones, E., McCartney, H., Beech, C., Palmer, I., Hyams, K., & Wessely, S. (2003). Flashbacks and post-traumatic stress disorder: The genesis of a 20th century diagnosis. *British Journal of Psychiatry, 182,* 158–163.

Jones, K. (2004). September 11 in the Emergency Room: Brief disaster intervention and compassion stress. In A. Pandya & C. Katz (Eds.), *Disaster psychiatry: Intervening when nightmares come true* (pp. 37–52). Hillsdale, NJ: Analytic Press.

Kacandes, I. (2003). 9/11/01 = 1/27/01: The changed posttraumatic self. In J. Greenberg (Ed.), *Trauma at home: After 9/11* (pp. 168–183). Lincoln, NE: University of Nebraska Press.

Kaplan, E. A. (2005). *Trauma culture: The politics of terror and loss in media and literature.* New Brunswick, NJ: Rutgers University Press.

Kardiner, A. (1941). *The traumatic neuroses of war.* New York: Paul B. Hoeber.

Keane, T., Kaloupek, D., & Weathers, F. (1996). Ethnocultural considerations in the assessment of PTSD. In A. Marsella, M. Friedman, E. Gerrity, & R. Scurfield (Eds.), *Ethnocultural aspects of PTSD: Issues, research, and clinical applications* (pp. 183–205). Washington, DC: American Psychological Association.

Kilgannon, C. (2005, June 12). Years later, a final goodbye to a firefighter lost on 9/11. *New York Times.*

Kinzie, J. (2005). Cambodians and massive trauma: What we have learned after twenty years. In D. Knafo (Ed.), *Living with terror, working with trauma: A clinician's handbook* (pp. 119–134). Lanham, MD: Jason Aronson.

Kleinman, A. (1988). *The illness narratives: Suffering, healing and the human condition.* New York: Basic Books.

Kleinman, A., & Desjarlais, R. (1995). Violence, culture, and the politics of trauma. In A. Kleinman (Ed.), *Writing at the margin: Discourse between anthropology and medicine* (pp. 173–189). Berkeley: University of California Press.

Kleinman, A., & Kleinman, J. (1997). The appeal of experience; The dismay of images: Cultural appropriations of suffering in our time. In A. Kleinman, V. Das, & M. Lock (Eds.), *Social suffering* (pp. 1–23). Berkeley: University of California Press.

Knafo, D. (2004). (Ed). *Living with terror, working with trauma: A clinician's handbook.* Lanham, MD: Jason Aronson.

Kogan, I. (2004). The role of the analyst in the analytic cure during times of chronic crises. *Journal of the American Psychoanalytic Association, 52*(3), 735–757.

Kolbert, E. (2002, May 20). A hole in the city. *New Yorker,* 71.

Kretsch, R., Benyakar, J., Baruch, E., & Roth, M. (1997). A shared reality of therapists and survivors in a national crisis as illustrated by the Gulf War. *Psychotherapy, 34*(1), 28–33.

Kupfer, D., First, M., & Regier, D. (Eds.). (2002). *A research agenda for DSM-V.* Washington, DC: American Psychiatric Association.

Kutz, I., & Bleich, A. (2005). Mental health interventions in a general hospital following terrorist attacks: The Israeli experience. In Y. Danieli, D. Brom, & J. Sills (Eds.), *The trauma of terrorism: Sharing knowledge and shared care, an international handbook* (pp. 425–437). Binghamton, NY: Haworth Press.

Lachkar, J. (2002). The psychological make-up of a suicide bomber. *Journal of Psychohistory, 29*(4), 349–367.

Lake, M. (2005, May 2). *Virtual reality heals 9/11 wounds.* Retrieved July 31, 2005, from http://www.cnn.com/2005/TECH/04/29/spark.virtual/index.html.

Lamprecht, F., & Sack, M. (2002). Posttraumatic stress disorder revisited. *Psychosomatic Medicine, 64,* 222–237.

Langer, L. (1997). Social suffering and Holocaust atrocity. In A. Kleinman, V. Das, & M. Lock (Eds.), *Social suffering* (pp. 47–65). Berkeley: University of California Press.

Langewiesche, W. (2002). *American ground: Unbuilding the World Trade Center*. New York: North Point Press.

Lapham, L. (2002, November). Audible silence. *Harper's Magazine*, 8–11.

Laub, D. (1995). Truth and testimony: The process and the struggle. In C. Caruth (Ed.), *Trauma: Explorations in memory* (pp. 61–75). Baltimore: Johns Hopkins University Press.

Lear, J. (1990). *Love and its place in nature*. New York: Farrar, Straus & Giroux.

Lee, S., & Kleinman, A. (2001). Professional psychiatry in its political contexts: A response to Robin Munro. *Journal of the American Academy of Psychiatry and the Law, 30*, 120–125.

Lewis-Fernandez, R. (1996). Cultural formulation of psychiatric diagnosis. *Culture, Medicine and Psychiatry, 20*(2), 133–143.

Leys, R. (2000). *Trauma: A genealogy*. Chicago: University of Chicago Press.

Lifton, R. (1967). *Death in life: Survivors of Hiroshima*. New York: Random House.

Lifton, R. (1978). Advocacy and corruption in the healing profession. In C. Figley (Ed.), *Stress disorders among Vietnam veterans: Theory, research and treatment*. New York: Brunner/Mazel.

Lindsay, K., & Gordon, L. P. (1989). Involuntary commitments to public mental institutions: Issues involving the overrepresentations of blacks and assessment of relevant functioning. *Psychological Bulletin, 106*, 171–183.

Linenthal, E. (2001). *The unfinished bombing: Oklahoma City in American memory*. New York: Oxford University Press.

Lipton, E. (2005, April 3). At the limits of science, 9/11 ID effort comes to end. *New York Times*.

Lisle, D. (2004). Gazing at Ground Zero: Tourism, voyeurism, and spectacle. *Journal for Cultural Research, 8*(1), 3–20.

Littlewood, R., & Lipsedge, M. (1989). *Aliens and alienists: Ethnic minorities and psychiatry*. London: Unwin.

Litz, B., Gray, M., Bryant, R., & Adler, A. (2002). Early intervention for trauma: Current status and future directions. *Clinical Psychology: Science and Practice, 2*, 112–134.

Lori, A. (2005). *The survival of hope*. Retrieved May 9, 2005, from www.haaretz.com.

Louie, M. (2001, December 3). The 9/11 disappeareds. *The Nation*.

Lower Manhattan Info. (n.d.). Retrieved July 3, 2004, from www.lowermanhattan.info/news/.

Lowry, E., & McCleery, G. (2005). The American Red Cross and September 11th Fund mental health disaster response. In Y. Danieli & R. Dingman (Eds.), *On the ground after September 11: Mental health responses and practical knowledge gained* (pp. 187–197). Binghamton, NY: Haworth Press.

Luhrmann, T. (2000). *Of 2 minds: The growing disorder in American psychiatry*. New York: Knopf.

Malgady, R., Rogler, L., & Costantino, G. (1987). Ethnocultural and linguistic bias in mental health evaluation of Hispanics. *American Psychologist, 42*(3), 228–234.

Malkinson, R., Rubin, S., & Witzum, E. (2005). Terror, trauma, and bereavement; Implications for theory and therapy. In Y. Danieli, D. Brom, & J. Sills (Eds.), *The trauma of terrorism: Sharing knowledge and shared care, an international handbook* (pp. 467–477). Binghamton, NY: Haworth Press.

Marks, I., Lovell, K., Noshirvani, H., Livanou, M., & Thrasher, S. (1998). Treatment of posttraumatic stress disorder by exposure and/or cognitive restructuring. *Archives of General Psychiatry, 55*, 317–325.

Marsella, A., Friedman, M., & Spain, E. (1996). Ethnocultural aspects of PTSD: An overview of issues and research directions. In A. Marsella, M. Friedman, E. Gerrity, & R. Scurfield (Eds.), *Ethnocultural aspects of PTSD: Issues, research, and clinical applications* (pp. 105–129). Washington, DC: American Psychological Association.

Marshall, R., Galea, S., & Kilpatrick, D. (2002). Letters to the editor. *Journal of the American Medical Association, 288*(21), 2683–2685.

Marshall, R., & Suh, E. (2003). Contextualizing trauma: Using evidence-based treatments in a multicultural community after 9/11. *Psychiatric Quarterly, 74*(4), 401–420.

Martin, S. (2002). Thwarting terrorism. *Monitor on Psychology, 33*(1).

Maser, J., Kaelber, C., & Weise, R. (1991). International use and attitudes toward *DSM-III* and *DSM-III-R*: Growing consensus in psychiatric classification. *Journal of Abnormal Psychology, 100*(3), 271–279.

Masson, J. (1998). *The assault on truth: Freud's suppression of the seduction theory*. New York: Pocket Books.

Mattingly, C., Lawlor, M., & Jacobs-Huey, L. (2002). Narrating September 11. *American Anthropologist, 104*(3), 743–753.

McCann, I., & Pearlman, L. (1990). Vicarious traumatization: A framework for understanding the psychological effects of working with victims. *Journal of Traumatic Stress, 3*(1), 131–149.

McGlaughlin, J. (1981). Transference, psychic reality and countertransference. *Psychoanalytic Quarterly, 50*, 639–664.

McNally, R. (2003). Progress and controversy in the study of posttraumatic stress disorder. *Annual Review of Psychology, 54*, 229–252.

Miliora, M. (2000). Beyond empathic failures: Cultural racism as narcissistic trauma and disenfranchisement of grandiosity. *Clinical Social Work Journal, 28*(1), 43–53.

Miller, J. (2002). Affirming flames: Debriefing survivors of the World Trade Center attack. *Brief Treatment and Crisis Intervention, 2*(1), 85–94.

Miller, M. (2003). Working in the midst of unfolding trauma and traumatic loss: Training as a collective process of support. *Psychoanalytic Social Work, 10*(1), 7–25.

Miller, N. (2003). Reporting the disaster. In J. Greenberg (Ed.), *Trauma at home: After 9/11* (pp. 39–47). Lincoln, NE: University of Nebraska Press.

Mirabito, D., & Rosenthal, C. (2002). *Generalist social work practice in the wake of disaster: September 11 and beyond*. Florence, KY: Thompson Custom Publishing.

Mitchell, J. (1983). When disaster strikes . . . The critical incident stress debriefing process. *Journal of Emergency Medical Services, 8*(1), 36–39.

Mitchell, S. (1993). *Hope and dread in psychoanalysis*. New York: Basic Books.

Mitchell, S. (1997). *Influence and autonomy in psychoanalysis*. Hillsdale, NJ: Analytic Press.

Moghaddam, F., & Marsella, A. (Eds.). (2004). *Understanding terrorism: Psychosocial roots, consequences, and interventions*. Washington, DC: American Psychological Association.

Moran, M. (2003). Trauma-response strategies still missing in action. *Psychiatric News, 38*(23), 42–43.

Morikawa, A. (n.d.). *Interviews with family members of World Trade Center attack victims*. Unpublished manuscript.

Myers, D., & Wee, D. (2005). *Disaster mental health services*. New York: Brunner-Routledge.

Nacos, B. (2002). *Mass-mediated terrorism: The central role of the media in terrorism and counterterrorism*. Lanham, MD: Rowman & Littlefield.

Nader, K., & Danieli, Y. (2005). Cultural issues in terrorism and in response to terrorism. In Y. Danieli, D. Brom, & J. Sills (Eds.), *The trauma of terrorism: Sharing knowledge and shared care, an international handbook* (pp. 399–410). Binghamton NY: Haworth Press.

National Association of Social Workers. (2002, November/December). Chapter convenes social work community to discuss impact of attack. *Currents 47*(3), 3.

National Center for Health Statistics. (n.d.). Classifications of diseases and functioning & disability. Retrieved June 14, 2002, from www.cdc.gov/nchs/.

National Crime Victims' Rights Week. (n.d.). *The history of the crime victims' movement in the United States.* Retrieved August 15, 2005, from www.ojp.usdoj.gov.

National Institute of Mental Health (NIMH). (2001). *Research in response to the terrorist acts in America.* Retrieved July 5, 2004, from http://grants1.nih.gov.

National Institute of Mental Health (NIMH). (2002). *Mental health and mass violence: Evidence-based early psychological intervention for victims/survivors of mass violence. A workshop to reach consensus on best practices.* Washington, DC: U.S. Government Printing Office.

Naturale, A. (2005). The New York State mental health response to 9/11/01: Project Liberty. In Y. Danieli & R. Dingman (Eds.), *On the ground after September 11: Mental health responses and practical knowledge gained* (pp. 536–540). Binghamton, NY: Haworth Press.

Nemiah, J. (1989). The varieties of human experience. *British Journal of Psychiatry, 154,* 459.

New York City Department of Mental Health and Hygiene. (n.d.). *Medical Reserve Corps/NYC. 2003.* Retrieved October 9, 2006, from www.nyc.gov.

New York City Department of Mental Health and Hygiene. (2003). Post-traumatic stress disorder. *City Health Information, 22*(1), 1–4.

New York State Office of Mental Health. (n.d.). *New York State Office of Mental Health's response to the World Trade Center disaster.* Retrieved July 21, 2005, from www.omh.state.ny.us.

New York State Office of Mental Health. (n.d.). *2005–2009 statewide comprehensive plan for mental health services: Appendix 5: Project Liberty services and delivery.* Retrieved August 3, 2005, from www.omh.state.ny.us.

New York State Office of Mental Health. (2006). *Project Liberty Regular Services Crisis Counseling Assistance and Training Program final report: June 15, 2002–December 31, 2004.* Albany, NY.

New York University. (2006). *How prepared are we, New York?* New York: New York University.

New York University. (n.d.). *Center for Catastrophe Preparedness and Response.* Retrieved July 21, 2006, from www.nyu.edu/ccpr.

Norris, F. (2002). Disasters in urban context. *Journal of Urban Health, 79*(3), 308–314.

Norris, F., Friedman, M., Watson, P., Byrne, C., Diaz, E., & Kaniasty, K. (2002). 60,000 disaster victims speak: Part I. An empirical review of the empirical literature, 1981–2001. *Psychiatry, 65,* 207–239.

North, C., & Pfefferbaum, B. 2002. Research on the mental health effects of terrorism. *Journal of the American Medical Association, 288*(5), 633–636.

Obeysekere, G. (1985). Depression, Buddhism and the work of culture. In A. Kleinman & B. Good (Eds.), *Culture and depression: Studies in the anthropology and cross-cultural psychiatry of affect and disorder* (pp. 134–152). Berkeley: University of California Press.

O'Donnell, M. (2003, October 4). Scientologist's treatments lure firefighters. *New York Times,* A1.

Oldham, J. (2004). Commentary on "A national longitudinal study of the psychological consequences of the September 11, 2001 terrorist attacks: Reactions, impairment, and help-seeking": Preparing for terrorist attacks: An ongoing challenge. *Psychiatry, 67*, 167–169.

Oliver-Smith, A. (1996). Anthropological research on hazards and disasters. *Annual Review of Anthropology, 25*, 303–328.

Ong, A. (1995). Making the biopolitical subject: Cambodian immigrants, refugee medicine and cultural citizenship in California. *Social Science and Medicine, 40*(9), 1243–1257.

Perilla, J., Norris, F., & Lavizzo, E. (2002). Ethnicity, culture, and disaster response: Identifying and explaining ethnic differences in PTSD six months after Hurricane Andrew. *Journal of Social and Clinical Psychology, 21*(1), 20–45.

Petryna, A. (2002). *Life exposed: Biological citizens after Chernobyl*. Princeton, NJ: Princeton University Press.

Pfefferbaum, B. (2006). Disasters in the 21st century: Lessons from Project Liberty. *Psychiatric Services, 57*(9), 1251.

Pfefferbaum, B., North, C., Bunch, K., Wilson, T., Tucker, P., & Schorr, J. (2002). The impact of the 1995 Oklahoma City bombing on the partners of firefighters. *Journal of Urban Health, 79*(3), 364–372.

President's New Freedom Commission on Mental Health. (2003). *Final report to the President*. Retrieved July 21, 2005, from www.mentalhealthcommission.gov.

Prince, R. (1998). Historical trauma: Psychohistorical reflections of the Holocaust. In J. Kestenberg & C. Kahn (Eds.), *Children surviving persecution* (pp. 43–53). New York: Praeger.

Psychotherapists for Social Responsibility (n.d.). Retrieved July 19, 2006, from www.psr.org.

Raines, H. (2003). Foreword. In *Portraits: 9/11/01* (pp. vii–viii). New York: Times Books.

Ramirez, A. (2006a, May 22). New Yorkers' disaster preparedness falls short, study finds. *New York Times*, B2.

Ramirez, A. (2006b, September 8). Polls show drop in assurance since the attacks of Sept. 11. *New York Times*, B6.

Reissman, D. (2004). Commentary on "A national longitudinal study of the psychological consequences of the September 11, 2001 terrorist attacks: Reactions, impairment, and help-seeking": New roles for mental and behavioral health experts to enhance emergency preparedness and response readiness. *Psychiatry, 67*(2), 118–124.

Renick, O. (1993). Analytic action: Conceptualizing technique in light of the analyst's irreducible subjectivity. *Psychoanalytic quarterly 62*, 553–571.

Rhodes, L. (1991). *Emptying beds: The work of an emergency psychiatric unit*. Berkeley: University of California Press.

Ribowsky, S. (2005). Challenges in identification: The World Trade Center dead. In Y. Danieli & R. Dingman (Eds.), *On the ground after September 11: Mental health responses and practical knowledge gained* (pp. 77–82). Binghamton, NY: Haworth Press.

Rich, F. (2002, August 31). Slouching towards 9/11. *New York Times*.

Rich, F. (2005, October 31). One step closer to the Big Enchilada. *New York Times*, C12.

Rife, J. (2002, April 28). Brighter days ahead: Post 9/11, it's a long journey back to work for commuters. *Times Herald-Record*, 65.

Roberts, S., Flannelly, K., Weaver, A., & Figley, C. (2003). Compassion fatigue among chaplains, clergy, and other respondents after September 11th. *Journal of Nervous and Mental Disease, 191*(11), 756–758.

Rogler, L. (1999). Methodological sources of cultural insensitivity in mental health research. *American Psychologist, 54*(6), 424–433.

Roland, A. (1988). *In search of self in India and Japan*. Princeton, NJ: Princeton University Press.

Rosack, J. (2002). Experts question extent of 9/11 mental health consequences. *Psychiatric News, 37*(20), 1.

Rosenthal, J. (2002, September 1). 9/11: Finding utility and respect in the dictionary of disaster. *New York Times Magazine*, 28.

Rosenwald, G., & Ochberg, R. (1992). Introduction: Life stories, cultural politics, and self-understanding. In G. Rosenwald & R. Ochberg (Eds.), *Storied lives: The cultural politics of self-understanding* (pp. 1–18). New Haven: Yale University Press.

Rosner, D., & Markowitz, G. (2006). *Are we ready? Public health since 9/11*. Berkeley: University of Calif. Press.

Roth, B. 2004. Large group destruction: A group analyst at Ground Zero. In D. Knafo (Ed.), *Living with terror, working with trauma: A clinician's handbook* (pp. 429–448). Lanham, MD: Jason Aronson.

Roth, M. S. (1987). *Psycho-analysis as history: Negation and freedom in Freud*. Ithaca, NY: Cornell University Press.

Saakvitne, K. (2002). Shared trauma: The therapist's increased vulnerability. *Psychoanalytic Dialogues, 12*(3), 443–449.

Salis Gross, C. (2004). Struggling with imaginaries of trauma and trust: The refugee experience in Switzerland. *Culture, Medicine and Psychiatry, 28*, 151–167.

Salmon, J., & Sun, L. (2001, December 19). Victims at risk again: Counselors scramble to avert depression, suicides, after 9/11. *Washington Post*, A1.

Satel, S. (2002, July 26). New Yorkers don't need therapy. *Wall Street Journal*.

Saul, J. (2005). Promoting community resilience in lower Manhattan after September 11, 2001. In Y. Danieli & R. Dingman (Eds.), *On the ground after September 11: Mental health responses and practical knowledge gained* (pp. 470–478). Binghamton, NY: Haworth Press.

Schafer. R. (1983). *The analytic attitude*. NY: Basic Books.

Schauben, L., & Frazier, P. (1995). Vicarious trauma: The effects on female counselors working with sexual violence survivors. *Psychology of Women Quarterly, 19*(1), 49–64.

Schlenger, W. (2005). Psychological impact of the September 11 terrorist attacks: Summary of empirical findings in adults. In Y. Danieli, D. Brom, & J. Sills (Eds.), *The trauma of terrorism: Sharing knowledge and shared care, an international handbook* (pp. 97–108). Binghamton, NY: Haworth Press.

Schlenger, W., Cadell, J., Ebert, L., Jordan, B., & Batts, K. (2002a). Letters to the editor. *Journal of the American Medical Association, 288*(21), 2685.

Schlenger, W., Cadell, J., Ebert, L., Jordan, B., Rourke, K., Wilson, D., et al. (2002b). Psychological reactions to terrorist attacks: Findings from the national study of Americans' reactions to September 11. *Journal of the American Medical Association, 288*(5), 581–588.

Schuster, M. A., Stein, B. D., Jaycox, L. H., et. al. (2001). A national survey of stress reactions after the September 11, 2001, terrorist attacks. *New England Journal of Medicine, 345*, 1507–1512.

Scott, J. (2003). Introduction. In *Portraits: 9/11/01* (pp. ix–x). New York: Times Books.

Sebald, W. G. (2003). Air war and literature. In *On the natural history of destruction*, pp. 1–104. New York: Random House.

Seeley, K. (2000). *Cultural psychotherapy: Working with culture in the clinical encounter*. North-vale, NJ: Jason Aronson.

Seeley, K. (2001, November 11). *Serial psychotherapy and cultural subjectivity*. Paper presented at Psychoanalysis Across the Disciplines, Rutgers University, New Brunswick, NJ.

Seeley, K. (2005a). The listening cure: Listening for culture in intercultural treatment. *Psychoanalytic Review, 92*(3), 431–452.

Seeley, K. (2005b). The psychological treatment of trauma and the trauma of psychological treatment: Talking to psychotherapists about 9/11. In N. Foner (Ed.), *Wounded city: The social impact of 9/11* (pp. 263–289). New York: Russell Sage Foundation.

Seeley, K. (2005c). Trauma as a metaphor: The politics of psychotherapy after September 11. *Psychotherapy and Politics International, 3*(1), 17–27.

September 11 Digital Archive. (n.d.). *Documents, flyers*. Retrieved May 15, 2006, from www.911digitalarchive.org.

Sept. 11 victim IDed. (2007, May 17). *Metro*, 2.

Shephard, B. (2001). *War of nerves: Soldiers and psychiatrists in the twentieth century*. Cambridge, MA: Harvard University Press.

Sherman, M. (1996). Distress and professional impairment due to mental health problems among psychotherapists. *Clinical Psychology Review, 16*(4), 299–315.

Silvan, M. (2004). Do we do what we think we do? Implicit theories in the analyst's mind. *Journal of the American Psychoanalytic Association, 53*(3), 945–956.

Silver, R., Poulin, M., Holman, E., McIntosh, D., Gil-Rivas, V., & Pizarro, J. (2005). Exploring the myths of coping with a national trauma: A longitudinal study of responses to the September 11th terrorist attacks. In Y. Danieli, D. Brom, & J. Sills (Eds.), *The trauma of terrorism: Sharing knowledge and shared care, an international handbook* (pp. 129–141). Binghamton, NY: Haworth Press.

Silverman, L. (2004, March). *Shared meaning and the language of disaster*. Paper presented to the American Psychological Association, Division 39, Miami.

Soldz, S. 2007. In protest of APA torture stance, author returns award. *Common dreams.org news center*, Aug. 27. www.commondreams.org/archive/2007/08/26/3414.

Somasundaram, D. (2005). Short- and long-term effects on the victims of terror in Sri Lanka. In Y. Danieli, D. Brom, & J. Sills (Eds.), *The trauma of terrorism: Sharing knowledge and shared care, an international handbook* (pp. 215–228). Binghamton, NY: Haworth Press.

Somer, E., & Saadon, M. (1997). The assassination of Yitzhak Rabin: Resonance of a national tragedy in psychotherapy. *Psychotherapy, 34*(1), 34–43.

Sommers, C. & Satel, S. (2005). *One nation under therapy: How the helping culture is eroding self-reliance*. New York: St. Martin's Press.

Sontag, S. (1977). *Illness as metaphor*. New York: Picador.

Southwick, S., & Charney, D. 2004. Commentary on "A national longitudinal study of the psychological consequences of the September 11, 2001 terrorist attacks: Reactions, impairment, and help-seeking": Responses to trauma: Normal reactions or pathological symptoms. *Psychiatry, 67*(2), 170–173.

Spiegel, A. (2005, January 3). The dictionary of disorder: How one man revolutionized psychiatry. *New Yorker*, 56–63.

Spiegelman, A. (2004). *In the shadow of no towers*. New York: Pantheon.

Stein, B., Elliot, M., Jaycox, L., Collins, R., et al. (2004). A national longitudinal study of the psychological consequences of the September 11, 2001 terrorist attacks: Reactions, impairment, and help-seeking. *Psychiatry, 67*, 105–117.

Stoller, E. (2005). The crying game: Coping with compassion fatigue post-September 11. In Y. Danieli & R. Dingman (Eds.), *On the ground after September 11: Mental health responses and practical knowledge gained* (pp. 461–463). Binghamton, NY: Haworth Press.

Stolorow, G., & Brandchaft, B. (1994). *The intersubjective perspective*. Northvale, NJ: Jason Aronson.

Stone, J. (2005). Foreword. In Danieli, Y. & Dingman, R. Introduction. In Y. Danieli & R. Dingman (Eds.), *On the ground after September 11: Mental health responses and practical knowledge gained* (pp. xlvii–il). Binghamton, NY: Haworth Press.

Strozier, C., & Gentile, K. (2004). Responses of the mental health community to the World Trade Center disaster. In D. Knafo (Ed.), *Living with terror, working with trauma: A clinician's handbook* (pp. 415–428). Lanham, MD: Jason Aronson.

Sturken, M. 2004. The aesthetics of absence: Rebuilding Ground Zero. *American Ethnologist, 31*(3), 311–325.

Summerfield, D. (1999). A critique of seven assumptions behind psychological trauma programmes in war-affected areas. *Social Science and Medicine, 48*, 1449–1462.

Susser, E., Herman, D., & Aaron, B. (2002). Combating the terror of terrorism. *Scientific American, 287*(2), 52–62.

Tarantelli, C. B. (2003). Life within death: Towards a metapsychology of catastrophic psychic trauma. *International Journal of Psychoanalysis, 84*, 915–928.

Taylor, S., Thordarson, D., Maxfield, L., Federoff, I., Lovell, K., & Ogrodniczuk, J. (2003). Comparative efficacy, speed, and adverse effects of three PTSD treatments: Exposure therapy, EMDR, and relaxation training. *Journal of Consulting and Clinical Psychology, 71*(2), 330–338.

Thakker, J., & Ward, T. (1998). Culture and classification: The cross-cultural application of the *DSM-IV. Clinical Psychology Review, 18*(5), 501–529.

Therapy Dogs International, Inc. (n.d.). *A dog will love you forever*. Retrieved July 25, 2005, from www.tdi-dog.org.

Thomas, N. (2002, April 13). The lure of trauma: The call of the unconscious. Paper presented to the American Psychological Association, Division 39.

Toner, R., & Connelly, M. (2006, September 7). 9/11 polls find lingering fears in New York City. *New York Times*, A1.

Tosone, C., & Bialkin, L. (2004). Mass violence and secondary trauma: Issues for the clinician. In S. L. Straussner & N. Phillips (Eds.), *Understanding mass violence: A social work perspective* (pp. 155–167). Boston: Allyn & Bacon.

Trachtman, R. (1999). The money taboo: Its effects in everyday life and in the practice of psychotherapy. *Clinical Social Work Journal, 27*(3), 275–288.

Truman, B. (1997). Secondary traumatization, counselor's trauma history, and styles of coping. *Dissertation Abstracts International, 57*(9-B), 5935.

Twemlow, S. (2004). Psychoanalytic understanding of terrorism and massive social trauma. *Journal of the American Psychoanalytic Association, 52*(3), 709–716.

Tylim, I. (2004). Skyscrapers and bones: Memorials to dead objects in the culture of desire. In D. Knafo (Ed.), *Living with terror, working with trauma: A clinician's handbook* (pp. 461–475). Lanham, MD: Jason Aronson.

U. S. Department of Homeland Security (n.d.). *Ready America*. Retrieved August 22, 2005, from www.ready.gov/America/.

U. S. Department of Homeland Security (n.d.). *Ready kids*. Retrieved August 22, 2005, from www.ready.gov/kids/.

van der Kolk, B. (2002). Posttraumatic therapy in the age of neuroscience. *Psychoanalytic Dialogues, 12*(3), 381–392.

van der Kolk, B., & van der Hart, O. (1995). The intrusive past: The flexibility of memory and the engraving of trauma. In C. Caruth (Ed.), *Trauma: Explorations in memory* (pp. 158–182). Baltimore: Johns Hopkins University Press.

Verdery, K. (1999). *The political lives of dead bodies: Reburial and postsocialist challenge*. New York: Columbia University Press.

Vlahov, D. (2002). Urban disaster: A population perspective. *Journal of Urban Health, 79*(3), 295.

Vlahov, D., Galea, S., Resnick, H., Ahern, J., Boscarino, J., Bucuvalas, M., et al. (2002). Increased use of cigarettes, alcohol, and marijuana among Manhattan New York residents after the 9-11 terrorist attacks. *American Journal of Epidemiology, 155*, 988–996.

Volkan, V. (2001). September 11 and societal regression. *Mind and Human Interaction, 12*, 196–216.

Waizer, J., Dorin, A., Stoller, E., & Laird, R. (2005). Community-based interventions in New York City after 9/11: A provider's perspective. In Y. Danieli, D. Brom, & J. Sills (Eds.), *The trauma of terrorism: Sharing knowledge and shared care, an international handbook* (pp. 499–512). Binghamton, NY: Haworth Press.

Wakefield, J., & Spitzer, R. (2002). Lowered estimates – but of what? *Archives of General Psychiatry, 59*, 129–130.

Watters, C. (2001). Emerging paradigms in the mental health care of refugees. *Social Science and Medicine, 52*, 1709–1718.

Weimann, G. (2005). The theater of terror: The psychology of terrorism and the mass media. In Y. Danieli, D. Brom, & J. Sills (Eds.), *The trauma of terrorism: Sharing knowledge and shared care, an international handbook* (pp. 379–390). Binghamton, NY: Haworth Press.

Weine, S. (1999). *When history is a nightmare: Lives and memories of ethnic cleansing in Bosnia-Herzegovina*. New Brunswick, NJ: Rutgers University Press.

Weine, S., Kulenovic, A., Pavkovic, I., & Gibbons, R. (1998). Testimony psychotherapy in Bosnian refugees: A pilot study. *American Journal of Psychiatry, 155*(12), 1720–1726.

Westen, D., Novotny, C., & Thompson-Brenner, H. (2004). The empirical status of empirically supported psychotherapies: Assumptions, findings, and reporting in controlled clinical trials. *Psychological Bulletin, 130*(4), 631–663.

Widiger, T., Frances, A., Pincus, H., Davis, W., & First, M. (1991). Toward empirical classification for the *DSM IV*. *Journal of Abnormal Psychology, 100*(3), 280–288.

Wirth, H. (2003). 9/11 as collective trauma. *Journal of Psychohistory, 30*(4), 363–388.

Wong, N. (1984). Psychological aspects of medical illness. *Bulletin of Menninger Clinic, 48*, 273–278.

Wunsch-Hitzig, R., Plapinger, J., Draper, J., & del Campo, E. (2002). Calls for help after September 11: A community mental health hotline. *Journal of Urban Health, 79*(3), 417–428.

Yaeger, P. (2003). Rubble as archive, or 9/11 as dust, debris, and bodily vanishing. In J. Greenberg (Ed.), *Trauma at home: After 9/11* (pp. 187–194). Lincoln, NE: University of Nebraska Press.

Yehuda, R. (1999). Biological factors associated with susceptibility to posttraumatic stress disorder. *Canadian Journal of Psychiatry, 44*, 34–39.

Yehuda, R. (2000). Low cortisol and risk for PTSD in adult offspring of Holocaust survivors. *American Journal of Psychiatry, 157*, 1252–1259.

Yehuda, R. (2002). Posttraumatic stress disorder. *New England Journal of Medicine, 346,* 108–115.

Yehuda, R., & McFarlane, A. (1995). Conflict between current knowledge about posttraumatic stress disorder and its original conceptual basis. *American Journal of Psychiatry, 152*(12), 1705–1713.

Young, A. (1995). *The harmony of illusions: Inventing post-traumatic stress disorder.* Princeton, NJ: Princeton University Press.

Young, A. (2001). Our traumatic neurosis and its brain. *Science in Context, 14*(40), 661–683.

Young, J. (2003). Remember life with life: The new World Trade Center. In J. Greenberg (Ed.), *Trauma at home: After 9/11* (pp. 216–222). Lincoln, NE: University of Nebraska Press.

Zadroga, J. (2007, May 25–28). Who is a 9/11 victim? *Metro,* 1.

Zimbardo, P. (2003, February 28). The political psychology of terrorist alarms. *APA Online: APA Divisions.* Retrieved August 30, 2006, from www.apa.org.

Zimering, R., Munroe, J., & Gulliver, S. (2005). Secondary traumatization in mental health care providers. *Psychiatric Times, XX*(4), 43–47.

Zoellner, L., Fitzgibbons, L. & Foa, E. (2001). Cognitive-behavioral approaches to PTSD. In J. Wilson, M. Friedman, & J. Lindy (Eds.), *Treating psychological trauma and PTSD* (pp. 159–182). New York: Guilford Press.

Index